LIBRARY

In memory of

Catherine E. Boyd

Professor of History
at Carleton 1946-1966

The Lost Italian Renaissance

The Lost Italian Renaissance

HUMANISTS, HISTORIANS, AND LATIN'S LEGACY

Christopher S. Celenza

THE JOHNS HOPKINS UNIVERSITY PRESS
BALTIMORE AND LONDON

*This book has been brought to publication with the generous assistance of the
Lila Acheson Wallace–Reader's Digest Publications Subsidy and the
Craig and Barbara Smyth Fund for Scholarly Programs
and Publications.*

ᘒ

The Johns Hopkins University Press
2715 North Charles Street
Baltimore, Maryland 21218-4363
www.press.jhu.edu

Library of Congress Cataloging-in-Publication Data

Celenza, Christopher S., 1967–
The lost Italian Renaissance: humanists, historians, and Latin's legacy /
Christopher S. Celenza.
p.   cm.
Includes bibliographical references and index.
ISBN 0-8018-7815-2 (hardcover : alk. paper)
1. Renaissance—Italy. 2. Renaissance—Italy—Historiography. 3. Humanism—
Italy. 4. Humanism—Italy—Historiography. 5. Italy—Civilization—
1268-1559. 6. Italy—Civilization—1268-1559—Historiography. 7. Histori-
ography—Italy—History—To 1500. I. Title.
DG445.C38 2004
945'.05'072—dc21   2003012858

A catalog record for this book is available from the British Library.

For Ronald G. Witt

Contents

Preface and Acknowledgments   ix

Introduction: A "Lost" Renaissance and a "Lost" Literature   xi

CHAPTER ONE
An Undiscovered Star: Renaissance Latin and the Nineteenth Century   1

CHAPTER TWO
Italian Renaissance Humanism in the Twentieth Century:
Eugenio Garin and Paul Oskar Kristeller   16

CHAPTER THREE
A Microhistory of Intellectuals   58

CHAPTER FOUR
Orthodoxy: Lorenzo Valla and Marsilio Ficino   80

CHAPTER FIVE
Honor: The Humanists of the Classic Era on Social Place   115

CHAPTER SIX
What Is Really There?   134

Appendix: The State of the Field in North America   151

Notes   157

Index   205

Preface and Acknowledgments

THERE EXISTS a wealth of relatively unstudied Latin material highly relevant for the history of Renaissance Italy in all its aspects. There are some classificatory handbooks and new publishing initiatives focusing on these texts, and scholars have been examining and commenting on them for some time. Still, there is no one resource that offers an understanding of how this material came to be comparatively understudied, what it can teach us about the Italian Renaissance, and why it is unique and worthy of sustained attention now. This book is intended to meet that need and, in addition, to move beyond concerns specific to Renaissance studies. Emphasizing as it does the way nineteenth-century nationalist assumptions shaped the study of the fifteenth-century Italian Renaissance, the book makes an important (though by now unsurprising) point about scholarly disciplines across the board: they are heavily indebted to tradition, achieve a taken-for-granted status within one or two generations, and sometimes need reexamination and refocusing so that they can remain vital.

Parts of chapter 1 were published in the *Journal of the History of Ideas* 62 (2001): 17–35. Parts of chapter 4 appeared in *Modern Language Notes* 119 (2004); in *Italian Renaissance Cities: Artistic Exchange and Cultural Translation,* edited by S. Campbell and S. Milner (Cambridge: Cambridge University Press, 2004); and in *Marsilio Ficino: His Theology, His Philosophy, His Legacy,* edited by M. J. B. Allen and V. Rees (Leiden: Brill, 2002). I thank the editors of the two journals, the Syndics of Cambridge University Press, and Brill for permission to reprint.

In writing this book, I have benefited considerably from the generosity and encouragement of institutions and people. Michigan State University, to which I here record my thanks, provided an intellectual home and financial support from 1996 onward. I conceived the book while a fellow, in 1999–2000, at Villa I Tatti, the Harvard University Center for Italian Renaissance Studies in Florence, to which I owe thanks for that remarkable year. While I was there, its then Director, Professor Walter Kaiser, read and critiqued early drafts, as did my colleagues at the Center, especially Luca Boschetto, Stephen Campbell, Georgia Clarke, Isabella Lazzerini, Maureen Miller, and Stephen Milner. It pains me greatly that a very dear friend and mentor, Salvatore Camporeale—long associated with Villa I Tatti—died as this book was completed. He read and commented on most of it, and if the book conveys even the smallest fraction of his humanity, generosity, and engagement with scholarship, it will be a success. Many others read part or all of the book and contributed to it more than they know; these readers include William M. Calder III, Craig Gibson, Kenneth Gouwens, John M. Headley, Elizabeth McCahill, John Monfasani, Charles M. Radding, Rosemary Trippe, and Ronald G. Witt. The two readers for the Johns Hopkins University Press, John Marino and Edward Muir, offered advice that shaped the book in fundamental ways, as did Henry Y. K. Tom, Executive Editor at the Press. To all of these interlocutors I extend my warmest thanks. And of course, *errorum huius libri culpa est mea sola.*

I would like to conclude these acknowledgments by singling out and thanking two people. My wife, Anna Harwell Celenza, has read every paragraph of this book countless times, has improved it by her careful attention, and has been with me every step of the way. Finally, Ronald G. Witt, to whom this book is dedicated, has—by his learning, intellectual vitality, openness, kind wit, and gentle grace—inspired me ever since I first met him years ago.

Introduction

A "Lost" Renaissance and a "Lost" Literature

A FEW YEARS AGO in Florence, I found myself in a villa at a reception after an academic lecture. The villa is beautifully placed: it sits on a small hill over the Arno River, from which vantage point you have a glorious, postcard-style view of all of the city's most famous monuments: Brunelleschi's Dome, the Medici-sponsored Church of San Lorenzo, the Palazzo della Signoria with its elegant tower above the building's rusticated, rough-hewn stone. Even from a distance, you can't miss the monuments as they rise above the little city's hustle and bustle, and few can fail to be impressed. At a certain point during this reception, I fell into conversation with a senior Renaissance scholar, an American who had published much and seen a lot over the past half century. His graduate education and early career had been in the late 1950s and early 1960s, he told me, and the one thing he remembered most when he thought back on the scholarly climate of the day was that there was debate: debate about what the Italian Renaissance was, debate about its legacy, debate about how far it extended socially, and so on. At present, he went on, there just isn't any debate. Those sorts of questions had never really been definitively answered. Instead, they fizzled out, as things do in academia, and now, although there was much being published in the field, there wasn't much engagement with the larger ideas that had propelled all that debate in the first place. Upon reflection, I realized he was right, and I resolved to write this book.

What was the senior scholar talking about? To understand him we have to ask the basic question, Was there an Italian Renaissance? This question has been debated since the sixteenth century in many different guises, but it was discussed with especially great intensity from the early twentieth century onward in the United States. There had been no major new interpretation of the Italian Renaissance since the Swiss scholar Jacob Burckhardt had published his famous book on the subject in the nineteenth century. He stressed that the Italian Renaissance saw the birth of the modern individual and the liberation of humanity from the repressive shackles of medieval, group-oriented mentalities. Italian thinkers, turning to the ancient Roman and Greek past, found a new way to conceive of themselves: not as members of a corporate group but as individuals. This break was felt not only in literature and the arts but also in statecraft and society at large, Burckhardt had maintained. The Italian Renaissance represented the time when Europeans began to become modern.

Burckhardt advanced this interpretation of the Italian Renaissance in 1860, and it gradually became the dominant one. However, despite the strength of Burckhardt's interpretation of the Renaissance, neither he nor subsequent scholars had access to the complete range of sources to study the period, largely because of the nature of the source material, much of which was written in Latin and had not yet been clearly cataloged, let alone edited or translated. More will be said about this limitation, but for now suffice it to say that scholars who were interested in the field simply could not do what scholars always do: check the sources for themselves. What remained of Burckhardt's interpretation was the idea that the Renaissance marked the beginning of modernity. What was lacking was a comprehensive collection of sources.

Other fields in premodern Europe did not, with rare exceptions, suffer the same fate. Classical studies, for example, had been the cornerstone of the German educational system since the early nineteenth century. The discipline therefore naturally benefited from the great push toward cataloging, inventorying, and editing that characterized the academic efforts of the later nineteenth and early twentieth centuries. This distinctive period saw the foundation of all the great series of classical texts and of the systematic gathering together of *fragments*—bits that were scattered throughout ancient sources but relevant to disciplinary concerns. This and related enterprises ensured that classics had its sources attended to. Of course, even today someone will occasionally find a new line or two from an ancient comedy in an Egyptian papyrus; but for the most part, by the early twentieth century, most important extant sources for classics were at least well edited, if not always translated into many modern languages. And in the meantime, in the early twentieth century, medieval studies came into its own as an academic discipline and was especially vigorous in the United States. Its sources had not been given the same degree of attention initially as classical sources, but, just one small step behind classicists, medievalists cataloged, edited, and made their sources available. So, by the early twentieth century, although the editions were sometimes cumbrous and difficult to use, interested medievalists had access to relatively well-tended sources that pertained to the intellectual climate of the Middle Ages.

The sources for the Italian Renaissance, however, were always regarded as less than important, and this is the idea I explore in chapter 1. Nineteenth-century intellectuals, by and large, were convinced that only a native language could be a true vehicle for the expression of real culture. When this idea merged with the rise of nationalist conceptions of history, the systematic large-scale study of Renaissance Latin was doomed. Italian Renaissance intellectuals had their own reasons and concerns for writing in Latin, not Italian, but because of the often cursory glances nineteenth-century scholars accorded their work (much of it in manuscript or unreliable early printed editions), Renaissance thinkers were stigmatized as having retarded the development of Italian culture. The "lost" Italian Renaissance has to do with intellectual history.

The "lost literature" encompasses Renaissance Latin texts that were "skipped" because of nineteenth-century interests foreign to the Renaissance itself. The Renaissance, conceived as a period, is a broad time span, which one could extend from the late thirteenth to the mid–seventeenth century. But the lost literature I am discussing is more specifically grounded in time. It consists of Latin works in prose and poetry (mostly prose), as well as vernacular works which, because they were seen as "tainted" in the wake of nineteenth-century prejudices, also went ignored, all of them the products of what I term the *long fifteenth century*. Indeed, from about the mid–fourteenth to the early sixteenth century, certain factors can be singled out as marking an organic whole.

There is, especially in the early fifteenth century in Florence, then throughout Italy, a real belief in the notion that one could renew and renovate contemporary culture by reviving, turning toward, and ultimately judging oneself against classical antiquity. One could accomplish this end by, among other things, writing in a new Latin, unlike medieval church Latin, which would reflect the idealized purity of style and eloquent expression that this revived antiquity symbolized. Especially until about the middle of the fifteenth century, this dream was vibrantly, almost naively alive. As the century wore on and this new culture spread, more critical examinations of language were accompanied by the evolution of different social spaces in which intellectuals operated; and by the early sixteenth century, there were important thinkers and theorists in Italy, such as Pietro Bembo, who began examining the Italian vernacular with the same critical intensity and acumen formerly accorded to Latin. But by then, the educated throughout European society assumed a basic knowledge of antiquity and competence in the new Latin; and gradually, along with discoveries both natural and linguistic that seemed to challenge the ancient literary past, the notion that one could not only imitate but also surpass the ancients gained hold. In literary and intellectual terms, the Italian Renaissance extends from, say, the lifetime of Petrarch (1304–74) to the early sixteenth century, and it is from this period that the "lost literature" primarily stems. A portion of this literature has been edited and translated. Much of it, however, survives only in manuscript, and the rest can be found in early printed editions from the late sixteenth and seventeenth centuries, editions that—in their ordering, principles of selection, and inevitable omissions—often reflect the concerns of their compilers as much as the original work they contain.

As to the question of the existence of the Italian Renaissance, the level of debate waned in the mid–twentieth century, primarily because new, seemingly more pressing problems presented themselves. The question is still open for debate, but to understand the problems undergirding it, we have to situate matters in the larger context of the historiography of Europe broadly conceived. A short while after the waning of the debate concerning the existence of the Renaissance—let us say in the late 1950s—Italian Renaissance historians in the United States became captivated by the notion known as *civic humanism* formulated by the historian Hans Baron. In chapter 2 I address this historiographical issue briefly, but for now it is enough to know that, to a postwar America proud of its democratic heritage, the notion that the Florentine Renaissance had given birth to the modern idea of popular government was very appealing, as was the linking of ideas to concrete political events in what seemed to be an "objective" way.[1] Much subsequent scholarship in Italian Renaissance intellectual history dealt with the idea of civic humanism—proving it, disproving it, examining it critically. So there was a bit of interest in making Renaissance sources available that were pertinent to this specific theme, but there was no large-scale systematic effort undertaken to do so, let alone to widen the purview to texts not directly relevant to the problem of civic humanism.

Soon, however, American historians en masse were overtaken by a new trend in historiography that began in France in the 1920s and eventually made its way across the Atlantic Ocean. This was social history, which tried to recover parts of the past that did not tend to be recorded in official (political or diplomatic) sources or intellectual tracts. Social historians aimed to study the lives and mentalities of everyday people who had escaped traditional forms of documentation. They pointed out, quite rightly, that these underrepresented groups needed study if we were to have a complete picture of the past and transcend what had been a century-long preoccupation with political and institutional history with an occasional glance toward (an idealized) "high" culture. Those who did this type of work, the first social historians, were breaking with the past and doing revolutionary scholarship that was not always initially appreciated. Moreover, in the United States, the move to social history proved to be in harmony with the political beliefs of many academics coming of age in the 1960s. Although this sense was not always consciously articulated, social history became the "right" kind of history to be doing. Practicing social history came to serve as a sign that one was socially engaged and willing to turn from the grand narratives of political history to focus instead on those who had been slighted by the grand narrative tradition. The turn toward social history occurred, let us say, in the 1960s and 1970s and by the 1980s was the norm. Social historians went from being a minority to the majority among academic historians in the United States, and doing social history became a safe way to engage in an established field with relatively settled canons of research and method: Thomas Kuhn's normal science, in which, rather than asking new questions, one is—often quite usefully—solidifying established answers to old ones and smoothing out the rough edges.[2] Meanwhile, a number of pathbreakers appeared in various fields. Who were they?

In the historiography of western Europe, they were the people who began to combine social history with intellectual and cultural history; they asked social questions about intellectuals, and they used traditional intellectual sources to illuminate social history. They were people like Walter Burkert in classical studies, who uncovered new dimensions of the power of religious ritual by combining highly developed philological skills with anthropological questions, or Peter Brown, whose field-shaping work on late antiquity began with a well-known biography of Augustine, which set that early Christian thinker in a social context in a way not attempted previously. In medieval studies, one saw the emergence of Caroline Walker Bynum in the early 1980s, who, in studying monastic communities, asked questions regarding gender and the construction of sexuality, using texts that formerly would have fallen to scholars conditioned by long practice not to pose those sorts of problems. In a field very close to Italian Renaissance studies, that of Reformation studies or, more broadly, early modern Germany, Heiko Oberman transcended heroic teleological narrative and saw the medieval roots of much Reformation thought. In the study of the French revolution, Lynn Hunt formulated the problem by focusing on the construction of public symbolic discourse, and she seamlessly wove together the previously diverse strands of documentary history, art history, and intellectual culture.[3] Although this notion of writing a multileveled history of society had important antecedents in modern historiography, these scholars all effected fundamental reorientations in their fields by combining perspectives that had hitherto been seen as the provinces of separate academic subdisciplines.[4]

One could continue and add the names and work of numerous authors in many different fields who combined intellectual and social history in innovative ways. But the underlying motif in the work of all of these scholars was that they paid equal and sophisticated attention to *both* sides of the problem. A scholar who perhaps by inclination was in sympathy with the goals of social history nonetheless used intellectual historical sources; and a philologically oriented scholar, whose primary inclination was to study texts, realized that he or she could not offer an intuitively satisfactory account of the intellectuals under study by examining texts in a social vacuum. Instead one had to take the useful step, after reading the texts, of posing the sorts of questions that social historians had grown accustomed to asking. In Italian Renaissance studies, however, although there has been no shortage of brilliant, virtuosic work, there are no analogous boundary-crossing figures, and until recently, few scholars have attempted to bridge the divide.[5] Why? Because in this field, the division between social and intellectual historians grew starker than in any other, for reasons touched upon throughout the first three chapters of this book.

Owing to this separation, there is another key area in which Renaissance studies have remained behind other fields, and that is in what I would like to call *deep historiography*. If we glance at classical studies, we see that there has been an ongoing tradition, at least since the late nineteenth century, of sustained reflection on the way the discipline has proceeded. From early pioneering works by Sir John Sandys and Ulrich von Wilamowitz-Moellendorff, to Rudolph Pfeiffer, to a twentieth-century titan like Arnaldo Momigliano, to contemporaries like Mary Beard, Luciano Canfora, William Calder, Hellmut Flashar, Marcello Gigante, Glenn Most, Annabel Robinson, and many other excellent scholars, classicists have always remained alert to their field's great practitioners and have with increasing sensitivity documented the contexts in which many of the scholars who have shaped classical studies actually practiced.[6] Medievalists have been a few steps behind classicists, as they were with respect to the editing of sources, but in the last two or three decades they have produced remarkable work on the history of medieval studies as a discipline. R. Howard Bloch, Norman Cantor, Gabrielle Spiegel, John Van Engen, Stephen Nichols, Kathleen Biddick, Patrick Geary, Christopher Gerrard, Robert Morrissey, and numerous others have shed light on the evolution of their field, masterfully documenting how medieval studies changed from an early-nineteenth-century romantic fascination with an imagined chivalric past to a source-based academic discipline with its own concerns and problems in the twentieth century.[7] As to the study of the scholars who have worked on the Italian Renaissance, the study of Jacob Burckhardt is of course an exception; Burckhardt, the writer of the most important work in the field, has had a sizable literature devoted to him.[8] There is also the volume, still unsurpassed, of Wallace Ferguson, who covered the evolution of the interpretation of the Renaissance from the period itself to the early 1940s.[9] And J. B. Bullen has recently examined a number of key nineteenth-century writers on the Renaissance.[10] Beyond that, there have been numerous studies concerning Hans Baron; and there have been many recent interesting articles regarding the historiography of the Italian Renaissance as a whole, but they have tended to be synoptic in purview, covering a wide range of fields within the Renaissance.[11]

One thing seems clear: the more systematic and full are the collections of sources, the more a discipline can bring more than a tiny circle of hyperspecialists into its orbit, and the more it has room to reflect on its existence *as* a discipline. In this sense, its scholars can also more easily incorporate ideas and methods from other disciplines that can usefully transform their own. But the sources are the key. If they are not there, or worse, if they are there but not easily accessible, stagnation is inevitable.

And here is where we return to the questions of the Renaissance. Did it exist? Of course: no one could deny that there were groups of early modern thinkers who believed they were living in a time of cultural rebirth, that this movement began in Italy, and that other parts of Europe gradually partook of this malleable, multifaceted, movable feast. To deny that the perception of rebirth existed would be an Orwellian erasure of a documentable past language, even given the lamentable state of preservation of much Renaissance source material.

The more difficult question concerns the Renaissance's nature and importance. Here we enter into problems, especially if we consider the questions that social historians have justifiably been asking for a long time. For it is undeniably the case that, even if some of the cultural forms that the Renaissance inspired made their way eventually to many segments of society—what Peter Burke has recently called the "domestication" of the Renaissance—the movement was one predominantly created and shared by Europe's socioeconomic elites and more specifically by its intellectuals.[12] In this sense, the key problem has to do with both the social function and the importance of intellectuals.

As for the social function of intellectuals, chapters 3 to 5 of this book are concerned with precisely this problem. Chapter 3 attempts to bridge the divide between social and intellectual historians of the Renaissance by proposing a theoretical framework to understand communities of intellectuals. My central presupposition is that intellectuals are important if we want to understand society; as a group they are no more important than other segments, but no less, either. They frequently serve as linchpins in understanding fundamental societal concerns, such as the development of religious orthodoxy, as I show in chapter 4. Or they will often function themselves as proto–social historians, giving exacting and interesting observations of their own and surrounding social milieus, as I demonstrate in chapter 5, which deals with humanist views of honor. Even if one is the most socially oriented of social historians, there is nothing virtuous, at five centuries' remove, about ignoring intellectuals. They are a key source of information about the life of the past, and yet they have not entered the narratives of the development of early modern Italian society, at least not on their own terms.[13]

Italian Renaissance intellectuals, the best of them, also have an importance beyond merely documenting social relations: a number of their works still can speak to us today. A century and a half after Jacob Burckhardt wrote his influential book, we now know that the idea of an Italian "Renaissance" cannot be understood in a totalizing way. The surviving evidence from the period shows that in many categories that are important to modern history-writing—economics, political systems, and social dynamics—there was no sharp upheaval or rebirth in European culture. What one sees over the long term is instead continuity of social relations and political patterns that, with inevitable local variations, continue until the eighteenth century, when the rise of newspapers, the full flowering of capitalism, and powerful, competing, notionally secular nationalisms changed the world forever. But there is a small group of thinkers whose work does represent something distinct, yet not fully understood, and part of this book's purpose is to open a door to understanding this material.

All of this speculation will be useless within a generation or two unless we attend to the source problem and its wider implications, and this is the concern of the book's final chapter and a short appendix. The lost literature is unique: to understand it, we must think carefully about the textual legacy we possess and conceive of a Renaissance philology that is sensitive to the multifaceted source material the Renaissance presents us, a philology that is not a mere imitation of classical philology but a practice that is sui generis. The lost literature has a definable importance: beyond certain key fifteenth-century writings that can be considered masterpieces, there are innumerable works that, collectively, bring later figures like Machiavelli, Castiglione, and many others into clearer view, as well as offering other stimuli to further thought. Finally, the period within which the lost literature was produced has an identifiable end: chapter 6 emphasizes this fact as well, delineating this terminus from a number of different perspectives. The appendix goes on to explore some aspects of the editing and translating dimension of the problem: what has been done, what is being done, and what is available for English readers.

Although in the book's first two chapters I deal with certain scholars who have written on the Italian Renaissance, this is an opportune time to point out that this is not a book about the historiography of early modern Italy, even about its Anglophone variety. Economic historians, from Frederic Lane and Raymond De Roover to Marvin Becker and Richard Goldthwaite and social and political historians like Gene Brucker, Samuel Cohn, Lauro Martines, Anthony Molho, David Herlihy, Nicolai Rubinstein, and Richard Trexler all have written works of immeasurable importance in fleshing out the contours of early modern Italian life.[14] Importantly, too, all have inspired and trained a number of students, many of whom have gone on to study the structuring of early modern Italian families, the place of women within early modern Italian society, the place of workers, the nature of crime in early modern Italy, and so forth.[15] But in this book I want to talk specifically about how scholars have read the writings of Italian Renaissance intellectuals and then suggest how we might reconceive the study of these lost Latin writings and thus understand their true importance. This lost literature is not lost absolutely, as we shall see. Rather, it is lost comparatively. That is, if we compare the study of equivalently important sources in other fields like medieval and ancient studies, we will see that we can call this Latin literature "lost" without straining the meaning of the word.

One last note: at some points in this book I will seem to be contesting certain received notions, especially those which in the United States have been (in my view) uncritically filtered through the lens of a poorly understood, deracinated German idealism. But I am not throwing the baby out with the bath water. From Plato onward, one of the central tenets of most Western theories of knowledge has been that to know something, you have to be able not only to practice it but also to give an account of it, to explain it. I suppose I found that as time went by and I had published a bit in the field, I was able to "do" Renaissance intellectual history, but I became less sure of what I *was* doing, of why Renaissance intellectual history was important, and of where it stood in the historiographical tradition. In writing this book, I have been trying to find answers to those questions.

The Lost Italian Renaissance

CHAPTER ONE

An Undiscovered Star

Renaissance Latin and the Nineteenth Century

The rapid progress of humanism after the year 1400 paralyzed
native impulses. Henceforth men looked only to antiquity for the
solution of every problem, and consequently allowed literature to
sink into mere quotation.

JACOB BURCKHARDT, *The Civilization of the Renaissance in Italy*

HOW CAN IT BE that the nineteenth century's most influential
historian of the Italian Renaissance, Jacob Burckhardt, could write in
such a way concerning Renaissance humanism, the central intellectual movement of the period? Why are there times in his great and well-known work *The
Civilization of the Renaissance in Italy* when he seems almost regretful that Italian
humanists chose to write most of their work in Latin, not Italian? With respect
to Burckhardt himself, the answers are complex. He saw the writing of history
neither as a dry, antiquarian exercise nor as a study of inevitable forces, disconnected from worldly human action; rather, history was a guide for the future of
literature, art, and culture broadly conceived.[1] He sought to explain his material
in ways that would connect with his audience. Understanding the assumptions
of this audience is the goal of this chapter, which can be summed up in a question: Why in the nineteenth century — the era of great encyclopedic projects —
was Italian Renaissance Latin almost completely passed over? The answer is that
two elements came together in such a way that Renaissance Latin was never

even seen as a possible field of serious inquiry for many European intellectuals. First, there existed a belief inherited from the Enlightenment regarding language, to wit, that only a native tongue could truly express the essential genius of a people. When this assumption regarding language merged with the second factor, the rise of nineteenth-century nationalist historiographies, Renaissance Latin was doomed.

"Gentlemen, nations are thoughts of God." This is the way Leopold von Ranke (1795–1886) used to begin his history courses in Berlin, Jacob Burckhardt (1818–97) later remembered.[2] While Ranke himself was concerned primarily with documentary history and the evolution of the modern state, he was also part of a larger trend in the German-speaking world that sought to identify, in the study of the past, the spirit, or *Geist,* of a given era or people, a project that had been theorized by Hegel (1770–1831). Ranke and others, like Johann Gustav Droysen (1808–97) and August Böckh (1785–1867), taking their point of departure from Barthold Niebuhr (1776–1831) and more immediately and practically from Wilhelm von Humboldt (1767–1835), saw themselves as self-consciously transcending Hegel, basing their ideas in documentary sources as opposed to a priori theorizing.[3] Certain assumptions were similar, however, none more so than presuppositions relating to the *Volksgeist,* and although Ranke and his successors recognized the complexity of Europe's evolution *as* Europe, most assumed that the separate nations had separate national characters. This is not to say that Ranke was relentlessly teleological; history was made in the process of the unfolding of events. He saw as his primary mission the documenting and understanding of modernity, a view that, despite their later divergences in practice, Burckhardt shared.[4] The goal was, following Niebuhr's approach in classical studies, to present history in an appealing way and in a manner useful to modernity.[5] This was bound up with a larger set of movements, encompassing the search for national identity and a tendency toward locating essential characteristics of a "people."[6] One of these characteristics was language, and a central preoccupation of scholars became the manner in which culture expressed itself through language, even as classical philology was becoming "the first historical discipline, the model for all other historical sciences" and the general view of scholarly fields as separate, specialized entities was growing.[7]

In their concern with language as a vehicle for cultural transmission and as a reifying characteristic of a people, nineteenth-century scholars were the heirs of the many-faceted Enlightenment. Ideas of a plurality of cultures had flourished;

as it was put in the *Encyclopédie*, the great project of Denis Diderot (1713–84) and Jean le Rond d'Alembert (1717–83), language expressed the "genius of a people."[8] If all peoples could have an equal sensitivity to the relationship between words and things, a universal language might have been possible: "but the difference in climate, character, and temperament makes it such that all of earth's inhabitants are neither equally sensitive nor subject to the same emotions [*également affectés*]. Since different idioms are born because of the different genius of each people, one can thus decide that there will be nothing universal [i.e., with respect to language]. Could one really give each nation the same character, the same sentiments, the same ideas of virtue and vice . . . ?"[9] This recognition of a plurality of distinct cultures, along with the concomitant realization that forms of cultural expression would differ, meant the decline and fall of the notion that there ever could have been a universal language, one common to all people. Wilhelm von Humboldt, the architect of early-nineteenth-century university reforms in Germany, wrote that every language possessed its own inner form that, as Umberto Eco has put it, expressed "the vision of the world of the people who speak it."[10] In other words, language as a vehicle of expression was influenced by upbringing, environment, and culture, all of which were proper to individual nations. When one came to the highest sorts of artistic products, only a native tongue could truly be a vehicle for national genius.

Hand in hand with this conception of language went an evolutionary historiographical paradigm. Here, on the one hand, one sees a fusing together of the Enlightenment recognition of the plurality and evolution of cultures and the attendant biological metaphors applied to history.[11] The metaphors used are those of growth: approach (to an ideal), perfection (the ideal, "mature" state), and decline (a falling away from the perfected state). As an appropriate mid–eighteenth century antecedent of this view, we might cite the influential art historian and aesthete Johann Joachim Winckelmann (1717–68), who wrote famously that the only way for modern Germans to become great, or even inimitable, was precisely to imitate ancient artworks, and especially those of the Greeks; aspects of ancient Greek life that he saw as distasteful he explained away, asserting that they represented immature phases of the classical ideal, which was conceived as a balanced state of harmony that, in aesthetic terms, produced perfect beauty.[12] These tendencies and these sorts of explanatory mechanisms continued as the monumental projects of nineteenth-century historiography grew.[13]

Concomitantly, we see the development of a culture-oriented nationalist historiography in the German tradition, exemplified early on by Johann Gottfried von Herder (1744–1803) but coming to maturity in the middle of the nineteenth century.[14] Here, the final object of historical evolution is the nation, the expression of a people in organized, coherent form, a notion one encounters frequently in Ranke and those in his wake and which extends even to popularizing authors like W. H. Riehl and Gustav Freytag.[15] With respect to Theodor Mommsen (1817–1903) and Burckhardt, for example, Arnaldo Momigliano put it well:

> The new antiquarianism of the nineteenth century, like that of the seventeenth and eighteenth centuries, was an answer to Pyrrhonism, but unlike the earlier antiquarianism it claimed to be able to penetrate beyond phenomena into the spirit of a people and the structure of an organization. It was a study of antiquity revised in accordance with romantic notions of national character and the organic state, which in its turn paved the way for the sociological investigation of the ancient world introduced by Max Weber.[16]

The two general concerns just treated—an essentializing view of language along with the development of an evolutionary historiographical paradigm—were felt in the study of classical scholarship in the German world. In the first half of the nineteenth century, the Prussian research university became the Germany-wide norm. Along with its rise, *Altertumswissenschaft,* the study of classical antiquity, was given great weight. The study of classics was part and parcel of what was termed the *new humanism,* which reached back to Goethe and Schiller and gradually became the basis for German education at the level of the elite high school, the *humanistisches Gymnasium;* here, the aim was to provide a salutary classical education to future citizens.[17] Classics also became the heart and soul of the philosophical faculty of the University of Berlin (about which more will be said in chapters 2 and 3), and classical philology was its highest and purest manifestation.[18] As one of the practitioners of *Altertumswissenschaft,* Friedrich Wilhelm Ritschl (1806–76), put it, its goal was "to reproduce the life of classical antiquity."[19] Philology was born, or rather, reborn: the proper object of study for the classical philologist was . . . everything. Friedrich Gottlieb Welcker (1784–1868), whose most famous student was Karl Marx, approached the study of the ancient world with a *Totalitätsideal* in mind.[20] To master an ancient author meant not only a mastery of ancient languages but also a knowledge of literary history and tradition, local factors, and the history of philosophy. Barthold

Niebuhr had thought it should be his greatest triumph, were he able to bring antiquity once again to life;[21] and August Böckh spoke of achieving a "knowledge of antiquity in its entire breadth."[22] It was as if the poignant dream of early-fifteenth-century Florentines had been reborn: to translate a text effectively, Leonardo Bruni had written in the first decades of the fifteenth century, you had to understand "all its lines and colors."[23] To translate a culture, one had to know all its artifacts.

To succeed in this enterprise of cultural translation, however, one had to proceed systematically, to collect everything, to amass corpora—of texts, inscriptions, and archaeological sites. One needed all the evidence, and one needed it scientifically gathered, a method to which great impetus was given by Friedrich August Wolf in 1795 in his *Prolegomena to Homer*. Wolf, the great philologist, was one of the founding members of the philosophical faculty at the University of Berlin.[24] Moreover, one could not ignore one's colleagues in this enterprise: scholarship became both cooperative and competitive, as scholars worked in teams and published their results.[25] With a well-developed theory behind it and massive institutional support, the machine of organized scholarship coalesced, formidable in its size, breathtaking in its amplitude. Later in the nineteenth century, in 1890, the great historian of Roman law Theodor Mommsen would coin the term *Grossforschung* to designate the sorts of project that "could not be accomplished by a single individual but had to be directed by one."[26] The term described a situation already well established in the world of German *Wissenschaft*. Yet, even as the progress of German humanistic *Wissenschaft* grew apace, the nineteenth century was not without its debates. Even by the middle of the nineteenth century, there was a sense in which this tradition had already grown moribund, or at least had outstripped its original aim, which was to provide a *klassische Bildung*. Instead of offering a universal, spiritually rich education based on the study of the classics, higher education in classics seemed to become weighed down by increasingly more precise, specialized scholarly concerns.

Partly, this was due to analogies, usually implicit, that were made between the humanistic disciplines and the natural sciences and the concomitant burgeoning of highly specialized disciplines. The spectacular successes of German natural sciences by the mid–nineteenth century, especially chemistry and biology, led the humanistic disciplines inexorably to try to replicate the sense of certainty that the natural sciences offered. Subspecialties in the humanities were created ad infinitum, it seemed to many, and in the process the unified mission of the early nineteenth century—around which the modern research university was born—receded from view.[27] These disciplinary divisions were reinforced by one of the most conservative elements possible in the progress of research: the creation of departments, institutes, and programs in universities. Once one is created, it develops its own traditions, canons of research, and so on: in short, it never goes away. In any case, there were those who complained about these tendencies.

Beyond complaints of pedantry, however, a more formidable attack was launched, this time on some of the very basic foundations upon which this edifice rested. In his *Birth of Tragedy*, Nietzsche made the case that one found the essence of the ancient Greek genius by focusing on what he saw as a binary split in human psychology between Apollonian (rational) and Dionysian (unfettered and emotional).[28] For Nietzsche, his contemporaries had made the mistake of overstressing the Apollonian and ignoring the Dionysian and so had lost the true importance of ancient Greek culture. If they only knew, he posited, how the ancient Greeks had really lived, his buttoned-up colleagues would be shocked; Socrates became in his view less the hero of rationalism and more an overdrawn representative of an exaggerated Apollonian archetype, whose very style of thought led to a misapprehension of the Greek aesthetic in its totality.[29]

Nietzsche's work was greeted with silence, at least by then senior classical scholars.[30] In some sense, of course, Nietzsche was right that his contemporaries had sought—perhaps overmuch—to make the ancient Greeks too like themselves: The statement of Georg Friedrich Schoemann (1793–1879) on religion in antiquity, "Everything truly religious is related to Christianity," speaks volumes on the mentalities of the period.[31] Yet Nietzsche's ideas too were undergirded, fundamentally, by notions of separate national or at least ethnic characters, despite his dislike of the contemporary Prussian uses of nationalism as a shaping political force.[32] Part of the result of Nietzsche's attack is well known. Under the influence of Mommsen and then, even more importantly, Mommsen's son-in-law Ulrich von Wilamowitz-Moellendorff (1848–1931), who had in his early career responded directly to the *Birth of Tragedy* in a famous polemical review, *Altertumswissenschaft* was revived in the second half of the nineteenth century.[33]

Some took inspiration from some of Nietzsche's ideas, integrating them into their scholarship: Burckhardt, for example, shared with Nietzsche the notion that "great men," consciously or unconsciously, were key shaping factors in the progress of history (rather than functionaries in the service of immaterial historical "forces"); Burckhardt's lectures on Greek civilization may even have helped Nietzsche along in this regard.[34] Eventually others, most notably Wilhelm Dilthey (1833–1911), tried to draw distinctions between the natural and the human sciences, emphasizing that the one studied the phenomena of nature, while the other investigated the whole mental life of humanity. But in the end it was the institutionally enfranchised methods of Grossforschung that carried the day.[35] Scholars like Mommsen, Wilamowitz, and numerous other classicists opposed Nietzschean "antiphilology," and German scholarship, with its propensity for Grossforschung and its strong, titanic-seeming professorial leaders, continued to move forward. The assumptions about national identity and the place of language had been solidified, on whichever side of the ideological fence one sat. This background has had a lot to do with the manner in which the classical tradition has been perceived, even up to our own day.[36]

Because of the place a classical education began to hold in the German-speaking world, and because of the institutional support readily available in the world of the German research university, classical antiquity provided fertile ground for late-eighteenth- and nineteenth-century scholarship. While there had been a vigorous tradition of classical scholarship in Europe since the fourteenth century, it was in the nineteenth century that the above-mentioned tendency to create large-scale, systematic collections had issue: recognizably modern critical editions of the texts of major classical authors were undertaken. It was then, too, when encyclopedic plans were conceived and eventually implemented to create series of classical works, plans that were made manifest in the creation of the Teubner series of classical texts, founded in 1849, and its eventual early-twentieth-century *aemuli* on both sides of the Atlantic.[37] The *Oxford Classical Texts* series, for example, was founded in the late 1890s. Editorial agreements were sent out to twenty editors in 1897, and the first volumes began appearing in the early twentieth century. The *Loeb Classical Library* was founded in 1910, owing to the impetus of James Loeb. The *Corpus Scriptorum Latinorum Paravinianum* was founded on the initiative of Carlo Pascal of the University of Pavia in 1915. And *Belles Lettres* has been publishing its series of classical texts, the Série Grecque and the Série Latin (both part of the "collection des Universités de France"), since 1920.[38] This tendency was mirrored in patristic studies and in the twentieth century in medieval studies, both of the latter areas helped along by the industry of religious communities.[39] Yet, in the superstructure that the architects of these canons created, there existed interstices through which certain aspects of intellectual history were destined to fall. One of these aspects was Italian Renaissance thought, for a variety of reasons.

It is certainly surprising, given the phenomenal energy and dedication that scholars have brought to editing various works, that at the outset of this third millennium we still have no corpus of Renaissance Latin authors and that we lack any series of texts that is as complete, relatively speaking, as those that exist in medieval and classical studies.[40] Strange indeed, since the Renaissance must still be acknowledged as having bequeathed to us many of the positive and negative elements of ideological, philosophical, and literary modernity. Why is it that Renaissance Latin literature has for so long been placed at a second rank?

One must reach back to the above-mentioned Enlightenment ideas concerning the nature of language, which exert influence even today. Language, individual to every nation, expressed the "genius of a people," each one individual and distinctive: as nineteenth-century nationalist historiographies multiplied and romantic European perceptions of the past were conditioned by them, it was natural what the focal points would be. It was appropriate to invest energy in ancient, "classical" Latin and Greek literature, for those languages were native, natural tongues; it was fitting to investigate medieval documentary culture, for it helped illuminate the origin of European nations. However, the Italian Renaissance vogue for writing in classicizing Latin could not be appreciated in the same way: it was not a native tongue, nor did it express the "genius of a people." It is unsurprising that for a long time, Renaissance humanists, far from being appreciated as original thinkers, were blamed for having retarded the development of Italian prose and culture.[41]

An interesting inroad into "Enlightened" views regarding the Renaissance cultivation of Latinity is provided by Edward Gibbon, who toward the end of his *Decline and Fall of the Roman Empire* has some interesting and illuminating comments to make about the predilection for antiquity that Renaissance thinkers all shared. Gibbon himself was so devoted to the "pure" vision of Greek and Roman antiquity that he recognized first the beneficial effects exposure to the breadth of antiquity must have had on the "barbarians in Europe," who "were immersed in ignorance," whose "vulgar tongues were marked with the rudeness and poverty of their manners." Clearly men such as these reaped benefits from the study of antiquity: "The students of the more perfect idioms of Rome and Greece were introduced to a new world of light and science; to the society of the free and polished nations of antiquity; and to a familiar converse with those immortal men who spoke the sublime language of eloquence and reason." Their taste was refined, their genius elevated; "yet, from the first experiment, it might appear that the study of the ancients had given fetters, rather than wings, to the human mind. However laudable, the spirit of imitation is of a servile cast; and the first disciples of the Greeks and Romans were a colony of strangers in the midst of their age and country."[42]

Still, Gibbon clearly admired Renaissance Italians, precisely because they served as a cultural conduit for the purity and idealized perfection of the bearers of "the more perfect idioms of Rome and Greece." He even appreciated their taste for memorization and imitation, for an "artist" cannot "hope to equal or surpass, till he has learned to imitate, the works of his predecessors."[43] Other contemporary or slightly later thinkers, especially those who studied Renaissance thinkers in more detail and who cultivated Romanticism's love of the heroic individual, would not be so generous in their estimations of Renaissance humanists.

Through Renaissance humanists' adoption of classicizing Latin, Friedrich Schlegel wrote in 1815, a good number of poets "were lost to their language and nation."[44] Thus in his discussion of Renaissance writers, he omits Latinists, covering only those who wrote in the vernacular.[45] Schlegel's Swiss contemporary Simonde de Sismondi did the same. In his *Histoire de la renaissance de la liberté en Italie,* he highlighted the fourteenth-century revival of classical antiquity by Petrarch and others, suggesting, however, that the merit of their having transmitted classical literature must be weighed against the loss to developing Italian culture: without their zeal we would not possess many of the great works of antiquity, but "on the other hand, they turned their back on their own age in favor of erudition; imagination was curtailed, genius disappeared, language itself was retarded, abandoned as too vulgar in favor of Latin. . . . and pedantry submerged national originality."[46]

In a highly influential nineteenth-century historical work, Ranke's *History of the Popes,* these tendencies are also on view as he discusses the Italian revival of antiquity in the fifteenth century: "It would however be an exaggeration to represent this as the development of an original philosophical spirit; to talk of the discovery of new truths and the utterance of great thoughts. Men sought only to understand the ancients; they did not attempt to surpass them. Their influence was less powerful in stimulating to productive intellectual activity, than in exciting to imitation." But then, "This imitation was pregnant with the most important consequences to the civilization of the world. Men strove to rival the ancients in their own tongues." Yet this was still too restricted, too limited: "To whatever perfection this direct imitation of the ancients in their own languages was carried, it could not embrace the whole field of intellectual activity. It was essentially inadequate and unsatisfactory, and was too commonly diffused for its defects not to become obvious to many. A new idea sprang up; the imitation of the ancients in the mother tongue."[47] Then Pietro Bembo (1470–1547) arrived on the scene. In Ranke's view, his merit was not so much his Latin or his poetry in Italian but his attempt to regulate the Italian vernacular, which would excite the imagination of Ariosto.[48] For Ranke, the real contribution of the revival of antiquity could not be felt until a native tongue, Italian, came into play. And even still, there were limits, since "the genius of modern literature could not expand its wings with full freedom while bound down by the rules of classical composition. It was under the dominion of laws essentially foreign and inappropriate to its nature."[49] In his view, the revival of antiquity was momentous but ultimately limited by the practice of imitation.

In Ranke's wake, Georg Voigt saw the humanists as similarly hampered by imitation and believed that they "produced scarcely anything independent and nothing that was not surpassed in the next century."[50] He took a dour view of the humanists throughout his work and believed that their devotion to antiquity was fundamentally misguided: "In the event, antiquity could only be material for education, not an element of life; knowledge of antiquity could raise spirits pedagogically in many ways, as they were raised hitherto, but it could not make modern hearts beat in the same way that the heart of a Plutarchan hero or a Livian ancient Roman would have done. The study and the real life of these worshipers of antiquity must have come into a marvelous conflict."[51]

Voigt's is an interesting case, in that he reflects the contemporary nationalist view that Italians blocked the progress of their native culture when they insisted on writing in a nonnative tongue. Beyond this, however, he also reflects a particular tendency since the days of the late eighteenth century to see an essential cultural relationship between "German" (i.e., Prussian) culture and the idealized culture of ancient Greece over against the flaws of ancient Rome. The German language was viewed as structurally similar to ancient Greek, and the notion that ancient ("Classical," i.e., fifth-century B.C.) Greece represented a strong political system was also quite important. For instead of a system that

tended toward a unified empire (i.e., Rome), bent on conquest but sadly neglectful of its intellectual life, ancient Greece represented a community of inter-
dependent but ultimately free city-states, in which each citizen's cultural development was important and indeed related to day-to-day life. One needed
wit, training, and a rhetorically sophisticated philosophical outlook to function
in the assembly of a city-state, whereas one needed little more than strength,
might, and endurance to function within the Roman Empire. Hence, when it
came to Greco-Roman antiquity, real genius was Greek and Greek alone.[52]

So, for Voigt, Renaissance Italians, indebted ultimately as they were to ancient Roman styles of thought, could never really make any original contributions. "The very philosophy of the Romans had not, even in the eras of Cicero
and Seneca, exerted any sort of refreshing influence on life, and was really always
only a popularizing of Greek systems. Was this really, in its reheated form, now
supposed to form great politicians and martyrs to truth?"[53] The relative paucity
of Italian humanists who knew Greek well meant that they could only have
limited access to the real, Greek, greatness of antiquity. Voigt was willing to
concede to the humanists significant achievements in the realms of Latin grammar and orthography, classical text editing and textual commentary, even epi-
graphy. However, when it came to poetry and prose, they were lost. Since in
poetry "they do not find the object of poetry in itself and in the real world" but
rather in Roman antiquity, they remain at the level of formalism." Prose was
similarly hampered.[54]

No comment of Voigt's could be more illustrative of his Platonically influenced ideal view of cultural development, inherited from the days of Winckelmann, than this set of judgments on the rhetorical culture of the Italian Renaissance humanists: "The preacher believes he is so holy as his words, a political
speaker or author believes that he is truly enthused by his material, if he can
speak enthusiastically. . . . It was in this way, then, in these high-minded circles,
that morality was thoroughly taken away from simple conscience and transferred to a world of seeming."[55] *Eine Welt des Scheines,* a world of seeming, that
is, as opposed to being, or essence: for Voigt, the Italian humanists, by not following the proper course of their natural national development, had become
mere sophists, persuaded that the world they constituted with language was the
real world.

Voigt's contemporary, Jacob Burckhardt, the greatest, most synthetically
minded of nineteenth-century Renaissance historians, and himself a pupil of

Ranke in Berlin, put it most succinctly, summing up *opinio communis* in the passage with which this chapter began: "The rapid progress of humanism after the year 1400 paralyzed native impulses. Henceforth men looked only to antiquity for the solution of every problem, and consequently allowed literature to sink into mere quotation."[56] I should highlight that Burckhardt here is suggesting an objection that a reader might have to his relatively extensive treatment of humanist Latin literature; Burckhardt's sentiment thus is all the more revelatory of the thought-world he inhabited and reflective of the underlying assumptions that he shared with his intended audience. For Burckhardt and those who followed him, as most did for the next century, this developmental freezing of the national literature was not altogether a bad thing: it was necessary that the humanists cast their nets deep into the sea of antiquity, for it was there that they found the submerged, shipwrecked roots of the modern individual. Emblematic is Burckhardt's statement at the end of a lengthy exposition of humanist Latin poetry: "By what has been said hitherto we have, perhaps, failed to convince the reader of the characteristic value of this Latin poetry of the Italians. Our task was rather to indicate its position and necessity in the history of civilization."[57] The necessary factor to which Burckhardt alludes is the revival of antiquity, which, combined with the Italian *Volksgeist,* made Renaissance Italians, in his often repeated phrase, "the first-born among the sons of modern Europe."[58]

It is noteworthy that Burckhardt shares many of the same assumptions concerning the essential national characters of the figures under study, for in many ways he saw himself as turning away from the seemingly empiricist, politically oriented project of Ranke and his immediate successors. Burckhardt's study of *Kultur,* civilization, was immediately related to contemporary concerns and was part of his own, Basel-oriented backlash against the statist, Prussian, teleological political history so easily allied to a then-embryonic modernism and the advancement of technologically inclined state formation. Burckhardt's view that the real source of modernity was found in the aristocratic city-state world of Renaissance Italy mirrored his own complex but ultimately quite positive feelings for his own small, aristocratic city-state, Basel. He saw, in the Renaissance "discovery of the world and of man," something that might lead himself and his fellow Baselers toward their own cultural and artistic destiny; he saw, in other words, an accommodation with modernity that would in fact lead to a second Renaissance. In a way this concept represented a revival of the earlier conception of Winckelmann and Wilhelm von Humboldt, that a thorough grounding in the classics would lead to a community of truly free individuals. Yet, for Burckhardt and others like him, the proper setting for that sort of individual could only be found, ultimately, in a relatively small city-state, not in an empire such as Prussia, wittingly or unwittingly, was becoming.[59]

Because of his intimate involvement with Basel, Burckhardt can be seen as inhabiting quite a different mental world from that of Ranke. Burckhardt needed to find something positive about the literary production of the Italian humanists, and as we have seen, this element was in fact the essentially "modern" spirit that undergirded their work. The fact that they looked toward antiquity for inspiration was actually their most forward-looking tendency. Yet, despite Burckhardt's love for the spirit of the Italian humanists, his assumptions concerning Renaissance literature were well in line with those of his contemporaries. Since the Italian humanists chose to write in a nonnative tongue, their contribution to culture had to be primarily on the ideological, not the literary, plane. Later interpreters, John Addington Symonds for example, shared this tendency to see the lack of progress in Italian literature as a necessary trade-off, ample recompense for the gifts the Renaissance did give to the development of modern consciousness.[60] However, one thing that stands out in this view is the tendency not to take the *Latin* literary production of Renaissance humanists and philosophers all that seriously, as if their general spirit was important but their writings were not, since Latin was a nonnative tongue. This led to the absence of any series of Renaissance Latin texts equivalent to the great series of classical texts mentioned above.

One need only bring to mind authors like Joseph Conrad or Vladimir Nabokov to realize that literature of great profundity can be written in a tongue not one's own. Closer to home, one can also think of scholars like Erwin Panofsky, Arnaldo Momigliano, and Paul Oskar Kristeller, who wrote much of their work in nonnative languages and yet made contributions of great value and sagacity.[61] Of course, the five authors just mentioned adopted languages that in their day were still living, still spoken. Nevertheless, Latin was much more alive for Renaissance thinkers than for us; and Latin's status as a "dead" language makes its Renaissance revival all the more "alive" from our perspective, since it became a crucial instrument around whose use countless ideological positions often crystallized. The centrality of Latin also lent the question of usage a distinctive aesthetic, one liable to be influenced by dominant intellectual figures who became arbiters of proper Latin, as much, one suspects, by the force of their personalities as by their purity of style. Latin was a central element of intellectual discourse in Renaissance culture, and we cannot know that culture without it. However, as Italian literary scholarship took modern form in the nineteenth and twentieth centuries, Renaissance Latinists fell unjustifiably through the cracks, only to be saved to some extent in the twentieth.

All humanistic scholars, either implicitly or explicitly, give more weight to certain aspects of the past and less to others. Nineteenth-century historians and philologists had certain principles concerning what was important. The coming together of these principles led to what Pierre Bourdieu would call a *habitus,* that is, a complex and intersubjective web of concerns and assumptions shared by a group of people. The *habitus* yields (again in Bourdieu's terms) a *doxa,* an unspoken, taken-for-granted realm of opinion that defines the parameters of the possible within which actors in a given historical environment can operate.[62] Renaissance Latin fell outside the realm of the possible in the nineteenth century, for it did not represent an essential locus of linguistic perfection. This is ironic in the case of the Renaissance since the foundations for more systematic study of certain Renaissance Latinists—Italian ones, anyway—had been laid in the eighteenth century, by Italians interested in their medieval and Renaissance past. None of these was greater than Lodovico Antonio Muratori (1672–1750), whose twenty-five-volume *Rerum italicarum scriptores* gathered together many texts, Latin and otherwise, from a broadly defined Middle Ages (c. 500–1500) and served as an inspiration for other such projects. Nonetheless, his was a conception governed by the notion that there was an Italian nation, which he essentially equated with the peoples of the Italian peninsula; and the Renaissance Latin sources that he printed were those that were self-consciously historical—the histories of Florence by Leonardo Bruni and Poggio Bracciolini, for example. Although Muratori respected both the Renaissance turn to classical Latin and its proponents for their learning, it was not part of his enterprise to focus on Renaissance Latin texts as such; in his view, they were a small part of a much larger and more organically encyclopedic historical project.[63] In any case, by the mid–nineteenth century the norms and ideals had changed: the balance, in terms of scholarship, had shifted decisively, and new assumptions were in the air.

In the early 1830s, Ranke taught in his courses that historians ought to focus attention on the nations "that have played a preeminent, active role in history.

We should concern ourselves with the influence which these nations have had on one another, with the struggles they have waged with one another, with their development in peace and war."[64] If one transposes this sentiment to languages as representative of nations and of national genius, it is not hard to see how and why the above developments occurred. In their systematizing impulse to create corpora of inscriptions, to form series of texts, in short to develop a "scientific" philology, most nineteenth-century humanistic scholars did not deem the Latin literary production of the Renaissance worthy of sustained attention. Like an undiscovered star, Renaissance Latin sat at the outer edge of nineteenth- and early-twentieth-century consciousness, shining brightly yet just out of view.

During the often tormented times of the early twentieth century, two brilliant scholars, Eugenio Garin and Paul Oskar Kristeller, would recognize this great gap in historical knowledge. It is to the story of these two foundational interpreters of the Renaissance that this study now turns.

CHAPTER TWO

Italian Renaissance Humanism in the Twentieth Century

Eugenio Garin and Paul Oskar Kristeller

It is the concern of scholars and thinkers to uphold and to develop the precise concept of liberty and to build its philosophical theory; and this is the contribution which should be expected from us in the complex work of the restoration and revival of the liberal ideal and tradition.

BENEDETTO CROCE, *La teoria della libertà*

In the organization of institutions of higher education everything depends upon retaining the principle that knowledge must be considered as something not yet wholly discovered and never entirely discoverable, and that it must incessantly be sought as such.

WILHELM VON HUMBOLDT, *"Über die innere und äußere Organisation der höheren wissenschaftlichen Anstalten in Berlin"*

THE CULTURAL AND EDUCATIONAL environment in Europe in the first decades of the twentieth century was dramatic, fertile, and dangerous. The relation of the individual to the state, the nature of the nation, and the place of education in the formation of citizens were hotly debated. The backdrop to these discussions was an evolving modernism that encapsulated the shattering of belief in absolute progress and philosophical continuity by war, new developments in the theory and practice of natural science, the linguistic turn in philosophy, and rapidly changing canons of the arts.[1] The seeming speed of cultural change and the drama and excitement of the various perspectives on culture and civic life must be foregrounded if we are to understand the two major theoretical outlooks that have shaped modern scholarly opinion on the intellectual history of the Italian Renaissance, outlooks best represented in the work of Eugenio Garin (1909–) and Paul Oskar Kristeller (1904–99).

Both Garin and Kristeller transcended the nineteenth-century textual legacy (or lack thereof) explored in this book's first chapter, and they vigorously incorporated in their work much of the Latin source material that past historiography had ignored; they opened the way for themselves and for other scholars to make great inroads into Renaissance culture. The methods of investigation that each employed, however, are representative of two very different approaches not only to the Renaissance but to life itself, and each approach was conditioned by the tumultuous times in which our authors came to maturity and the gradual responses they developed in consequence. Aristotle wrote that the best sort of tragedy involves characters who are notable and basically good, but who at one time or another make an error of judgment that will lead them from happiness to misery.[2] The careers of our two central characters in this chapter were not so dramatic, perhaps, but the story is not without some tragic elements. For although these two scholars saw far beyond the available conceptual fields that each had inherited, the scholarly paradigms they adopted and fostered failed to create a long-lived field of study (in the North American academic world at least), to such an extent that the field they created is now on the verge of disappearing. Only by comprehending them in context can we come to an understanding of why their two distinctive ways of viewing the Italian Renaissance — so different in fundamental assumptions yet both so important — have not been appreciated to the extent they deserve.

At its most basic level, the difference in outlook between Eugenio Garin and Paul Oskar Kristeller is the difference between diachrony and synchrony, between philosophical historicism and philosophical idealism. The first tradition stresses dynamism and change in historical explanation; the second looks for immutable, universally true ways of explaining. The first can by definition never be absolute or all-encompassing in its explanatory power, because it must seek to describe process and dynamism in history, in a word, to explain how point A got to point B; to do this you must consciously make choices about what to omit. The second tradition strives instead to find a way to explain an epoch, a literary tradition, or an intellectual movement in a universal way, to take a cultural snapshot that tries to encompass every nook and cranny of a movement, to make statements that cannot, insofar as possible, be contradicted by specific examples. The first is antimetaphysical and attempts to locate trends within the inevitable pluralities of history; the second is primarily metaphysical and looks for absolute Ideas, for unity as opposed to plurality. The cultural and philosophical environment in Italy at the outset of the twentieth century was very important as background for our two thinkers. As we shall see, two Italian thinkers, Benedetto Croce and Giovanni Gentile, were of vital importance—for Garin, obviously, because he was a part of the Italian environment that Croce and Gentile had done so much to shape, and for Kristeller because, in flight from National Socialism, he spent some of the most important and formative years of his then young scholarly life in Italy, having earned the respect and patronage of Gentile. Croce and Gentile, too, diverged in their attitudes concerning the nature of history, and they can be seen as important influences on our own two protagonists. In what follows I shall discuss Croce and Gentile as background, then move on to a consideration of the thought of Garin (with a short detour) and Kristeller.

A word of caution: when one discusses influences, backgrounds, environments, and the like, it is tempting to fall into the trap of monocausal explanations, as if, because a thinker studies with scholar X, he therefore must think and write like X, or because she works in environment Y, her own production will be transparently affected by Y. This is decidedly not the perspective here. Rather, both Garin and Kristeller should be seen as individuals simultaneously shaping and shaped by their environments and struggling to carve out intellectual positions in a many-faceted cultural and intellectual field.[3]

Backgrounds: Giovanni Gentile (1875–1944) and Benedetto Croce (1866–1952)

Too little known outside of Italy, these two figures were of titanic importance in shaping the intellectual life of Italy in the twentieth century and must inevitably form the background to a discussion of Eugenio Garin and Paul Oskar Kristeller. What did Croce and Gentile share? How did they differ?

At the broadest level, Croce and Gentile both reflected the Europe-wide trend of immanentism, a philosophical movement which, in general terms, stands in opposition to most ancient and medieval thought. An immanentist philosopher locates absolutes in various realms of human experience, rather than in transcendent divinity, whether that divinity is represented by Plato's forms, Aristotle's prime mover, or the Judeo-Christian God. Immanentism had become self-conscious as a movement with Immanuel Kant (1724–1804), Georg Wilhelm Friedrich Hegel (1770–1831), and other German idealists, although, as Croce, Gentile, and others recognized, there were certainly Renaissance-era predecessors to them. In fact one of the major projects of both Croce and Gentile, when they turned their attentions to the Italian Renaissance, was to find Italian antecedents to immanentist styles of thought, thereby illuminating the forgotten contribution of the Italian nation to modernity. And both located the central genius of the Renaissance in the idea that Italian Renaissance thinkers were the first Europeans to turn from transcendence to immanence, even if the thinkers themselves were not always wholly conscious of the revolutionary break they were effecting.[4] Croce and Gentile, however, both rang particular changes on the immanentist theme, and as time went by their thought separated dramatically, with Croce verging more toward immanentism and Gentile recapturing a kind of transcendentalism in his devotion to what he called "actual idealism." A question of long standing has been to what extent each influenced the other, and it now seems pretty well accepted that Gentile was a greater influence on Croce than vice versa. So in individuating the two, it is best to begin with Gentile, even though he was the younger of the two thinkers.

Gentile, born in Sicily, had his university education at Pisa, studying with Donato Jaja and through him coming into contact with the work of Bertrando Spaventa, a professor at the University of Naples and a Hegelian.[5] Gentile began as a student of literature but quickly moved to philosophy. A revelatory early work is Gentile's second book, a critical study of Karl Marx from a Hegelian perspective.[6] There we see Gentile's belief that Marx had erred by concentrating too much on history as process, which tended to reduce art and religion to offshoots of history—to make them epiphenomena, rather than what Gentile believed they were: manifestations of the human Spirit, which Gentile conceived as an immanent absolute. Gentile then came to know Benedetto Croce, and the two began their long friendship and collaboration. In 1914 Gentile was awarded the chair that Jaja had occupied at the University of Pisa, and then in 1917 he moved to a professorship at the University of Rome. In 1922 he became the first minister of education of the Fascist regime; then, upon resigning, he helped in the founding and became the first head of the National Fascist Institute of Culture. He was assassinated by Communist partisans in Florence in April 1944. He was an academic insider as well as a public intellectual, concerned with both education and the specifically Italian philosophical tradition. He was also a powerful philosophical thinker.

In this capacity, Gentile believed in what he called the Spirito, or Spirit, a universal force immanent in all humanity that transcended religion and was continually evolving. He was strongly indebted to Hegel, and in fact Gentile's "Spirito" is similar in most ways to Hegel's "Geist." Gentile called his type of philosophy "actual idealism," by which he meant that his style of thought merged a concern for finding universal absolutes with the particular, phenomenological world. We are percipient beings, he suggested, and we perceive the world around us as separate from us, as if we are outside of the reality of nature, looking in. This, however, is a fundamental mistake, according to Gentile, which makes us "less than the earthworms that creep about unnoticed by the foot that crushes them."[7] To think this way, maintaining an essential separateness from the world—in other words, to say that our subjectivities are fundamentally separate from the objective nature with which they interact—is to say that "we are nothing, because we do not belong to reality."[8] Instead, Gentile wished to evolve a philosophy that transcended the subject-object dichotomy. He believed that he had done this with his "actual idealism," and he was convinced, moreover, that his philosophy was the natural outgrowth of Western philosophy, the next step in the evolution of human Spirit. For Gentile, *philosophy* equals *the history of philosophy* (as it had for Hegel), which is to say that the story of the unfolding of philosophical thought is in fact the story of human spiritual evolution. Thought, for Gentile, *is* reality, not something standing outside of reality.

Christianity was an important part of this story, because it included human will and agency in shaping the world.[9] For the pre-Christian ancients, to solve the problem of plurality meant to posit a world of transcendence. But the true message of Christianity, in Gentile's opinion, was that if the divine will were to be fulfilled, it required human concurrence: "though I have the gift of prophecy, and understand all mysteries, and all knowledge . . . and have not charity, I am nothing," Saint Paul had written.[10] The charity of which Paul spoke was to Gentile an act of human will, and we human beings were essential to the equation of reality. Instead of positing a transcendent divinity whom we could never approach, we were required to collaborate, literally to work together with divinity. Gentile wanted to show that there was no real division between us and divinity, that in fact the transcendental distinction was effaced and divinity and humanity were one.

In Gentile's view, Christianity had been on track to do this early on, but with Augustine (354–430) it went astray and reverted to the subject-object transcendentalism of the ancient world. When Augustine, blinded by the concept of omnipotence as a category, suggested that God's grace was necessary for salvation and was a gift that one could not earn, he essentially made humanity impotent, deprived human beings of control over their destiny, and abased human dignity before an unknowable transcendent absolute. For Gentile, Italian Renaissance thinkers, with their strong focus on the dignity of humankind, reawakened from the long slumber of the Middle Ages and redefined the problem; with them opened the "*regnum hominis* [reign of man]. . . . Even now we work to recognize or understand the free activity of man, which in the Renaissance was violently affirmed against the transcendental views of the Middle Ages."[11] Still, most Renaissance thinkers could not find the language to overcome the seemingly inherent transcendentalism of Western thought; their achievements were glimmering adumbrations of achievements of the human Spirit yet to be attained.[12] With Kant, real idealism was born. There was a synthesis between the thinking subject and the objective world, a synthesis that the act of thought itself represented.[13] For Gentile, however, even Kant made the mistake of allowing the different sorts of acts of thought to turn into concepts, to lose their character as *unities* of subject and object; thus Kant wound up turning these unities into concepts rather than acts.

Gentile responded with his philosophy of actual idealism, wherein the act of thinking itself does not just create reality; it *is* the only reality.[14] Influenced strongly by Hegel, Gentile suggested that the act of thinking is primarily dialectical and is a process that goes through different stages.[15] And thought evolves: its stages can be distinguished, and the evolution of the human Spirit is revealed and unfolded in the stages of thought that have evolved through history. Despite his many differences from Kant, he remained fundamentally Kantian in the sense that he believed it was the place of philosophy and philosophical reasoning to show demonstratively how reality is structured. He also shared the notion that philosophy as such was a regulative discipline, in the sense that, since all disciplines were looking for truth, and since philosophy was best at evaluating truth claims, it naturally stood at the top of all disciplines. Philosophy could, indeed must, achieve universal truths, even if these truths must always be understood as rooted in the actual world as it is experienced and configured by human beings. Importantly, this sort of philosophical speculation was thought to be adequately predictive: one could do things like found educational and societal systems on principles derived from the right sort of philosophical speculation.

There was a prophetic side to Gentile. He clearly believed that his own exposition of actual idealism represented the next and most important phase in the evolution of Spirit, and, as important, others believed him as well. He became a very public intellectual and was entrusted with weighty political responsibilities; he had an important hand in much of the educational reform associated with the Italian Fascist government (1922–44). We should keep in mind that some of the initial reforms that he carried out owed their origin to formulations he developed in concert with his older friend and collaborator, Benedetto Croce, when the latter was the minister of education in the last cabinet of Prime Minister Giovanni Giolitti. But it was Gentile who became, self-consciously, the "philosopher of Fascism."

In 1922 the Fascist Party took power in Italy and received full powers from the Italian Parliament in November of that year to carry out its educational reforms, which were effected the following year.[16] The reforms were certainly not as sweeping in practice as they were in theory, and many reforms simply represented the evolution of processes already under way. Still, changes did occur, and Gentile, who was made minister of education in 1923, was their primary author. As to secondary schools, an increased prominence was given to Latin across the board, that is, not only in the classical Lyceum-style school, but in the more technical sorts of schools as well. The Latin language was to be taught in such a fashion that it would reveal the inner life behind the text, not just the particularities of "sterile grammatical rules." At all levels, instructors were to teach the language so that it revealed and interacted with history, and history was to be taught in a way that emphasized Italy and the Italian nation, even as one recognized that Italy was situated within a plurality of other cultures.

Universities remained largely the same, at least at the outset, though one major reform that was already under way was in the idea of the university: a great autonomy was accorded to the universities themselves, taking an obvious cue from the nineteenth-century German idea of *Einsamkeit und Freiheit* — solitude and freedom to pursue research independent of close state control.[17] Students had more freedom in shaping their own curricula and faculty in designing them, though major officials were still appointees of the state. Unsurprisingly, as time passed, the demands of an increasingly totalitarian state necessitated more and more state intervention at all levels of education. Increasing centralization and the augmented prominence of religion in elementary and secondary education conspired to alter dramatically the spirit of much of the *riforma Gentile,* which, although acknowledging the importance of traditional religious instruction at the elementary educational level (toward the end of teaching basic morality), was secular in outlook, in a sense. That is, at the secondary level and higher, the original intent was to educate students in such a way that they would come to a truly philosophical understanding of the gradual evolution of the human Spirit and their own — and Italy's — place in that evolving story.[18] Nations are the tangible manifestations of Spirit, in Gentile's view, and they exist so that the ultimate in human liberty can be attained. The terms *human* and *liberty* have to be understood in distinct ways, however. A human being is one who partakes fully of the Spirit of humanity; not all citizens do this; not all attain, Gentile wrote as early as 1902, "to the actual exercise of that 'reason' (concrete, historical reason) that is recognized as the specific difference of humanity. They have the appearance of men, but not the substance, the spirit, the true humanity; and hence they cannot count as men. And they cannot, for example, make laws."[19] In other words, the many, to achieve true liberty, need strong leaders who understand how to guide them toward the immanent reality of the human Spirit. Gentile obviously partook of a very long tradition of philosophical idealism dating back to Plato, something we should keep in mind when we turn later to Kristeller.

Stepping back, we can see that, overall, this was the legacy of educational reform in early-twentieth-century Italy: more Latin, more consciousness of the Italian nation in history, more autonomous, German-style universities. As mentioned, some of the *riforma Gentile* originated with discussions between Gentile and Benedetto Croce, so it is appropriate now to turn to Croce and compare him with Gentile.

Croce, too, presents an interesting manifestation of the public intellectual and in many ways stands in contrast to Gentile.[20] For the most part, he lived outside of university circles, though he was comfortable among academics. He was a person of means, designing his own course of study and preferring for the most part to stay away from active political life, though he was made a senator for life in 1910 and, as mentioned, held for a short time the position of minister of education. He had great literary influence, however, and was as much a public intellectual as Gentile—more so, if we consider that his was the greater reputation outside of Italy.[21] In addition to founding the journal *La critica,* he had a long-standing association with the Italian publisher Laterza, a collaborative relationship that allowed him to exercise great influence in Italy and to be, as the decades wore on, an effective countervoice to Fascism.[22] His friendship and association with Gentile was perhaps the most important one of his life. At first, things were congenial. In the 1890s Croce had become a major figure on the Italian intellectual landscape, and when he decided to found *La critica* in 1903, he invited Gentile, then only twenty-eight years old, to collaborate with him as coeditor.[23] The two thinkers, however, evolved differently, and their opposition was made manifest in a well-known and at the time still friendly polemic that took literary form in 1913 and which Croce initiated. An early glimpse into Croce's opposition is provided by a letter he wrote to Karl Vossler, the German scholar of Italian literature, with whom Croce had a fifty-year-long friendship. The letter tells a lot, not only about the relationship that Croce and Gentile shared, but also about their different styles of thought, so it is worthwhile to pause for a moment and examine it.[24]

> I am going to work on philosophy only when I find the inspiration, because I don't like being a professional philosopher. On the other hand, you will have noticed that Gentile has taken a certain direction in his thought, which differentiates itself from mine because his thought tends to resolve everything into self-consciousness; and this direction already has quite a number of adherents. I am waiting in the hope that he matures or shakes off this momentary impulse before I argue with him; and if it dissolves by itself without my opposition and argument, so much the better. I haven't been inclined to oppose myself [to Gentile's tendency] because the opposition would turn on the lofty peaks of metaphysics—and this against a friend and collaborator who is to me *tamquam frater* [like a brother].

Croce opposes a philosophy that sees itself as self-sufficient, for it tends toward dogmatism:

The truth is that I believe the direction he has taken is harmful because it flattens all of life's oppositions and tensions, it weakens the energies of judgement, imagination, will, and winds up turning into a kind of mysticism.

His own mission was different, he confessed:

> My effort, instead, has been — within the ample bosom of unity — to allow all distinctions and oppositions to flourish and to found a system of judgments on life — a living system, one that changes with life itself but is constant in its changing. But this need, that I feel deeply, for a philosophy that is also *judgment,* is not felt equally by those of other temperaments, who are always looking for the peace of the soul in philosophy and who acquiesce in the immobile contemplation of the everlasting One.

The evolving intellectual opposition between the two would lead subsequently to political opposition and to an open break in 1925, when Croce wrote an anti-Fascist countermanifesto to Gentile's Fascist intellectuals' manifesto. Even in the early years, however, when the relationship between the two thinkers remained friendly, it is clear how differently they came to view the world. Gentile was the real philosophical idealist, who believed that there was a realm above that of everyday human activity, a level of reality in which truth and beauty reposed, to which only a real philosopher could have access. For him there was a hierarchy of disciplines; philosophy stood at the top, ponderous, grave, and, when practiced correctly, beyond dispute in the truth of its conclusions. Croce was different.

Croce's thought was distinguished by the fact that he was a philosopher of history who always retained a firm tie to an aesthetics grounded in the experiential realm of literary art; in effect, he was more of a real immanentist than Gentile. Like Gentile, Croce believed that universal truths could only be located in human experience. Process, change, and contingency always had to be figured into accounts of how the world worked and how things have come to be the way they are. Although he rejected most of Marx's relentless appeal to universal economic laws, the focus on process that was a part of Marx's legacy always remained with Croce.[25] In this sense, he was conditioned by his early association with Antonio Labriola, the Marxist historian whose lectures Croce attended in Naples in the late 1890s. Importantly, Labriola had stressed the notion that the goal of research was questioning, which he opposed to dogmatism. The scholar's task was not to come up with tidy generalizations summarizing an epoch or a historical phenomenon but rather to stimulate discourse and free thought, and even publishing had to be done in a certain antidogmatic way. As Labriola wrote in one of his most famous works, "the cult and dominion of words succeeds in corrupting and blotting out the real and living sense of things."[26] The function of an intellectual was the Socratic one of helping others learn to think freely, to think *socially,* and in the world of others.[27] This is the legacy Croce took from Italy's foremost Marxist thinker before Gramsci, though in the more structurally Marxist respects, Croce would turn away from Labriola.[28]

In his early career, Croce made his mark when he advocated and adapted the position of the literary scholar Francesco De Sanctis, that history was an art, not a science.[29] This led Croce to develop his influential theory of (predominantly literary) aesthetics, in which poetic intuition played a decisive role. Croce also decidedly and deliberately subordinated philosophy to history, and he resisted the appellation *philosopher.* In the words of David D. Roberts, Croce "concluded that although rigorous philosophizing remained essential, there could be no definitive, systematic philosophy."[30] History, with its dynamism and consciousness of the constancy of change, *became* Croce's philosophy. History deals with the actual world, but, as he wrote, "it is not so with philosophy, or, if you like, with the traditional idea of a philosophy which has its eyes fixed on heaven, and expects supreme truth from that quarter. This division of heaven and earth, this dualist conception of a reality which transcends reality, of metaphysics over physics" is the relic, for Croce, of an outdated transcendentalism, which itself was vanquished by the rise of historical criticism: "It can be said that once transcendental philosophy was subjected to historical criticism, philosophy itself ceased to enjoy an autonomous existence because its claim to autonomy was founded upon its metaphysical character."[31] This turn to historical criticism owes its origins, for Croce, to the thinkers of the Italian Renaissance and was fully realized in their true successor, Giambattista Vico.[32] And when discussing the problems of periodization in general, Croce recognized the usefulness and inevitable importance of schematizing history into periods, but he violently rejected the tendency to associate one univocal character to each period:

> [F]rom forgetfulness of the practical origin and empirical use of divisions by chronological periods arise inextricable controversies about the character of this

epoch or that, for example of the "Middle Ages" or of "humanism" or the "baroque" or "romanticism." A vain attempt is made to arrive at elaborate definitions which will embrace all the facts contained in these chronological partitions, whereas the real problem, in these cases, is to define the universal forms and modes of the spirit which the titles indicate. These cannot be confined within chronological limits, but by their nature are extra-temporal.[33]

The task of the historian is not to find the "essence" of a bounded chronological period, which Croce rejects as nonexistent. Rather, the historian must move deftly through time and, out of the many plural tendencies within a given time frame, draw attention to those that are most important; in short, the historian-philosopher must be conscious of the fact — in the tradition of Vico — that he is himself *creating*, rather than *describing*, history.[34]

Finally, for Croce, history was the history of liberty; and liberty was in many ways the key principle of human life, the immanent Spirit made manifest, and the manner in which Spirit continually evolved in the world of human beings. It would be an illusion, in Croce's view, to say that liberty can be oppressed, for even in periods of oppression, the seeds are sown for an awakening of liberty: "[W]hat then is the anguish that men feel for the liberty that has been lost, the invocations, the lost hopes, the words of love and anger which come from the hearts of men in certain moments and in certain ages of history? . . . these are not philosophical nor historical truths, nor are they errors or dreams; they are movements of moral conscience; they are history in the making."[35] Even though he turned from Marxism as a political philosophy, Croce retained the dialectical form of historical reasoning — Heraclitean in origin, really, though assuming modern form with Hegel, then being reified by Marx — which suggested that the unity of the world grew out of the deft emergence of Spirit that fashioned itself out of contradiction: epochs of one character were succeeded by epochs of a contradictory character, even as Spirit was gradually evolving, modernizing, and moving the world away from the false paradises of transcendence and toward the real world of praxis.[36]

In some ways, there were similarities between Croce and Gentile when it came to the responsibility of the historian looking back at the past, for Gentile too believed that one had to move diachronically and discern the past's most important aspects. But Gentile was never a friend of real dialecticism, and therein lies the real difference between them. Croce not only recognized but insisted upon the notion that countervailing tendencies were present not only as epoch succeeded epoch but also within epochs themselves. For Croce it would have been nihilistic to think that one could discern univocal stages of progress or divine a satisfactory teleology. History did not work that way, for Spirit manifested itself through conflict within conflict and could never be reduced to metaphysics. And for Croce, if he had a hierarchy of disciplines, history so conceived would have been at the top. For Gentile, in contrast, metaphysically oriented philosophy would have been at the top, and its goal was not to stop at the level of contradiction but rather to identify the contradictions and then resolve them.

Gentile became the institutional man of Italian Fascism, a well-known academic, a systematic philosopher who strove for a coherent immanentism based on action, undergirded by an unfolding, aprioristic logic, to the true principles of which philosophers alone were really privy. Croce remained an outsider, a self-consciously extrainstitutional man who chose to exercise his weighty intellectual leadership through privately run channels, who saw metaphysically oriented philosophy as decidedly subordinate to history, whose intellectual quest was to find "a living system, one that changes with life itself but is constant in its changing." To understand Eugenio Garin and Paul Oskar Kristeller fully, we will have to keep Croce and Gentile in mind, for they were important influences. It is not that Garin followed Croce exclusively nor Kristeller Gentile; the respective influences are rather to be located in a way of framing questions, a set of underlying concerns, and some fundamental presuppositions about what were seen as the most important emphases in conceiving Renaissance intellectual history. Overall, the most important difference between Garin and Kristeller is that Garin held a predominantly diachronic, historically oriented, immanentist outlook and Kristeller one of a synchronic, metaphysically oriented, transcendentalist idealism.

Diachrony and Synchrony: Eugenio Garin (1909-) and Paul Oskar Kristeller (1904-1999)

The diachronic approach, as I define it and as the Greek etymology of its name suggests, moves through time and seeks what is important in a given epoch for the future. Hence, in analyzing the Italian Renaissance, the intellectual historian will emphasize what he or she concludes is most important for the future, for modernity. How did the Renaissance adumbrate modernity, or even, how was the Renaissance modern? What, in the judgment of the historian, are the most important Renaissance attitudes toward the evolution of modern habits of thought? Who are the most important thinkers? These are the sorts of questions the diachronic approach leads one to pose, and Eugenio Garin's work is exemplary of this style of historical explanation. As we have seen above, this was a method dear to Croce, who believed the scholar should move through the vicissitudes and pluralities of time and note what is important in a given period, even as he recognizes that the tendencies he identifies as diachronically important are not the only identifiable ones.

The synchronic approach looks at things "all together in time" and attempts to take a kind of cultural snapshot of a given epoch. Theoretically, it looks less for the origins of modernity and more for the continuities with the past that a period possesses, as well as for a period's *self*-understanding. To be foregrounded here is the work of Paul Oskar Kristeller: out of the chaos of virtually untapped but relevant source materials that he found in Italian (and eventually European) manuscript libraries, he drew various elegant synchronic pictures of the period, creating theoretical frameworks that were as all-inclusive as possible. While Kristeller did not share many of Gentile's ideas and tendencies, in one respect he is strikingly similar: he too believed that traditional, "professional" philosophy was the highest and best form of thought. This love of metaphysical conceptualizing—for Kristeller very much in the tradition of Kant—was at the root of his research interests and of every major theoretical formulation that he evolved when approaching the intellectual history of the Italian Renaissance.

Eugenio Garin and Paul Oskar Kristeller are certainly not the only two major twentieth-century figures to have done influential work on Renaissance intellectual history, but they occupy poles on a kind of continuum within which much subsequent scholarship has positioned itself. Given what they were faced with, the lasting contributions of these scholars are immeasurable and of enduring value. It is also possible to see that these two major modes of conceptualizing Renaissance intellectual history have led to an impasse. Why did interest in Italian Renaissance intellectual history flag in North America? I suggest that both approaches, the diachronic and the synchronic, possess strengths but also undeniable weaknesses. The diachronic approach, on the one hand, can seem vague, since it necessarily leaves certain thinkers out of its larger accounts; blanket statements are made regarding a trend or an "-ism" (such as Renaissance humanism), but when one gets down to cases, one can always find contradic-tory examples that tend to render the larger point meaningless. The synchronic approach, on the other hand, can seem rigid, since it tends to freeze an often dynamic, developing movement in time, precisely by taking time and historical process out of its narratives.

One of the central problems of the Renaissance for both Garin and Kristeller was that of Renaissance *humanism*, as it has been for many other scholars.[37] What was it? What was its importance? Indisputably, one knew that there was, from at least the mid–fourteenth century onward, a tendency on the part of intellec-tuals to cultivate things that were believed to pertain to ancient, that is, Greco-Roman tradition, and that a label that had become attached to this tendency was *humanism*. Beyond that, interpretations varied greatly. Was humanism "philo-sophical"? Was it even itself a philosophy? Was it a literary movement? Was it a reawakening of the human spirit, a new view of what it meant to be human? Was it a revival of paganism? Was it a new way of conceiving Christianity? Was it a retarding factor on the development of Italian national culture or even on various modern forms of thought? As Garin and Kristeller came to maturity, scholarly accounts that embodied various of the just-mentioned positions were legion. Sometimes they were explicit about their underlying premises; more often than not the assumptions about the character of humanism were implicit: roiling beneath the calm surface of scholarly exposition lay turbulent vortices of national pride, disciplinary rigidities, and personal styles.[38] Both Garin and Kristeller wanted to resolve these ambiguities. Examining their two diverse ap-proaches to this problem will allow us most effectively to see how they differ.

Eugenio Garin has had a long academic career and has been very influen-tial, not only in Italian Renaissance studies, but in Italian intellectual life in general. The range of his work is remarkably broad: in addition to numerous works on the Renaissance, he has made major contributions to the history of thought from the Renaissance to the twentieth century, commenting on every-thing from the English Enlightenment—the subject of some of his earliest re-search—to the course of Italian philosophy in the twentieth century.[39] Garin was born in 1909; the formative years of his education were during the Fascist period in Italy, and he first encountered philosophy "officially" in 1923, in high school in Florence, just in time for the new curriculum of the *riforma Gentile*.[40] Although some of the "official" philosophy curriculum affected him, Garin, looking back from a distance of almost seventy years, said that it was through reading classical authors but especially other sorts of literature that he came to a real appreciation of what "philosophy" was. After encountering Dostoyevsky and Tolstoy, he writes: "I learned—or began to learn—not to look for philosophy only in books that proclaimed themselves philosophy books. I began to understand that philosophy—as I read later in Bertrand Russell—did not feed on itself alone, and that one of the ways of approach toward philosophizing is precisely reflection on the exemplary aspects of the various forms of human experience."[41] Early on, then, Garin sought to dissolve, rather than to accentuate, disciplinary boundaries. This concern would be especially evident in his interpretation of Italian Renaissance humanism, an interpretation that unvaryingly considered humanism as a movement of both literary *and* philosophical import, or rather, as a new way of thinking that was important precisely because it shattered then-existing disciplinary boundaries.

Soon thereafter, in 1925, Garin began university studies. He enrolled in the faculty of letters and became a philosophy major at the University of Florence; he was especially attracted early on by ethics and by the teachings of Ludovico Limentani. Through Limentani, Garin learned to appreciate "the inseparable link between a philosophy immersed in the 'conflicts' of individual and social life, and the richness of historical becoming." Limentani gave Garin "the sense of a way of doing philosophy and of making it face up to history." Garin, throughout his career, "attempted to remain faithful to his spirit."[42] Garin finished his university studies with exams and a thesis on English philosophy of the seventeenth and eighteenth centuries, which led eventually to a book in 1942.[43] These years, for Garin, meant also developing a method of reading. Because this method is in such contrast to Kristeller, it is worth quoting Garin's recollections at length:

> I became convinced that studying an author meant *reading him,* reading everything that he had left to us: to read every page of the author, every fragment, to such a point that one makes manifest every shadow of meaning, every internal tension, every minimal variation of tone, every echo of his reading, conversations, polemics, contrasts. For this method, it seemed fundamental to me to take the pulse of texts that appeared compact, to underline the variants of the sense of a term, recovering oscillations, uncertainties, conflicts.[44]

While close readings are also important to Kristeller, Garin's view is that it is necessary for the scholar to find internal tensions and contradictions in a text and that this in itself is a valuable method of proceeding. This, needless to say, is in stark contrast to the historiography of *synthetic* philosophy and has dialecticism at its very roots. As we shall see, Kristeller placed thinkers who were more synthetic on a higher rank, believing that synthetic philosophizing was in fact the highest form of reasoning. Garin's methodological stance does not necessitate that assumption.

Garin's study of figures from the English Enlightenment made him realize what a great debt they owed, even if it was often only implicit, to thinkers of the Italian Renaissance. This realization led him, eventually, to his study of Giovanni Pico della Mirandola (1463–94).[45] Most who have encountered the Italian Renaissance will have come across Pico, the Wunderkind of the Italian Renaissance, who proposed, in an open debate in Rome in 1486, to unite all knowledge. After Pope Innocent VIII forbade the debate, Pico was chastened, and some of the focus of his thought changed, as he joined the ranks of the Savonarolan party in Florence. In between, there had been polemics on all sides, dramatic events, and finally an early death. In short, in Pico's life as in that of few other Renaissance figures, one feels the overriding weight of one thing: *history*. When Garin came to realize the powerful imprint of history on Pico's life, he has suggested, another methodological point was solidified: he experienced the fall of an historiographical conception dear to the nineteenth and early twentieth centuries, that of "a philosophy of the sort that seemed totally rational, that grew on itself in a coherent line of reasoning, in which men and events are the bearers of a discourse that in itself is autonomous, even if, at times, there are pauses or 'irrational' offscourings, destined eventually to be individuated and expunged."[46] For Garin, in short, the rationalist tradition came to seem meaningless if divorced from history, if we understand *history* not as a progressive revelation of immanence but as a powerful force whose dialectical outlines were traceable but not deterministic. Especially since academic "disciplines" as they appear to us have not always existed with the same sorts of boundaries or presuppositions, to conceive of Italian Renaissance thought meant abandoning, insofar as possible, guiding assumptions regarding the nature of "philosophy." When, in the wake of the war, Garin set out to write a history of "Italian" philosophy, "the opportunity of looking for 'philosophy' in literature, in the natural sciences, in law, and in the moral sciences, became more and more evident."[47] Along the way, Garin realized the amount of unedited or incompletely edited Renaissance texts, and many of his scholarly efforts were devoted to making these texts available; from his early editions of Pico della Mirandola to his lengthy selection of Latin prose authors of the fifteenth century, Garin fostered the publication of little-known but important texts.[48]

Garin's own professional career began when he taught in a *Liceo*—an advanced high school—which he did in Palermo from 1931 to 1935, subsequently moving to a Liceo in Florence. From that time, 1935, until 1949, he taught contemporaneously at the University of Florence, in the Faculty of Letters.[49] He eventually moved on to become a professor at one of Italy's leading universities, the Scuola Normale Superiore di Pisa, and in the latter part of his career, he was the director of the Italian National Institute for Renaissance Studies, based in the elegant Palazzo Strozzi of Florence. He is now retired.

The most significant synthetic work among Garin's many writings on the Renaissance is an account of Italian humanism that was first published in German, a fact that deserves some explanation. In 1947 Ernesto Grassi, a prominent Italian intellectual who left Italy during the years of Fascism and settled in Switzerland, sponsored a publication of the German philosopher Martin Heidegger, with whom he had studied. The short treatise was entitled *Letter on Humanism,* and it took the form of an open letter that Heidegger had written to Jean Beaufret, in answer to Beaufret's question, "Comment redonner un sens au mot 'Humanisme'" (how to give back a meaning to the word *Humanism*).[50] To understand the importance of Heidegger's essay to our present purposes, we must highlight three factors.

First, Heidegger had throughout his career maintained the position that metaphysically based, aprioristic philosophy was at an end.[51] For him, thinkers such as Kant and Hegel, despite their immanentism and despite their many differences, nonetheless philosophized deductively, believing that one had to discern immutable principles to philosophize about the world as it is. For Heidegger, that sort of philosophizing was mistaken, since it was anthropological, in that the philosopher still starts from things that are present to him (things that, as Heidegger expressed it, were in the clearings of the forest, and not in the woods). German idealism was, in the final analysis, the last phase of the long deterioration of philosophy since the pre-Socratics, for it was after the pre-Socratics that philosophy concerned itself with beings and not with Being, or rather with "being that is present/there" (Heidegger's *Dasein*) and not with Being itself. For Heidegger, the real task was instead to discover what normally lay hidden from human beings, hidden in the woods: Being itself, which, although assumed and thus seeming to be close to our human experience, was actually far from actual articulation precisely because it seemed so close; instead it was hidden, and the postmetaphysical philosopher had to try to access it in its *Unverborgenheit,* its unhidden state.

In his *Letter on Humanism,* Heidegger suggested that, since any understanding of the term *humanism* began with some set of assumptions about human nature, it too was part of this age-old, essentially anthropological Western tradition now at an end: it had essentially no philosophical importance or distinction, since it too dealt with the limits of rational knowledge. In his *Letter,* we see, of course, that Heidegger, if he was aware of the vast variety of still little-known Renaissance texts, betrayed little knowledge of their existence. Nonetheless, his overriding judgment was that humanism was of no lasting importance philosophically. For Heidegger believes that we find the first humanism in ancient Rome, embedded in the term *humanitas,* the Latin translation of the Greek *paideia,* which for the Romans (so the argument goes) was a way to distinguish themselves from the barbarians and vaunt *Greek* culture as it was then taught in the Imperial period—in short, a very late and somewhat atrophied version of Greek culture: "But Greece was seen in its late manifestation and even this was seen in a Roman way." As to the Italian Renaissance, "the so-called Renaissance of the fourteenth and fifteenth centuries" was nothing more than "a *renascentia romanitatis*—a renascence of Romanness." A truer humanism was found in the eighteenth-century German reawakening of Greek mentalities, with thinkers "bei uns," such as Winckelmann, Goethe, and Schiller.[52] In this sentiment, Heidegger revealed the strong imprint of German idealistic neohumanism, with its propensity for Hellenism.

Second, Heidegger was a mentor of Kristeller to whom Kristeller retained a complicated lifelong loyalty, despite Heidegger's open endorsement of National Socialism. Third, in the years immediately after the Second World War, one of the problems that, as we have seen, both Croce *and* Gentile had raised was particularly alive: how had Italy and Italian traditions contributed to the evolution of European intellectual life? Thus, it is of great significance that Ernesto Grassi, having sponsored the publication of Heidegger, also sponsored the publication of Garin's synthetic account of Italian humanism. It signaled a volition on the part of certain Italian intellectuals to highlight the *philosophical* importance of Italian Renaissance humanism, which they believed had been veiled unduly by a newly arrived and overly revered metaphysical tradition, one that sought eternal instead of historicized truths and was based in Hellenizing, German, neohumanistic idealism. For historicists like Garin, this was a tradition to which Heidegger, despite his postmetaphysical agenda, was strongly indebted. Garin's work fit well with Grassi's aims, in that it was in effect a response to Heidegger and, in a larger sense, a response to German tradition. As we shall see, Garin also came to see his *Italian Humanism* as a rejoinder to Kristeller.

What was this important philosophical contribution made by the Italian humanists? In *Italian Humanism,* Garin argued that the best way to characterize Italian Renaissance humanism was as a fundamentally new way of thinking.[53] It was a movement whose essence was determined by its attitude toward the past, and this attitude had to do with understanding the ancients and cultivating them within their own historical environment. "The 'barbarians'," Garin wrote (meaning medieval and contemporary scholastic thinkers stigmatized by Renaissance thinkers as backward), "were not barbarians because they were ignorant of the classics, but because they did not understand them within the truth of their historical situation."[54] He goes on:

> So, in humanism one cannot, nor should one, distinguish the discovery of the ancient world and the discovery of man, because they were one and the same; because to discover the antique as such was to measure oneself in relation to it, to distance oneself from it, and to place oneself in relation to it. It meant time and memory, and a sense of human creation, of earthly work, and of responsibility. Not by chance were the greatest humanists in great part men of state, active men, accustomed to freely working in the public life of their time.[55]

The achievements of humanists were rooted and concretized in "humanistic 'philology,' which is consciousness of the past as such, a worldly vision of reality, and a human explanation of the history of men."[56]

Humanism, in other words, contributed a distinctive, activist ethos toward living in the world, and it did so by means of philology and rhetoric. Humanists, the important ones, were the thinkers who emphasized a break with the past, who, through meticulous scholarship, came to believe that Aristotle's logic was not the only logic, that the Bible could also be read for purely historical reasons, that, in short, ancient authorities were not the only authorities and that the past had a real, definable and identifiable historicity vis-à-vis the present. Humanist philology, by historicizing antiquity, came to a more modern view of what the doctrines of antiquity were: "thoughts of men, products of a certain culture, results of partial and particular experiences: not oracles of nature or of God, revealed by Aristotle or Averroes, but rather human images and contrivances."[57] Humanists were active, and they used their new understanding of their own relation to antiquity, gained by philological labor, to comment on and intervene in the world in which they lived. Those thinkers who did not fit this trend could be forgone, or if not forgone, relegated to a sort of second rank, since they did not contribute to the period's guiding genius.[58] It is a search for the guiding genius or main contribution of a period that drives a diachronically oriented historian, who sees it as his responsibility to isolate and represent what is most important about a period. Before we move to Paul Oskar Kristeller, we should examine briefly the work of another diachronic Renaissance historian, Hans Baron, whose influence on twentieth-century North American scholarship on the Italian Renaissance was immense, despite his never having held a permanent university position.[59]

Hans Baron (1900–1988) located the Renaissance's distinctive contribution in republicanism. He saw the years at the turn of the Quattrocento as a crucible of Western civilization, an archetypal conflict between freedom (represented by Florentine republicanism) and tyranny (represented by the encroachment of Milanese despotism) played out on the battlefield of the Italian city-states. Baron's thesis was clear: the Florentine war with Milan of 1402 was the central, pivotal event that led to the development of modern consciousness. As Florentine diplomats and rhetoricians readied for the Visconti assault, they came upon a felicitous marriage of efficacious political rhetoric and action. Nascent modern republicanism and civic freedom were buttressed by the classics, as Renaissance thinkers looked specifically to the Roman Republic for solutions to and paradigms for their modern problems. A new Latin prose style, based on Cicero, was the means by which these ideas concerning liberty were to be communicated. Under the pressure of war and struggle, there emerged in Florence a new theory that married classical studies to political ideology: civic humanism, which Baron termed as such as early as the 1920s.[60] This united an activist ethos to a specific conception about the place of the individual in politics. All citizens had the right and the duty to participate in the active governance of their state. Those who shared this conception were the important humanists, and all were judged against this yardstick.

Baron never claimed that there were not humanistically oriented intellectuals working for tyrants, nor, if one reads him carefully, does he even say that the

Renaissance was only or even primarily about republicanism. The overwhelming weight of his output, however, and the seemingly synthetic coherence of his civic humanism thesis made it clear what the most important legacy of the Florentine Renaissance was. We see that, in Baron's view, the historian could, indeed must, make *judgments* about past figures and past epochs. They are not all equal, and it is the responsibility of the historian to research the right figures, to place emphasis on the ones who contributed to the right trends, in order thereby to document the evolution of modernity and the contribution that the period under study, here the Renaissance, made to history's evolution. The paradigm is a formalist one, with familiar enough phases of approach, perfection, and decline. Petrarch (1304–74), for example, was characterized by Baron as having one foot in the Middle Ages and one foot in the Renaissance, a Moses who was allowed to see the promised land but not to enter.[61] Coluccio Salutati (d. 1406) was a famous humanist chancellor and was responsible among other things for creating a vital circle of leading humanists and, thanks to this circle's enthusiasm, for bringing Greek to the Florentine Renaissance.[62] He also wrote, in a famous treatise, *De tyranno (On the Tyrant),* that benign one-man rule, rather than republicanism, was, in an ideal world, the best sort of government; and in another work, the *De saeculo et religione,* he described the world of action with contempt, stressing the beauties of the contemplative life to a friend about to enter a monastery.[63] For Baron, then, these were "medieval," that is, nonrepublican, attitudes, which had to be fleshed out and discussed for what they were: a retrograde tendency against the advance of modernity.[64] The phase of perfection in Florentine humanism was reached with Leonardo Bruni (d. 1444), also a chancellor of Florence, whom Baron saw as a heroic figure, an avatar of republican freedom. Later phases of decadence were clearly discernible. And later areas of Italian history were then judged on the basis of the Florentine republican paradigm. Baron's views were extremely influential in the United States and represented a watershed moment in the historiography of the Renaissance. It was the first time in the history of the field that a scholar had made an argument, translatable in American terms, in which politics was so directly and intimately connected to culture: neither one was an epiphenomenon of the other, and they were unified in what seemed to be a powerful synthesis. Moreover, Baron took a stand on what the best aspects of modernity were and how those were found, at least ideologically, in the Florentine Renaissance: "participatory politics, constitutional government, and security for private property."[65] In a postwar United States of America, with the historical profession in the 1950s and early 1960s moving toward consensus vis-à-vis the importance of the values of the "free" versus the "totalitarian" world, Baron's views naturally attracted historians' attentions.[66]

However, soon after Baron's initial major works were published in the 1950s, scholars began to see problems in the sleek ship that he had built. Some questioned the sincerity of the Florentine intellectuals, the "civic" humanists, who were writing in praise of republicanism: were they simply expressing the ideology of Florence's ruling elite? What about the fact that Florence was far from a modern understanding of a republic, given the restricted nature of political participation, and seemed much closer to an oligarchy, with a relatively few ruling families sharing most of the power? How to understand the fact that a number of thinkers throughout Italy who shared the literary and cultural ideals of much of what humanism perforce represented—classicism, love of things ancient, disdain for scholasticism—nonetheless worked at the courts of despots and wrote just as enthusiastically in favor of one-man rule as Florentines did about republicanism? If the synthesis between classicism and republicanism was so powerful an organic unity, then why, when humanism spread elsewhere in Europe, was it not always or even often accompanied by republican politics?

Buffeted by winds of this strength, Baron's ship sprang a number of leaks, and—among specialized scholars working in the field—has now all but sunk. In its day, however, the ship traveled widely, and Baron's civic humanism thesis is a view still encountered in survey textbooks. In considering Baron himself, it is important to emphasize the social circumstances in which he wrote. Baron was part of the important diaspora of German-Jewish scholars who, forced from their own country, greatly enriched and transformed the cultures of Britain and the United States. As various scholars have noticed (most recently and exhaustively, Riccardo Fubini), Baron was a dedicated Weimar republican who saw this republic destroyed and was forced to leave it by the twentieth century's most hated tyranny, Nazi Germany.[67] It is unsurprising that he invested so much faith in the ideology of republicanism that the Florentines expounded and unsurprising as well that he cast the Renaissance as a dramatic struggle of freedom versus tyranny.

I have lumped Baron together with Garin because both are clearly diachronic in style: each starts with certain ideas about the nature of modernity, then seeks and emphasizes those aspects of the Renaissance that contributed to modernity.

Moreover, each was highly influential on subsequent historiography: Garin in Italy, Baron in the United States. They are, however, fundamentally very different sorts of historians. Baron was a political historian drawn into the orbit of cultural history in the tradition of the German luminaries Ernst Troeltsch and especially Walter Goetz.[68] Baron's theories about Renaissance humanism were not undergirded by complex philosophical ideas, nor by a philosophy of history.[69] The picture was relatively simple: an embattled, self-defined republic was threatened by a state with a fundamentally different-seeming political tradition; the immediate threat in 1402 crystallized intellectual developments that were brewing but previously inchoate; these developments were forced in a quantum way to come to literary fruition; and so the Renaissance, the real Renaissance of individual activist freedom, was born. The theory was simple and precise, it was teachable, and it seemed to engage politics and culture in a clear, cogent, and unified way. Eugenio Garin's diachrony, however, was much less given to quantum leaps and, in the tradition of Croce, could tolerate more ambiguities. For Garin, the Florentine war with Milan was of course important but could never in the Crocean tradition be given the explanatory weight Baron accorded it. Culture did not work that way: the global causes behind the emergence of the real spirit of freedom were never precisely isolatable in time, and the development of spirit was not linear and univocal but sinuous and complex; its agents in the subcelestial realm were not always even conscious of the epochal role they were playing. However, it was Baron's diachrony rather than Garin's more subtle version that made its way into American interpretations of Italian Renaissance intellectual history.

To return for just a moment to Eugenio Garin and his *Italian Humanism,* early on a revelatory moment occurs, when Garin, highlighting the importance of humanist philology, writes that "it is precisely that 'philological' attitude that, as an historiographical tradition which is today all too easily despised once saw, constitutes precisely the new 'philosophy,' or rather the new method of posing problems, which should not be considered, as a certain scholar believes, alongside of traditional philosophy, as a secondary aspect of Renaissance culture, but rather as itself effectively philosophizing."[70] There is a protest here: Garin is certain that Italian humanism, with its philological awareness and intense scrutiny of ancient Latin, was not only literary but *philosophical* in content. As such, it should not be dismissed as a retarding factor in Italian cultural development, nor as "merely" rhetorical. More importantly, as one sees from the footnote on that page, the "certain scholar" to whom Garin is referring is none other than Paul Oskar Kristeller.[71] Later in life, in the autobiographical memoir to which I have referred above, Garin characterized his own opinion on humanism in the following terms:

> Very far from—indeed, profoundly against—the thesis dear to Kristeller of a Renaissance humanism as a substantially grammatical fact, of a Renaissance which on the speculative plane was only a continuator of the Middle Ages, and as such, in truth, inconsistent, I have tried on the contrary to individuate its particularity precisely in the deep nexus of its multiple aspects, and above all in the conception of life, of man, and of man's activity. . . . Here, exactly, are the complex roots of modern civilization, without denying the deep connections of the preceding era, but also without attenuating the no less deep differences.[72]

Humanity and its manifestation in the lived world are the concerns of Garin, who renounces an overly metaphysical view of the history of thought. Although Kristeller is mentioned once or twice in Garin's memoir, he is in some sense conspicuous by his absence, and it is clear from the writings of both men that they had deep-seated differences, despite their cordial relationship. It is thus now an opportune time to turn our attentions to Kristeller, the opposite end of the continuum.

Kristeller's personal story is a dramatic one.[73] Like Baron, he was part of the German-Jewish diaspora of intellectuals caused by the rise of National Socialism in Germany. There is a poignant moment that Kristeller relates in a memoir published in 1994.[74] He tells that, when he was a little boy in Berlin, he once refused to shake hands with someone to whom he hadn't been properly introduced, and he offers this incident as an instance of a certain stubbornness that he says he possessed throughout his life. And there is one overriding idea that he clung to very stubbornly throughout his entire, often turbulent life, which he mentions in numerous places as providing a source of comfort and strength in a changing world. This is the idea of the superiority of a rationalist tradition in philosophical thought, which is the undergirding theoretical leitmotif of everything he ever wrote. He strongly associated this idea with the thought of Plato, Aristotle, and Kant; and it was Hellenic, not Roman, in origin. Also important was the general notion, which is part of this tradition, that there are stable realities in the universe that we can never access on earth but which we must nonetheless always strive to attain. Ultimately, it is on these stable realities that we predicate our truth claims, and even if we know that the things we discuss on earth can never be truly verified or compared against the eternally True, we nonetheless believe that the eternal truths exist and that our mundane truths correspond in some way to those larger realities.[75] Thus, when we make truth claims, we should make sure that they are as unambiguous and inclusive of varied evidence as possible, since even though we recognize the mutability of the human world, in our scholarship we should try to attain to the immutable and universally True.

To use the categories we have previously encountered, philosophically speaking, Kristeller was a transcendentalist, rather than an immanentist. Historically, however, he was very much an empiricist. Or to put it another way: metaphysically he was a Platonist, methodologically an Aristotelian. In this world, we should focus, Kristeller insisted, on problems we can hope to solve.[76] Philosophy dealt with higher truths; history was on a lower plane and dealt with the world of human beings: to have any hope of attaining to the world of universal truth, the historian must formulate solvable questions whose answers can account for all possible objections. This sort of orientation lends itself very well to a synchronic style of interpretation, precisely because of its love of universals.

And Kristeller's approach to humanism was indeed synchronic. For Kristeller, the problem with the term *humanism* was the problem of all "isms": whenever a specific definition was offered, so many exceptions could be found that the definition seemed so vague as to be useless. So he sought definitions that were grounded in Renaissance circumstances. The first problem was the word *humanism* itself, *humanismus,* which was not used in the Renaissance. In Kristeller's day, moreover, the word was employed in many varying senses; while it was used in conjunction with the Italian Renaissance, it was also often identified with phenomena as variegated as German idealism, humanitarianism, and the kind of pragmatism (often termed *secular humanism*) represented by John Dewey and others of his philosophical persuasion (some of whom were Kristeller's colleagues in the philosophy department at Columbia University).[77]

The problem was that these movements, in trying to find antecedents to their own views, would look back and find predecessors in the Italian Renaissance. The pictures they drew were often skewed toward their own views and could be accommodated only with great difficulty to the very varied, scarcely understood intellectual phenomena of the Italian Renaissance. Moreover, in the early twentieth century, scholars interested in the Middle Ages reacted strongly against what they saw as an unjustified tendency on the part of modern historians, from Jules Michelet and Burckhardt onward, to accept at face value the judgments of humanists regarding the lack of culture in the Middle Ages. When this "revolt of the medievalists" was complete, around 1930 or so, medievalists began finding humanism in the Middle Ages as well, in Thomas Aquinas (1225–74), among others.[78] By the time Kristeller was established, the term had become almost wildly equivocal and had so many different meanings that it seemed, in the end, to mean nothing. For someone of Kristeller's rationalist leanings, this was an intolerable situation. What to do?

Kristeller's goal was to try to find Renaissance-era meanings. Roughly contemporaneously, Kristeller and Augusto Campana, in separate articles, found that the word *humanism* was used for the first time by a German *Gymnasium* teacher in the first decade of the nineteenth century, to refer to a pedagogical system rooted in the Greek and Roman classics and dimly associated with the Renaissance.[79] Closer to home, they found that the word *humanist (humanista)* did exist in the Renaissance, in late-fifteenth- and early-sixteenth-century Italian university student slang. It referred to a teacher of the *studia humanitatis,* the humanities, whose five subjects included grammar, rhetoric, history, poetry, and moral philosophy (ethics). Here, then, was something grounded in contemporary categories. For Kristeller, humanism was identified with the gradual shift in interest among Italian Renaissance intellectuals to the five mentioned subjects and was properly seen not as a philosophy but as a phase in the history of the rhetorical tradition. This was buttressed by the sorts of employment opportunities that humanists found: they were secretaries to republics, to princes, to the pope, hired pens of all sorts; they were also teachers.

Kristeller's approach is synchronic because, again reflecting the Greek etymology of the word, it treats things "all together in time" (*sun chronos*) and does so in a double-faceted manner. First, and most importantly, it is all-inclusive. There was one thing and one thing only that a certain group of Renaissance intellectuals shared. This was a commitment, either implicit or explicit, to the branches of literature that fell under the rubric of the *studia humanitatis,* those five subjects mentioned above. These thinkers did not all share a certain political ideology (as one could highlight Florentine republican thinkers, one could just as well, and contemporaneously, have found litterateurs working at the courts of Renaissance despots); they did not all share a certain activist view of the world and of the place of humanity within it (one could find humanists, most notably

Petrarch, who were not always enthusiastic about life in the world); they did not all share certain religious or, indeed, antireligious views; and they did not all share the tendency to want to surpass the ancients (witness the Ciceronian movement, whose firmest adherents used in their own Latin writings no phrase not found in Cicero's). They only shared one thing: a commitment to the five mentioned subjects. In 1972 Kristeller wrote concerning the humanists, "[W]e must try to keep all their achievements in mind when we want to generalize, and must not merely overemphasize some features that have a special appeal for us, at the same time omitting others that may be less appealing or fashionable."[80]

The second reason Kristeller's approach is synchronic is that it compresses many developments in Renaissance intellectual life into a simple, easily understandable formula. It is as if Kristeller took a cultural snapshot of the humanist movement in the middle of the fifteenth century.[81] Or better, one might even say that in his account "time is suspended or abolished analytically, so that things that actually occur in the flow of time are treated as part of a uniform moment or epoch in which they simply coexist."[82] There is not much change in Kristeller's humanism. For example, as we now know from an excellent study by Benjamin Kohl, the five subjects of the *studia humanitatis* were not born from the head of Zeus as a unified cycle of disciplines. They evolved into one and in fact were not mentioned together until 1440, as part of the suggested library contents list that Tommaso Parentucelli, soon to become Pope Nicholas V, made for Cosimo de' Medici.[83] Moreover, at the school level at least, while humanist educators taught grammar, rhetoric, poetry, and history as separate subjects, moral philosophy was taught not as a subject in itself; rather, its lessons were epiphenomenal to the other subjects: moral lessons were drawn, but it was not a separate topic.[84] Still, Kristeller's point was that, implicitly or explicitly, there was a group from Petrarch's day onward whose literary practice was centered on the five mentioned disciplines.

In considering Kristeller's views, it is again useful to bring to bear certain social conditions.[85] Kristeller, like Baron, was constrained for the sake of his personal safety to leave Nazi Germany.[86] Before that, however, and as influential on his professional development, were Kristeller's early education and his university years. First and foremost, throughout his high school and university career, Kristeller studied with some of Germany's leading scholars, among whom we can name the great scholar of ancient Latin prose Eduard Norden; perhaps the greatest traditional German philologist, Ulrich von Wilamowitz-Moellendorff;

the intellectual historian Werner Jaeger, who would emigrate to the United States; and Ernst Hoffman, scholar of ancient and late ancient Platonism, under whose supervision Kristeller would write his dissertation on Plotinus.[87]

Encountering these men, Kristeller came into contact with what was, on balance, the preeminent scholarly tradition in the West: that of German *Wissenschaft*, which for a long time had had the ancient world at its heart. When this tradition was first elaborated in the late eighteenth century, it was the center of the "new humanism" so dear to the German intellectuals (like Wilhelm von Humboldt among many) who reformed German education and considered that the study of Greek antiquity was central to the development of the educated.[88] And as we have seen, even an existentialist like Martin Heidegger believed it was in the idealized ancient Greek (not Roman) world, that "real" humanism had occurred, the real renaissance of which happened not in fifteenth-century Italy but in eighteenth-century Germany. The tradition of Wissenschaft was further developed alongside the rise of the Prussian research university and was embodied in Wilhelm von Humboldt's view, partially cited in one of the epigraphs of this chapter. Wissenschaft—knowledge, science, academic research— had to be understood "in the deepest and widest sense of the word."[89] It had to correlate the search for objective knowledge on the part of the scholar with the subjective development of students; the principle of Wissenschaft must remain pure, and although the state must support Wissenschaft fully, it must seek not to intervene overmuch.[90] Finally, scholars must proceed industriously, despite the melancholy truth that knowledge is "never entirely discoverable." To devote oneself to Wissenschaft meant to have a vocation.

Higher Wissenschaft in the humanistic disciplines was not supposed to be overtly political. A major thrust of the university reforms at the outset of the nineteenth century was in fact to recognize the inherent importance of the humanistic disciplines. The three traditional "higher" professional faculties of theology, medicine, and law were in many ways inherently political and connected to the state; practicing recipients of degrees in all three fields, even theology, had to be licensed (the fathers of both Burckhardt and Nietzsche, for example, were both *Dorfpfarrer,* official town pastors). The nineteenth century, however, saw the rise of the conception that the disciplines that lay outside of the professional faculties, which included natural sciences as well as the humanities and which made up the "philosophical" faculty, should no longer be seen as subordinate to them. In 1808 the great biblical philologist Friedrich Schleiermacher said that since it was becoming clearer and clearer that all knowledge hangs together as one, the philosophical faculty was the place, finally, where all of this could be best understood, where it all ultimately came together.[91] Despite vicissitudes to come, by the late nineteenth century, German Wissenschaft had the character of a secular religion, and its exponents, the esteemed professors, were bearers of that religion.[92] In Kristeller's day, this tradition still existed.

This cannot be overemphasized: Kristeller came to scholarly maturity in a system in which professors, especially those who worked in the classical tradition, were revered. The best of them, the most inspiring, seemed to have a true vocation; they lived for Wissenschaft. We should also recall a concept that was coined in the late nineteenth century: that of *Grossforschung,* that is, the undertaking of a scholarly project so vast that no one person could do it but which needed a unifying mind to form its aims and to direct it.[93] The acceptance of this notion on a large scale and its institutionalization was behind the most productive phases of some of the great collaborative projects of editing: the *Monumenta Germaniae Historica,* for example, which all medieval scholars consult.[94]

Along with the rise of Grossforschung in the second half of the nineteenth century, there was also a change in the conceptualization of the humanities. The earlier nineteenth-century conception voiced by Humboldt and his colleagues had held that all disciplines other than the professional ones shared a certain "philosophical" core of truth and hence should be grouped in the same faculty, the *philosophische Fakultät.* By the second half of the century, however, the natural sciences, using the Grossforschung model, had attained unparalleled successes and high standing.[95] And as to the humanities, the more that evidence was gathered and studied in an organized fashion, the more one began to see analogies made to the natural sciences. Humanistic Wissenschaft had to try to attain to the same sort of certainty. Although Wilhelm Dilthey and a few others in the humanities reacted against this "scientific" trend (in the English sense of the word), it was a powerful, shaping idea.[96] The combination of these various tendencies meant that a prominent professor, one who had the energy and vision to see a scholarly field in its entirety, had to be present to guide the field's development. Philosophical idealism, reverence for the ancient (specifically Hellenic) world, appreciation for the power of a guiding idea set forth by a prominent intellectual, and, eventually, analogies to the natural sciences: these all formed part of Kristeller's intellectual background before his move to Italy.

As he was doing research on his dissertation during a limited stay in Italy in

1933, Hitler's racial laws were passed, and Kristeller realized that his hopes for a German university career had ended. He went back to Germany and worked for some months in Berlin, settling his affairs and corresponding with foreign scholars, in the hopes of having a career elsewhere.[97] He attracted the attention of Giovanni Gentile, with whom he shared a natural sympathy for the idealist tradition, as well as for the ideals of Grossforschung. Spurred on by this contact, Kristeller returned to Italy, where he spent six years, from 1934 to 1939. With Gentile's sponsorship, Kristeller taught in various capacities, and in his free time he investigated the manuscript holdings of the Italian libraries. It was during these years that he found a vast, poorly catalogued reserve of unexploited materials of almost unimagined extent: manuscripts of Renaissance texts, mostly Latin, which were unedited and largely unknown to scholars, even Renaissance scholars.[98] These unedited texts, he realized, could shed great light on the Renaissance and move its modern historiography from the plane of unsupported but appealing generalizations about the centrality of humankind and the active life to a more source-based, integral discipline. He grew to love working with manuscripts in an almost visceral way, treasuring the sense of discovery that his Italy- and later Europe-wide search afforded him, along with the memorable situations that working in varied environments among different people afforded.[99]

As we have seen, Garin, too, realized the extent and value of these sources, and they were at the center of much of his work. It took Kristeller, however, naturally inclined to the encyclopedic, Grossforschung model, to make the first-ever systematic effort to survey all the holdings of Italian, and eventually European and even worldwide, manuscript libraries that held material relevant for Renaissance studies. Kristeller kept detailed notes of all the libraries he visited, and the project connected with these visits lasted his entire life, issuing forth in the massive, six-volume *Iter Italicum,* as well as his *Latin Manuscript Books.*[100] Both projects have become indispensable resources for scholars working in Renaissance intellectual history. Through them, one can survey the holdings relevant to Renaissance intellectual, cultural, and social history that are present in Latin manuscript collections throughout the world, even those with incomplete or unprinted catalogs. With these projects, Kristeller transformed a field by opening up the amount of resources available to scholars. If the manuscript library situation was previously of the sort familiar to readers of Umberto Eco's *Name of the Rose*—where the function of a library was to protect and preserve information from the outside world—after Kristeller the information became democratized, since anyone, anywhere, who had access to a scholarly library could see in relative detail what relevant Renaissance materials were available on a global level. Kristeller clearly loved the manuscript heritage and wanted to see it diffused and understood as widely as possible. This very love, combined with the academic traditions he encountered in his career, also affected his thoughts on the problem of humanism in important ways. How so?

Kristeller was conscious of the shaping power of past historiography and understood the manner in which past prejudices could inform modern scholarship.[101] Thus he realized that it was possible that certain Renaissance thinkers had been "skipped" and, if they were not rescued soon, were in danger of disappearing.[102] Kristeller's general interpretation of humanism fosters manuscript study in a way that the diachronic approach never can, since the synchronic approach has the effect of "leveling," if one considers Renaissance intellectuals. In other words, if one focuses on all those who shared some sort of commitment to the five *studia humanitatis* and makes humanism thus defined the center of research, it is not so necessary to make value-based distinctions among humanists or indeed among other Renaissance thinkers such as Aristotelians or Platonists. That is to say, since their work en masse was almost entirely unknown, *all* Renaissance thinkers became worthy objects of study. Kristeller repeatedly said that despite offers, he refused to write a general history of Renaissance thought, because he believed we were not in a position to do it, given the poor state of the sources.[103] We just did not know enough about what Renaissance thinkers had written, even about the ones who by reputation at least were important, to be able to synthesize meaningfully. Kristeller's *Iter Italicum*, his *Latin Manuscript Books,* and his initiative toward founding the *Catalogus translationum et commentariorum* all testify to his belief that the sources had to be fully surveyed and eventually edited before they could be studied as parts of a visible whole.[104] Renaissance thought, for Kristeller, was Wissenschaft: ultimately unknowable, but something we must nonetheless strive to know.

Kristeller's drive toward synchrony was also fueled by a desire to make sure that important intellectual movements other than humanism (using his definition) did not go ignored and that as many intellectual trends as possible be included in any general picture of the cultural history of the Renaissance. This accorded with an overall synchronic tendency in his life's work. In his earliest major published work, his doctoral dissertation on the later Platonist Plotinus, Kristeller considers the problem of how to address the work of a past thinker, such as Plotinus: "The philosophical content of a doctrine or world view relates of course to its relationship to reality, which exists for all eras and also for us is equally able to be grasped, despite the distance in time and in spiritual authority."[105] He then recognizes the problem of the correspondence theory of truth: "First and foremost, it seems that we lack a secure measuring rod for reality, with which we could compare Plotinus's picture of reality."[106] How to transcend this problem? All we can do, Kristeller wrote in 1929, is stick to the texts: the truth of an analysis "lies in the persuasive meaning of the textual materials, in the same way that the truth of an hypothesis in natural science lies in the explanation of the [natural] phenomena.[107] Fifty years later, in a contribution to a volume of studies dedicated to Eugenio Garin, Kristeller wrote concerning the Renaissance:

> It is my belief that an historical period of such complexity cannot be described in a simple definition. . . . A historical period has its own particular physiognomy, and the attempt to identify that physiognomy must proceed one step at a time. If there is a definition to be formulated, that formulation must come at the conclusion of our study and not at its outset. . . . We must set ourselves the task of understanding and interpreting the entire period by examining each of its aspects, not only those we like.[108]

Philosophy, too, was subject to equivocal definitions, and any proper scholarly definition should attempt to be univocal. From the same Festschrift article:

> The task of defining philosophy seems still more difficult than the problem of the Renaissance, and every thinker or school offers a different definition. Like the history of other aspects of culture, the history of philosophy is usually written from the point of view of one particular philosophy; in building a case for the argument that certain thinkers from the past have been its precursors, each point of view usually gives little attention to thinkers or problems which are not related to it. Our goal should be to create a history of philosophy which comprehends everything which has at any time been considered a part of philosophy. In widening our perspective, such an aim could make us aware of problems and ideas worthy of our attention.[109]

In other words, in the case of a diverse phenomenon like Renaissance thought, univocity can only be achieved by a very broad definition. Our history of philosophy must be comprehensive, covering everything ever considered a part of philosophy. Again, one thinks of Wissenschaft: an ideal that can never be achieved but which is nonetheless the goal. However, according to Kristeller, not all forms of thought were philosophical. He goes on:

> Of course, it must be clear that philosophic thought may be seen in two lights: first, in its strictly technical and professional sense; and second, in a broader sense which goes beyond professional philosophy to include the largely philosophic thought found in the writings of poets, men of letters, theologians and scientists. The historian of philosophy must shed light on the development of professional philosophy, but if we are to understand Renaissance thought we must examine it in the broader sense, with particular attention to humanism, or we run the risk of defining philosophy in a way which would preclude its existence in the fifteenth century or, for that matter, in the twentieth.[110]

The notion of "professional" philosophy is important in understanding Kristeller's position vis-à-vis Renaissance philosophy and his refusal to grant Renaissance humanists the appellation *philosopher*. At first glance, *professional philosopher* seems to indicate an institutional, university-based philosopher. Thus, when one looks at Kristeller's oeuvre and some of the scholarly traditions he created, one is struck by the prominence of Renaissance Aristotelianism. Kristeller developed a famous position, to the effect that neither Renaissance humanism nor Platonism killed off scholastic Aristotelianism. Instead, the scholastic tradition throve in the Renaissance and even grew alongside humanism and Platonism; most times these traditions coexisted, and at the times when a preference for one or the other tradition was voiced, this should be seen as a disciplinary rivalry, much as different present-day academic disciplines have rivalries with one another.[111] This position, too, reflected Kristeller's unparalleled knowledge of Renaissance-era manuscript sources: in fact the number of unedited or poorly edited Aristotelian, scholastic manuscripts from the Renaissance era is far greater than the number of Platonic manuscripts and easily as large as the number of humanistic manuscripts, if we understand *humanistic* here along Kristeller's lines.[112] Again, one observes Kristeller's preservationist instincts shaping and conditioning his theoretical formulations. The material was out there, so all of it needed study.

The term *professional philosopher,* however, has a resonance beyond just *university-centered philosopher,* since we see that Kristeller also considered a Platonic philosopher like Marsilio Ficino (1433–99), who only taught very briefly at a university, not a humanist but a philosopher.[113] For Kristeller, professional philosophers are those thinkers who, founding their thought on the correspondence theory of truth, engage with the rationalist traditions of philosophy that he so appreciated, which he saw as stretching from Plato, through Aristotle, to Kant. Needless to say, this rationalist tradition leaves out a number of thinkers whom many would term philosophers, even professional philosophers: Marx, Nietzsche, twentieth-century analytic philosophers, and Richard Rorty, to name just a few.[114]

When we narrow our focus to the Renaissance era, it is striking that Kristeller, given his appreciation for contemporary etymologies, never carried out the same sort of study for the word *philosophy* or *philosopher* that he did for the terms *humanism* and *humanist.* If he had, he would have seen that there were humanists who referred to themselves also as philosophers and some who, in their antagonism toward metaphysically oriented philosophy, revealed minds very acute and seasoned in the philosophical tradition.[115] Why did Kristeller insist on placing the humanists on a lower rung on the ladder of scholarly disciplines? One of the most explicit formulations comes again, tellingly, in another Festschrift dedicated to Eugenio Garin. Kristeller stresses his notion that the humanists were mainly rhetoricians: "Although we may not endorse all of Plato's critique of rhetoric, we must maintain with him that there is a clear distinction between opinion and knowledge, and that philosophical as well as scientific and scholarly knowledge have a validity that is different from, and superior to, anything that rhetoric can offer."[116]

The real problem with Kristeller's notion here is this: nowhere is it written in stone that *philosophy* means only idealist philosophy, with metaphysics and ontology—the study of "pure," incorruptible being—at the top. Kristeller insisted on separating humanism from philosophy because philosophy, or his version of philosophy, claimed to aim at higher truths; but I think, frankly, that some of Kristeller's most ardent followers have not always realized that this very separation was a deliberate, self-consciously backward-looking, idealist *prise de position,* not a statement of an eternal ontological verity.[117] In other words, there have been respectable arguments against this position by philosophers, most notably Richard Rorty.[118] And ever since Greco-Roman antiquity, there have been two traditions, one predominantly literary and rhetorical, and the other predominantly metaphysical, both of which have claimed the name philosophy.[119]

Kristeller's love of metaphysically oriented philosophizing represents an old German tradition of appreciating the accomplishments of classical ancient Greece over against those of ancient Rome. "If we want to understand the history of thought and learning in the western Latin Middle Ages," Kristeller wrote, "we must first of all realize that it had its foundation in Roman, not Greek antiquity." And Roman literature, Kristeller noted, was "weak in philosophy."[120] Kristeller also said that part of what motivated the direction of his research was the early-twentieth-century "revolt of the medievalists," one aspect of which was to note the continuities between the Middle Ages and the Renaissance, rather than their sharp differences.[121] And the rhetoric that the humanists revived was medieval in origin, tied for Kristeller to the traditions of *ars dictaminis,* the "art of letter-writing" that underlay medieval Italian notarial practice.[122] When the humanists turned their verbally oriented attentions to rhetoric, they did not, as Kristeller saw it, transform the medieval tradition so much as adorn it with newer inheritances from fundamentally Roman sources. So, despite all his differences in method, presuppositions, and natural intellectual inclinations, in the end Kristeller's Renaissance humanism is, in one respect at least, similar to that of Heidegger: nothing more than a *renascentia Romanitatis,* a "renascence of Romanness" that could have little if anything to say that was philosophically momentous. Only those Renaissance thinkers who engaged with the high points of Greek genius, Plato and Aristotle, could be dignified with the name philosophers. Kristeller could never countenance the notion that, by self-consciously turning away from metaphysics, some humanists were actually making a philosophical statement.

It is worth noting that despite Kristeller's reverence for Hellenism, which he shared with Heidegger, Kristeller's lifelong project was anti-Heideggerian, in that Kristeller believed strongly in the metaphysically based philosophical tradition that Heidegger had rejected. Kristeller created a research program, in fact, that emphasized that our knowledge of the past could and should be based in sources. He believed that although we could not in our lifetimes reach a full or perfect knowledge of that past—indeed, that humanity could never attain perfect knowledge on earth—the mission to gather, assimilate, and interpret was nevertheless vital, in the belief that the mature fruits of that mission would somehow "correspond" with the world of eternal truth.

Kristeller did inherit from Heidegger the notion that there are in the universe realms of experience that are difficult to access in purely rational terms: hence Kristeller's fascination with Plotinian Neoplatonism, which (to simplify greatly) posits a supreme being unreachable except by mystical (for Plotinus ecstatic) experience. However, unlike Heidegger, Kristeller did not turn away from traditional rationalism. Richard Wolin has recently made a powerful and controversial statement that addresses the way Heidegger's secular Jewish students came to terms with their mentor's active involvement with National Socialism and seeming lack of contrition for that involvement.[123] Wolin does not treat Kristeller, but we can add Kristeller's case to the list; although Kristeller refrained from extended critique and self-indulgent consideration of the Heidegger problem, Kristeller's rationalist project was in effect a rebuttal *in practice* of Heidegger's antimetaphysicalism. On the negative side, this strong adherence to traditional rationalism meant that Kristeller's work remained unconnected in any meaningful way to twentieth-century philosophy. This is a perilous position for an intellectual historian, because without even cursory attention to contemporary philosophical and theoretical developments, one easily risks the accusation of practicing a scholarship that is no more than mere antiquarianism.

Kristeller's approach has been influential because it is clear, empirical, and universal. Instead of arguing over a necessarily subjective definition of humanism, scholars could finally sweep that question out of the way and get to work. And the main work was editing texts. Or it should have been. Now, some fifty years after Kristeller's general position on humanism was enunciated and popularized, we still have no systematic series of Renaissance Latin texts *with translations*.[124] Without translations, it is infeasible for university instructors to make the field interesting to younger students, both undergraduate and graduate. Also, the lack of translations has until recently precluded the possibility of the sort of interdisciplinary work that has been seen in classics and medieval studies (for example, that of Walter Burkert, Peter Brown, and Caroline Walker Bynum), in both of which fields it has long been the norm for social historians to use intellectual historical source material and vice versa.

The truth is that while Kristeller's general theory of humanism is endorsed by many scholars, it has not been fully accepted, or at least not accepted to such an extent that it has changed the practice of scholarship; scholars of western European history, including Renaissance scholars, still use the term *humanism* in widely varying ways. Kristeller believed that his theory grew organically from the manuscript source material, and in Kristeller's wake, many intellectual historians (and I refer here primarily to Anglo-American scholarship) have realized the importance of manuscript study for their research and have integrated study of little-noticed manuscripts into their work.[125] Few, however, have taken, say, a year from their careers and edited and, as important, translated a text, so that the canon of Renaissance authors could be expanded. One of the reasons for this is obviously related to the politics of scholarship in the American university system: one often hears the refrain that "editions don't count" when it comes to hiring and granting tenure.

But if Kristeller's theory in general has not found complete acceptance, there must be still another reason. This, I believe, is related to the truism that every generation must write its own histories and, in doing so, must continue to ask larger questions of diachronic significance. Part of the allure of the study of the past is explaining change. Kristeller's synchronic approach to the problem of Renaissance humanism, which is *empirically* the most inclusive, does have the effect of closing doors in this regard. One tends, as did Kristeller, to avoid focusing on trends within the larger movement, for fear that the trend under study will be conflated with the movement as a whole and in general to avoid asking larger questions.[126] It is both the blessing and the curse of Grossforschung: once the larger problem (in this case Renaissance humanism) is solved (here by Kristeller's "theory" of humanism), all that is necessary is for energetic minions to be ready to continue the gathering work that will solidify the larger hypothesis, thus making some of the fuzzy edges clearer—to perform Thomas Kuhn's "normal science."[127] This, however, can lead to stagnation: the humanities are not the natural sciences, and not all scholars are content to see themselves only as minions.

One of the flaws of classical German idealism, from roughly 1770 to 1840, was that it was never able, in its view of the state, to appreciate the needs of all social classes. When the cult of the Nation reached beyond the members of the upper strata of society who had, to all intents and purposes, invented it, some of the ideas that the idealists had formed—which were themselves parts of self-sustaining, larger, internally coherent philosophical outlooks—became vulgarized with tragic results in the twentieth century.[128] In the same way, perhaps, and in a much smaller arena, Kristeller's own, rigidly hierarchized idealism, in which Kantian philosophy stood at the top, led him to create a timeless, beautiful, self-sustaining world for the humanists. This idealism led him to de-emphasize the fact, however, that the humanism of the *studia humanitatis,* Kristeller's humanism, was a world that Renaissance thinkers rarely all inhabited at the same time and place; and his love of idealism compelled him to place the realm of language, history, human action, and change—a world inevitably messier and less consistent than that of metaphysics but no less important—on a decidedly lower level.

Yet, when one privileges the world of language and history, as did Eugenio Garin, one must, as rhetorically sophisticated thinkers often do, take positions, positions that inevitably exclude other ones from their purview. Garin naturally acknowledged the existence of humanists who worked at the courts of despots, as well as Aristotelians and other sorts of thinkers, and he made many contributions to the study of those groups throughout his long and distinguished career. Still, when it came to stating the primary importance of the Renaissance, he was convinced that the birth of the true sense of human liberty was paramount, and he found this most powerfully in the activist humanists of approximately the first half of the fifteenth century. This "liberty" meant a self-conscious sense of freedom from dogmatism, and it was undergirded by the intellectual freedom connected with the modern sense of history, with its sensitivity to the historicity of language and historical context. Garin's position does, however, tend to exclude institutionally enfranchised intellectuals or relegate them, much as the humanists themselves did, to a lower rank. In the final analysis, Garin is *making an argument* about humanism, whereas Kristeller is *classifying* it.[129] Garin is the historian, looking for a plausible explanation of a trend as well as its broader significance, Kristeller the philosophical taxonomist, separating things into natural kinds.

At the outset of this chapter, I cited Aristotle's *Poetics* to the effect that Aristotle's definition of a good tragic hero could help us understand the plights of Eugenio Garin and Paul Oskar Kristeller. There was a reason for this. We remember that a tragic hero must be notable in character and basically good; our two protagonists certainly were both of those things. Each was shaped by the rise of Fascism, a moment in European history that was unparalleled in its difficulties, and each responded in his theorizing about the Renaissance in a heroic and original way. Garin had to live through Italian Fascism, and by

now it should be clear that his experience finds a reflection in the way he theorized humanism, explicitly linking it to a fervent antidogmatism and a love of
intellectual liberty. In his autobiographical statement, he wrote, "Renaissance
humanism was of course strikingly distant, but it offered the possibility of reflecting seriously on the origins of the modern world, on politics, morals, science." Looking back from the distance of a half century, he continued, "it is well
not to forget what sort of a tormented entity Europe was between the two wars,
and then in the second world war—and what the Italian climate was between
'35 and '45, from the Ethiopian war to the catastrophe, and then to the Liberation."[130] Garin, on the one hand, had lived through a period when dogmatism
was put into practice; when it had ended, he, along with many others, felt a need
to understand how the previous fifty years had happened, to come to terms with
the indignity of having lived through a gradual but ever-increasing restriction
on intellectual freedom, along with all the compromises and sins of omission
that had entailed.[131] In his work on humanism, he highlighted those Renaissance
classicists who had stood for precisely what intellectuals living under totalitarian regimes cannot stand for: the freedom to question received ideas that are
phrased as eternal truths. His antimetaphysical stance regarding the relationship
of philosophy and history was also a central part of the historicist tendency in
postwar twentieth-century Italian philosophy, in which the imprint of Benedetto Croce and Antonio Gramsci was central.[132] Finally, Garin also represented
a proclivity toward activism in Italian intellectuals, which has an approximate
parallel in the activism of French intellectuals in the wake of the Dreyfus affair.

Kristeller, on the other hand, suffered the torment of having to leave his
homeland for no other reason than an accident of birth. Like many others, he
idealized the land he had lost, which, in his private cultural imaginary, became a
world where there was always a place for pure serenity tied to Platonic contem-
plation and the idealist tradition, removed from the world because it should be,
because politics and scholarship should not be mixed. In this latter respect, he
reflected a well-known tendency among German intellectuals to remove themselves from contemporary politics and to consider Wissenschaft and "enlightened" reason as a kind of faith: it was a faith born in the classical *polis* of Athens
(or in reaction to it, if one thinks of Plato), a faith that must be left uncorrupted
by the vagaries of mundane history, a faith, finally, that reflected the fact that
everything that has ever been done, as Kristeller once wrote, would "remain
alive in the memory of an infinite being for which the past as well as the future

is always present, and that is thus the greatest, the only true historian, and the keeper of the eternal tradition of which even our best human traditions, to use a Platonist phrase, are but shadows and images."[133]

It would be a mistake to suggest that the positions of Garin and Kristeller are the only ones available when it comes to talking about Italian Renaissance thought. So many brilliant scholars have contributed to the discussion that it would be superfluous to try to classify them, and any attempt to do so would turn this into a very different sort of book. It would also be a mistake not to recognize the dominant imprint of Garin and Kristeller on the field of Renaissance intellectual history or the fact that these two brilliant thinkers came out of specific times and places that affected their thought. And this must be said: European scholars may be surprised to hear this, but there are no more than a handful of institutions in North America where there are practicing scholars of Italian Renaissance intellectual history. There are many Italian and comparative literature departments, but their early modern specialists focus almost exclusively on vernacular literature (thereby omitting much of the fifteenth century); and there are many historians of early modern Italy, but their specialties are for the most part social, economic, or political history, and they have had little time for Italian Renaissance (especially fifteenth-century) intellectual life — except insofar as they have considered intellectuals and their work as epiphenomena of socioeconomic forces.

Given how many universities there are in North America, the absence of the Italian Renaissance as a field is striking, though not really surprising. On the one hand, neither Garin's nor Kristeller's positions on Renaissance humanism served to make the field a permanent fixture of American educational life; this fact, if anything, is the tragedy. And to tie up the slightly flawed Aristotelian metaphor, one can ask what was the tragic flaw of each scholar. In Kristeller's case perhaps it was a too-vehement adherence to traditional idealism, which led to an unwillingness to recognize both the power of history and the changing landscape of philosophy after Kant, and in Garin's case a kind of untranslatability. For although Garin's work has been translated into English, it has never really been culturally translated; if one is not aware of the way his work was part of a series of postwar debates on the structure, pedagogy, and direction of Italian culture, one is sometimes left in the dark if one is seeking a systematic picture of what he is trying to say.

Lest readers get the wrong idea, however, let it be stated that my own position toward the work of these two scholars is one of true admiration. Thinking of Kristeller, one is awed not only by how much he did, but also by how much of his time he devoted to intellectual moments with which he was not in sympathy, given his idealist predilections; he edited and made known texts of all areas of Renaissance endeavor, not just those he considered in the highest rank. As for Garin, one wonders how one thinker could indeed be so equally interested in so many different areas, from the Renaissance to modernity, and write and think about them so learnedly, on so many varied occasions and in so many different formats. Without Kristeller's synchronic vision, one could gain a superficial view of a multifaceted, very complex period; without Garin's diachrony, one might lose the forest for the trees. The fact that Renaissance intellectual history is so meagerly represented in the United States has little to do with Garin and Kristeller in themselves and more to do with academic sociological factors. As Peter Novick has sagaciously remarked, "no aspect of academic life is as taken for granted as the division of inquiry into separate disciplines—institutionally embodied as learned societies at the national or international level, as departments on individual campuses."[134] I am not unaware that what I term in this book the "field" of Italian Renaissance intellectual history is not a field at all, in North American disciplinary terms. Not quite literature (because not in the vernacular), not quite philosophy (because philosophy departments in the main do not respect the history of philosophy as an area of serious inquiry), not quite history (because superficially not germane to social, economic, and political history), the Latin writings of the Italian Renaissance—which are, collectively, its intellectual backbone—exist in a strange sort of limbo. The sources are there, but in North America at least, they have been "disciplined" out of existence.

In any case, as Garin and Kristeller were applying their remarkable talents to scholarship, many new developments occurred in the intellectual history of the twentieth century, developments that for the most part did not find their way into Renaissance scholarship, at least not explicitly. In chapter 3 I attempt to account for some of the most important twentieth-century intellectual trends and out of them to construct a set of theoretical positions that encapsulate and utilize the best elements of the diachronic and the synchronic traditions.

CHAPTER THREE

A Microhistory of Intellectuals

In a word, historians are involved in the effort to understand both
what something meant in its own time and what it may mean for
us today.

DOMINICK LACAPRA, *Rethinking Intellectual History:*
Texts, Contexts, Language

The fear of science, of "scientism," of "naturalism," of self-
objectivation, of being turned by too much knowledge into a
thing rather than a person, is the fear that all discourse will
become normal discourse. That is, it is the fear that there will be
objectively true or false answers to every question we ask, so that
human worth will consist in knowing truths, and human virtue
will be merely justified true belief. This is frightening because it
cuts off the possibility of something new under the sun, of human
life as poetic rather than merely contemplative.

RICHARD RORTY, *Philosophy and the Mirror of Nature*

ANY INTELLECTUAL HISTORIAN must confront prob-
lems of language and truth. It is imprudent for a scholar who is dealing
with ideas in the past to be disconnected from the ideas of the present, and too
many critiques of traditional models of truth and the way language reflects it
were advanced in the course of the previous century for us to ignore them.
These critiques have not found their way into Renaissance intellectual history,
by and large, so in this chapter I would like to come to terms with just what
we are doing when we talk about the past. First, I shall state the problem and

some of its iterations. Then, in the second section, I propose a model to resolve some of the difficulties.

What Is the Problem?

As we have seen in the previous chapter, the term *philosophy* had a very particular resonance for Kristeller. Like many of his era, strongly devoted to the German idealist philosophical tradition, Kristeller associated philosophy with the highest form of human reasoning and considered it a regulative discipline, one whose proper function was to serve as an arbiter of knowledge and whose rigorousness guaranteed its near-monopoly on the highest expressions of truth. Philosophy, thus considered, became a secular religion for many intellectuals, and rationalism, with Kant considered its ablest exponent, held great pride of place. An important underlying assumption of this tradition was that true statements articulated in properly deployed language "corresponded" with truths that were universal. The difficulty of defining just what those universal truths were, however, led to new avenues of inquiry. Toward the end of the nineteenth and at the beginning of the twentieth centuries, alternatives developed within the philosophical tradition, and the correspondence theory of truth gradually came under attack, as various thinkers implicitly or explicitly began to concentrate on problems of language and the way it could be said to represent reality. These discussions came to a head in the twentieth century, and in what follows I shall try to touch on some of the more salient arguments, with the final goal always being to extrapolate ideas that are useful in practice for Renaissance historians. The various thinkers we shall meet should be seen as signposts on a busy and crowded road, signposts that are nonetheless useful in helping us find our way toward our desired end: to discover what, in the many literary and philosophical debates of the twentieth century, can help us more effectively frame our scholarly questions pertaining to the Renaissance.

The early twentieth century saw a split between what are now termed *analytical philosophy* and *continental philosophy*. An important figure in the development of the analytical tradition was Gottlob Frege (1848–1925), who in his philosophizing attempted to reverse the basically Platonist position, strongly held also by Kant, that mathematics dealt with a priori truths. For Frege, instead, if these truths were a priori true, it was because we had created that system, and in fact mathematics itself was seen as a "projection into logical space of our own propensities towards coherent argument."[1] So even mathematics, the last bastion of universalism, could be shown to be an analytical human construct. Roger Scruton puts it well: "What appears as an independent realm of mathematical entities or mathematical truth, is simply a shadowy representation of our own intellectual powers."[2]

Even more important was Ludwig Wittgenstein (1889–1951), who at the end of his most famous work wrote, "[W]hat we cannot speak about we must pass over in silence."[3] This pithy quotation can serve as a symbol for us of one of Wittgenstein's main contributions: the idea, namely, that language itself was constitutive of reality and that there was no reality outside that of language. Ordinary usage was what determined meaning, and there was nothing outside of usage that could be addressed. In his later work, which he chose not publish in his lifetime, Wittgenstein amplified these ideas and focused more on the social aspect of language.[4]

Because of the difficulty in coherently describing the universal truths that were supposed to lie behind the pronouncements of language, philosophers gradually moved toward dissections of language itself, and then finally to the position that only language constituted reality. It was Wittgenstein, really, who led to the separation mentioned above, between analytic and Continental philosophy. Analytic philosophers, largely Anglophone (Wittgenstein had spent much time at Cambridge, studying there early with Bertrand Russell and later becoming a naturalized British subject), came to concern themselves more and more with language and logic, and as they did, their debates became quite specialized and grew so complex as to be out of reach of an educated and even very interested outsider. They saw their discipline as the handmaiden of natural science, viewing philosophy as a puzzle-solving enterprise designed to clarify the use of language;[5] and the history of philosophy grew less and less important, as analytic thinkers came almost completely to ignore all but their very immediate predecessors.

The debates about language had an important effect on Continental philosophy as well, but the responses developed were quite different, and the main tendency to emerge was the movement known as existentialism, well represented in both Germany and France. The central philosophical problem with which existentialists concerned themselves was an old one, that of existence versus essence. Existentialist philosophers believed that the search for eternal essences was a misguided one, since it was doomed to be unfulfillable; therefore one had to try to find a way to ground life instead in existence, life as it is lived, which is transitory.

The chief German representative of this position was Martin Heidegger, who as we have seen believed that metaphysically based philosophy was at an end. Despite the sententious claims of those who placed metaphysics at the top of the philosophical disciplines, this conception of philosophy was essentially anthropological and dealt with the being that presented itself to philosophers (the *Dasein*), rather than with true Being, which was hardly able to be adequately conceptualized.[6] The philosopher after metaphysics had to find strategies to access this "hidden" Being in its unhidden state, what Heidegger termed its *Unverborgenheit*. Tragically, accessing this hidden Being was difficult if not impossible to do, so that the project in some sense seemed doomed to failure, or at least, to endless continuation and unremitting change.

French existentialism was in line with some of the just-mentioned ideas, and I shall discuss it together with literary theory, since both are part of the same larger context. My discussion will lead to the prototypical example of literary deconstruction, exemplified by Jacques Derrida's critique of Lévi-Strauss. Too often, critical theorists are treated as oracular, their thoughts and even some of their individual statements interpreted in ways divorced from both their textual and social context. In this discussion, then, I shall situate the following thinkers in the context in which they might have seen themselves, that of an ongoing debate about the proper realm of knowledge and culture.

Jacques Derrida first came to prominence in France in the late 1960s. This is important as background to his work, because, as often happens, his theories are responses to what he saw around him as much as they are independent statements. He is identified as a poststructuralist, because he wrote in reaction to the structuralist movement, whereby social scientists took the lead from late-nineteenth- to early-twentieth-century linguists. The most important of these linguists was Ferdinand de Saussure (1857–1913), who argued that languages have an inner system, a structure that reflects certain basic realities. These realities could be perceived as a system of differences: words make sense because they are different from other words. Whatever the morphology of the individual language, with systematic work the linguist could reduce the language to its basic structure and see how its separate morphological elements fit the larger outline. This approach was transferred into what the French called the "human sciences," *les sciences humaines,* one of the most prominent of which was anthropology. Claude Lévi-Strauss was one of the social scientists who sought to transfer the paradigm of structural linguistics to culture broadly considered, partially because of a self-conscious dissatisfaction with the rationalist tradition in philosophy.[7] In well-known investigations of the Brazilian tribe the Nambikwara and other "primitive" civilizations, he applied the structuralist linguistic approach to his objects of investigation. Structuralism dominated French social scientific thought in the 1950s and 1960s, and the rhetoric by which it was attended was for some uncomfortably close to scientific, in the Anglo-American sense of the term. In other words, *les sciences humaines* promised the same sort of certainty offered by the natural sciences, and the structuralist paradigm worked its way into all aspects of French academic life, including the writing of history, as we shall see later in this chapter.

An important philosophical challenge was posed contemporaneously by French existentialism, especially well represented by Jean-Paul Sartre.[8] There was a sense in which the neopositivist rhetorical baggage with which structural social science was laden was unsatisfactory and seemed naive to some. The human sciences were just that, about human beings. How could human beings, cultures, be something almost quantifiable? Sartre's reexamination of the problem of existence versus essence proved a way to enter into controversy with structuralists. He suggested that the search for an "essential" human nature, indeed the search by humans for *essences,* was doomed to barrenness and was related to what he called bad faith, which meant for him any sort of deterministic belief that our radical freedom was restricted, or bounded by universal concerns outside our own existence. In other words, once you posit an essence, you abase human freedom before that essence. It was only by focusing on existence, and by living life with its inevitably agonizing choices, that people could find meaning. And this sort of living could never be reduced to a set of laws, structural or otherwise. Later in his life, Sartre adopted a kind of modified Marxism. This too is important, because it revealed a focus on group life and corporate choice and action; in the second part of this chapter, we shall see residues of this in the work of Pierre Bourdieu.

Derrida's critique was much more fundamental and more influential because it engaged the structuralists on their own ground. In his well-known critique of Lévi-Strauss, his basic position was that one does violence to reality by naming things. He carefully went through Lévi-Strauss's examination of the Nambikwara and, largely using the language of Lévi-Strauss himself, showed that there were any number of internal contradictions in the account of tribal life that Lévi-Strauss had constructed.[9] A famous example involved Lévi-Strauss's account, in the *Tristes Tropiques,* of the way he had coaxed forbidden information out of the Nambikwara children.[10] One child was angry with another, so she revealed the secret name of the child with whom she was angry. Lévi-Strauss then set the children against each other, so that he could hear and then understand their secret names. In his account he suggested that he had felt guilt, because he as an outsider had disturbed the hitherto unviolated, seemingly idyllic Nambikwara system of social relations. Like a post-Heisenbergian physicist observing a particle, Lévi-Strauss was suggesting that he himself had changed what he had observed by the very act of observation, thus imploding the innocent, simple, and guileless reality in which the tribespeople had been living. Derrida by contrast emphasized that, while it was true that the Nambikwara had been hitherto undisturbed, it was by no means clear that they were so innocent as Lévi-Strauss wanted to make them seem. If one analyzed Lévi-Strauss's account with precision, one saw that the tribespeople, too, could engage in treachery and practices of social dominance and hierarchy—exactly what, Lévi-Strauss had been arguing, they were unacquainted with prior to his coming. By thus deconstructing Lévi-Strauss's work, Derrida showed that many of the conventions of structuralist social science were self-invalidating. In his critique of naming, he showed how a given name can be seen as an unpersuasive representation of the thing described; Derrida thus helped launch a powerful critique of France's dominant intellectual culture in the humanities and the social sciences. But a problem, as was soon revealed in many discussions attendant upon deconstruction theory, was that it tends itself toward self-invalidation. If a scholar applies the same principles to his own work, it becomes difficult to make any assertions at all, because all assertions involve naming, of a sort. In fact, there are elements of Derrida's thought and approach that, if isolated, can lead to a kind of nihilistic, unhelpful skepticism vis-à-vis the possibility of descriptive writing about the past.

Meanwhile, another French thinker who has had enormous influence in American academia should be mentioned, and this is Michel Foucault. For us he is important primarily because of his notion of the *episteme,* by which he means a set of unarticulated assumptions that people share, inevitably embedded as they are in shaping power structures.[11] The *episteme* leads people to accept unquestioningly a given system of power relations and is expressed in what Foucault termed a *discourse,* that is, an internally coherent system of language that tended to reinforce the *episteme.* Most phenomena that Foucault investigated, from the history of prisons to insane asylums, early modern science to sexuality, were reduced to the omnipresence of power and the struggle among different groups to gain and exercise it. The fact that Foucault presented a way of thinking about assumptions that are unarticulated is important, but a problem, as even Foucault himself in his late work seemed to realize, was that the notion of the *episteme* leaves people essentially powerless before the mentioned unarticulated structures of power. Everything is reduced to power, and it is difficult to escape from the ruling power structures that make up the *episteme* in which one finds oneself embedded. As such, again, we find it difficult to explain change—which, most reasonable people will concede, exists—and more difficult still to apply Foucault consistently to historical phenomena other than those he investigated.

So what is the problem? The problem is that the course of philosophy and theory in the twentieth century has led to a radical destabilizing of the notion that seemingly true statements refer to unambiguously true things. In one sense this is a very old position and is reflected in ancient skepticism as well as in certain forms of medieval nominalism. But to take comfort, as many do, in a "nothing is new under the sun" mentality is deceptive, because if there is anything that history teaches us, it is that context is important.

The fact that these forceful objections have all occurred so recently is significant, because as philosophers and theorists were eroding a number of traditional presumptions about the nature of assertion and truth, many of the cataclysmic events of the twentieth century seemed to show a real-world reflection of this dissatisfaction, even as twentieth-century thought was also obviously a response to the events. The century of genocide, of the atomic bomb, and of widespread freedom-restricting totalitarianism was a signal disappointment, coming as it did after centuries of "rationalistic" progress. Perhaps the evolution of traditional subject-object rationalism, in its *inevitably* linked context of the growth of Western societal institutions, was no progress at all. In this sense, the problems with which philosophers of language and theorists have wrestled are entirely new: the combination of their content with their context makes them distinct from anything that has come before. How then does one find a way out of this impasse, toward the end of practicing a meaningful, noncynical, sort of inquiry?

We have choices before us. The first necessary choice is to transcend the extreme skepticism of some varieties of deconstruction. Self-contained systems can never be won over by argument, so the question becomes one of utility. Even if we cannot prove demonstratively that complete philosophical skepticism is unfounded, we must realize that it is the obligation of scholars to find ways of looking at the past that *both* go beyond throwing up one's hands and surrendering to ideology *and* are undergirded by useful assumptions about the world as we understand it today. This does not mean, however, that our consideration of theory is useless, because such careful reflection can help us think more muscularly and flexibly. Even if one disagrees with some of the claims put forth by various theorists, consideration and understanding of their arguments can help scholars to foreground aspects of the past that might not hitherto have come so easily to light and to articulate those newly lighted objects of thought in a fashion that is intellectually more agile and more suited to our own time. In what follows, I suggest that we can accomplish this task by incorporating theories drawn from the philosophy of science and of language which have been evolved as answers to the sorts of language-based objections that I have previously outlined. Then we can add to the mix the kinds of questions that social historians have asked, as we try to develop a system of talking about Renaissance intellectuals.

As to language, we must consider the work of a philosopher who came out of the analytic tradition, only to turn against it, to an extent, and make very valuable arguments about the way in which philosophizing should be conceived. This is Richard Rorty, who in much of his work has been concerned to combat modes of thought that he terms, collectively, *representationalism*. Bjørn Ramberg formulates the concern particularly well:

> For thirty years or more, Richard Rorty has worked to break the grip on analytic philosophy of two problem-defining assumptions. The first is the Kantian idea that knowledge, or thinking generally, must be understood in terms of some relation between what the world offers up to the thinker, on one side, and on the other the active subjective capacities by which the thinker structures for cognitive use what the world thus provides. The second is the Platonic conviction that there must be some particular form of description of things, which, by virtue of its ability to accurately map, reflect, or otherwise latch on to just those kinds through which the world presents itself to would-be knowers, is the form in which any

literally true . . . statement must be couched. Together, these comprise what Rorty calls representationalism.[12]

Rorty himself took his cue from thinkers with whom the analytic tradition wrestled and whom it finally discarded. As Rorty writes, "Wittgenstein, Heidegger, and Dewey are in agreement that the notion of knowledge as accurate representation, made possible by special mental processes, and intelligible through a general theory of representation, needs to be abandoned."[13] Existentialism and pragmatism provided his starting points: existentialism, in that it taught him that the search for essences that one could describe using language was doomed at certain levels to inconsistency; pragmatism, in that it inculcated in Rorty a need for the philosopher to interact with the world as best it could be perceived and contribute to debate in useful ways.

In a sense, Richard Rorty represents a pragmatic counterpart to Jacques Derrida. A distinct advantage of Rorty's thought is that he moves in constructive, relatively clear ways beyond the difficulties of deconstruction. Once one has dissected the shaky assumptions behind representationalist styles of thinking, what next? Where is one to go from there? Rorty is not advocating an alternative view of human epistemology; instead, he is changing the set of questions: "To assert the possibility of a post-Kantian culture, one in which there is no all-encompassing discipline which legitimizes or grounds the others, is not necessarily to argue against any particular Kantian doctrine, any more than to glimpse the possibility of a culture in which religion either did not exist, or had no connection with science or politics, was necessarily to argue against Aquinas's claim that God's existence can be proved by natural reason."[14] A frequent objection to deconstruction is that it leads to a kind of nihilism in which, since nothing can be asserted as unequivocally or unproblematically true, dogmatic ideology is taken as a substitute. Rorty has transcended this problem by focusing on consensus and conversation, embracing the notion that philosophy and its use of language is therapeutic, rather than regulative.

To understand this last sentence, we must trace a few broad developments. One of the legacies of the later Renaissance was the revival and forceful articulation of ancient skepticism, buttressed by the rediscovery of the work of Sextus Empiricus and, more importantly, by the needs of the era.[15] Due to his critical spirit and the precise Jesuit education he received, René Descartes (1596–1650) found himself preoccupied with skeptical arguments, and in what is perhaps his most famous work, the *Discourse on Method,* he came up with a "foundationalist" solution.[16] Let us say that all our knowledge of the world around us has as a starting point the senses, in that they are the necessary mediating factor by which we gather impressions of the outside world, out of which we construct what we believe we know. But we are aware that the senses are fallible, and we are often confronted with two people perceiving the "same" thing, the same object of sense, radically differently. What if, right now, all your senses were failing you at once, and you weren't where you (perhaps mistakenly) think you are, but somewhere else? Confronted with the possibility that you cannot *know* that all your senses are not failing you at once, can you even be sure that you exist? Descartes's famous answer, of course, was, in chapter 4 of the *Discourse,* "Cogito, ergo sum" (I think, therefore I am). In other words, there was one thing that on pain of absurdity one could not deny, namely that one was thinking and as such was a thinking *being,* one who existed. So Descartes had a "foundation" upon which he could build other philosophical positions, which he did with such brilliancy that he is by common consent considered the founder of modern philosophy.

What this meant, again speaking broadly, was that epistemology, the theory of knowledge, became a major preoccupation of philosophers. Philosophy became *about* knowledge and knowing, and knowledge seemed to be what all disciplines (natural sciences and humanistic disciplines alike) were interested in gaining. Since all disciplines were at some level about gaining knowledge, and since philosophy was about critically examining the attainment of knowledge, philosophers, especially after Kant, considered their discipline a master-discipline that oversaw and adjudicated the claims and arguments of the others. Kant, in approaching these problems, came to believe that in our quest to know the world, we are faced with two factors: the "thing in itself," the immediate object of our quest for knowledge, and, in a larger perspective, the intuitive knowledge that there is a totality of things in the universe, even if we can never completely know that totality. The "thing in itself," the *Ding an sich,* for Kant, was discrete and could never, by definition, be known in itself. We could, however, know it for us, in our own realm. And our intuitive knowledge that there does exist a totality of things (that, in short, we can conceive of infinity without knowing infinity) served as a guarantee that our subjective but certain knowledge corresponded with the more ideal, absolute realm of truths.[17]

Given the strength of Kant's ideas, it is no accident that, in the course of the

Humboldtian foundation of the Prussian research university, which we have touched upon repeatedly, the *philosophische Fakultät* was considered the most prestigious and that all disciplines save the "professional" schools of theology, medicine, and law were grouped under the name philosophical. Wilhelm von Humboldt's view concerning Wissenschaft and higher education represented the translation into institutional terms of Kant's theories about knowledge.[18] As we have seen, Paul Oskar Kristeller explicitly voiced this traditional view concerning the superiority of philosophy, and it should now be clear that the notion that "rationalistic" philosophy was superior was a guiding, organizing principle in his own work. He and many others have believed that the best sort of philosophy in some sense mirrored the purest, most uncorrupted sorts of truth.

Richard Rorty's concern has been to overcome the notion of philosophy as a search by thinking subjects to "represent," in the sense of "mirror," the objective world. Instead, Rorty adds to the mix the notion of interpretive communities. As Jürgen Habermas has put it (in a partial critique of Rorty), Rorty "replaces the two-place relation between representing subject and represented object with a three-place relation: the symbolic expression, which accords validity to a state of affairs, for an interpretive community."[19] This formulation is applicable and important for intellectual historians, if conceived in this way: The language one uses to describe the world in which one is interested (the Renaissance, say) is symbolic in that it evokes rather than represents the past; it gives validity to the past world one is trying to evoke; and it makes sense within an interpretive community, fellow scholars, at a given moment in time. One returns to the interconnected themes of consensus and conversation: for Rorty, a philosopher is supposed to be part of a conversation that leads to the development of useful consensuses. It is in this sense that he transcends nihilism, in that a given position will not function within a given community if it is not of the sort to garner consensus. This position is "relativistic" in the sense that one is speaking of concerns that are "relative" to a certain time and place, but not nihilistic in that it is the free (and not dogmatic) expression of opinions—as in a true conversation—that creates the needed consensus at a given time. It is in this sense that he wants to conceive of philosophy as something therapeutic rather than regulative: philosophy is no longer a master-discipline but one voice, and a very important one, among many in our quest to evoke, understand, and finally participate in the world in which we find ourselves.

This approach is useful for intellectual historians for at least two reasons. First, and most obviously, when we have a justified conviction that certain set scholarly paradigms are not responding adequately to our interpretive needs, we should not, for the sake of loyalty, feel compelled to repeat them endlessly. Rather we should try to understand them as part of a conversation in which we are allowed to participate. Second, thinking of the enterprise of scholarship in this conversational, inherently collaborative way should offer a clue, perhaps, as to how we can try to depict the past. This is crucial if we are dealing with intellectuals, who themselves were participating in conversations within interpretive communities, for it is those interpretive communities that intellectual historians now should be trying not to "represent," but to evoke. Intellectuals in the past lived as we do, within interpretive communities. How can we understand their world? Through what lenses can we see the past? In the second section of this chapter, I propose that we must think collaboratively and bridge the gap in Italian Renaissance studies, which is wider than in almost any other historical field, between social and intellectual historians.

A Microhistory of Intellectuals

Social historians of early modern Italy have been brilliantly adept at incorporating various aspects of social science theory and, on occasion, literary theory in their work. A number have integrated theoretical approaches from anthropology, which in turn has led to one of the most fruitful avenues of social historical inquiry: microhistory. In a recent article surveying North American work on early modern Italy, Edward Muir discussed microhistory, suggesting that it was a perspective that "attempts to abandon all teleological and anachronistic assumptions about the course of history in favor of the microscopic examination of a small group, a tightly circumscribed event, or an individual, with a goal of discovering elements of cultural or social practices that are invisible to the wide-angle lens of more macrohistorical techniques, especially quantitative ones."[20] It is rare, however, to see microhistorians venture into intellectual history; the "small group" is never a small group of intellectuals, the "tightly circumscribed event" will never be an event connected in any way with intellectual history, and the "individual" is rarely an early modern intellectual, that is, someone who wrote at least part of his or her work in Latin. To understand why intellectuals are absent (speaking broadly) from microhistorical accounts that deal with early modern Italy, we must contextualize microhistory's emergence as a field; in doing so, we shall see that the appearance of microhistory represents a historiographical parallel to the poststructuralist turn in literary theory and the philosophy of language, as sketched above.

In French historiography, structuralism emerged in the *Annales* movement, which, Peter Burke has suggested, can be divided roughly into three phases: the founding generation, the years of institutional acceptance, and the post-1968 period.[21] To grasp the movement's evolution, we must reach back to the journal founded in 1929 by Lucien Febvre and Marc Bloch, which in its first version was entitled *Annales d'histoire économique et sociale*. Febvre, whose early interest was the sixteenth century, and Bloch, a medievalist, were dissatisfied with then-prevailing modes of political and institutional history and with a unitary, ever forward-marching conception of time.[22] Instead of a history reduced to chronology—to sequences of leaders, regimes, intellectuals, or events—they sought instead to bring the layered and diverse nature of time into relief. A merchant's time might be different from a farmer's time, which might in turn be other than a laborer's time, and so on. The seasons, local social norms with respect to life stages, the climate, the physical landscape: these and other features served as springboards for what Fernand Braudel would later call an *histoire totale*, a "total history" that would reach beyond events and instead articulate the enduring structures that shaped human life in the past.[23]

The interdisciplinary excitement and the feeling of newness of these early years is easy to understand. Bloch and Febvre had met as young colleagues in Alsace, at the refounded, out-of-the-way (from a Parisian perspective) University of Strasbourg, itself newly recovered from Germany in the First World War.[24] Febvre wrote to his good friend Henri Berr that at Strasbourg there was a "feeling of solidarity, union, exchange, that one could not have in the same measure anywhere."[25] "Here at Strasbourg," wrote Febvre to the respected Belgian medievalist Henri Pirenne, "it is no chimera: every week we work together, professors of all the literary disciplines, without asking each other what is our specialized degree."[26] For Febvre and Bloch, this type of collaboration led to a desire to found a journal that was both readable and as fruitfully interdisciplinary as the Strasbourg environment. By 1928 they had found a publisher, and the journal's first issue appeared early in 1929. By the early 1930s, both men had made their move to the center of French intellectual life, Paris; Febvre to the Collège de France, Bloch to the Sorbonne. The movement became institutionalized during the 1930s and 1940s. Bloch died heroically, fighting for the French resistance in the Second World War, and Febvre published his famous work, *The Problem of Unbelief in the Sixteenth Century: The Religion of Rabelais*, in 1942. As Peter Burke points out, Febvre wrote this work in frustrated response to a recent edition of Rabelais, whose editor, Abel Franc, seemed to make the great sixteenth-century satirist a forerunner of Enlightenment-era free thinking with respect to religion.[27] Exhibiting an acute literary sensibility, Febvre documented that the contemporary charges of "atheism" leveled against Rabelais were nothing more than stock smears; the religious question was far from an either-or proposition in the French sixteenth century, and study of how Rabelais existed *in community* was needed to gain a fuller understanding than Franc had provided. Febvre's work showed that though the *Annales* approach began with a desire to break through disciplinary traditions by including economic, sociological, and anthropological insights, its first-generation magnate was a refined intellectual historian first and foremost. Thereafter Febvre became the head of the sixth division of the *Ecole Pratique des Hautes Etudes*, a division planned to carry out *Annales*-style research.

At this stage, the *Annales* movement had become a school, enfranchised and powerful, a Gallic mirror of German *Grossforschung*, as Braudel took over real direction and large-scale, necessarily collaborative projects were initiated.[28] Italian microhistory constituted a reaction primarily to the presuppositions, doctrines, and methods developed during this "school" period, which, under the symbolic and actual leadership of Fernand Braudel, became the hotbed of French structuralism. For Braudel, the economy in its broadest sense represented the vantage point for viewing history. In the three-volume study known to English readers as *Civilization and Capitalism, 15th-18th Century*, Braudel saw history as an edifice. He envisioned a structure with a ground floor of physical geography: the earth and the unwritten customs and social patterns that derive from its use; this is material culture, which makes up the structure of everyday life. On the next story up reside the organized sorts of exchange activities, such as the local markets, trade fairs, and sea-trade networks that make up economic life. And permeating the structure's plan and in a sense existing above, or atop the stories are the mechanisms of capitalism. These include a global reach on the part of organized economic interests, monopolies both de jure and de facto, and—for Braudel—the realization that capitalism cannot ever entirely control the two lower spheres of economic activities (material and commercial) but rather recapitulates them almost ontogenetically.[29] Braudel's magisterial vision encompassed the entire sphere of human activity, both metaphorically and literally, in that he wanted to think about the world as a whole, not just European civilization.

One more fact is necessary for a full understanding of *Civilization and Capitalism*. In a later memoir, Braudel suggested that the aging Febvre had strongly encouraged him to write this work and that Febvre had seen it as one part of a two-man collaborative history of the early modern world.[30] The other partner was to have been Febvre himself, and Febvre, who died before doing so, was to have provided the intellectual historical side of the picture. In a sense that some have not always taken into account, Braudel's *Civilization and Capitalism* was to have been one-half of a partnership between a sophisticated, societally integrated intellectual history and the more long-term socioeconomic views traditionally associated with the *Annalistes*. Indeed, the *Annales* movement originally did not intend to exclude intellectuals but to think about them in a new, essentially anticanonical way. As testament to this dimension of the *Annales* approach, there is the work of Febvre and Bloch, of course, but also the searching studies of Jean Delumeau on early modern Europe, Jacques LeGoff on (everything under the sun, but especially) medieval intellectuals, and Roger Chartier on the history of the book.[31]

Braudel's structuralist, long-term, macroeconomic approach, however, was the direction in which the *Annales* tradition and its various *equipes* were heading in the 1960s, and the problem known to sociologists as the *structure-agency dilemma* inevitably came into relief. On the one hand, environment and context always "structure" people's lives, especially in the loose sense that one's field of vision and sense of possibilities are shaped by the circumstances in which one is placed. On the other hand, we proceed in our own lives as if we can make choices, and we behave, it seems, as if our choices make a difference; the very activity of our lives implies that each human being functions on the assumption that he or she has "agency" with respect to the surrounding world. The Braudellian *Annaliste* model of "total history" gave great weight to structures but seemed to fit people into those structures less as choice-making actors and more as anonymous factors in a larger equation. In the final, post-1968 generation of *Annaliste* research, the structuralist moment was rethought in France, even as important legacies of the original *Annales* project remained vigorous.[32]

It is now an opportune time to turn to a direct response to French *Annales*-style structuralism, which occurred in Italy in the 1970s: microhistory.

Braudel's intriguing metaphor of the house suggested an edifice with delineated but connected stories, a complicated structure with an inside and an outside, in the environment even as it constituted its own environment. But, the emerging microhistorians wondered, were there any people in the house?[33] Microhistorians were reacting to the *Annales* style of approaching history, which they felt limited scholars' attention to real people and, as importantly, kept those who were formerly marginalized by history still on the margins. The first microhistorians were also reacting against Marxist historiographical tradition, which had also—and often coterminously with the *Annales*—favored "macro" style, overly determinative approaches.[34] Though dissatisfied with much of Marxist method, they retained the Marxist sympathy for the lower socioeconomic strata of society, for E. P. Thompson's "poor stockinger and 'obsolete' hand-loom weaver" who needed to be rescued "from the enormous condescension of posterity."[35] Italy, with such a rich and relatively untapped stock of archival materials, especially inquisitorial records, became the prime laboratory for a new method of thinking about the marginalized in history. This method was first and foremost prosopographical; that is, the researcher's task was to find names and trace them throughout a body of archival source material. Second, one was to narrate the tale; one's writing was to be, as much as possible, unencumbered by larger assumptions or models, and most of all, the impersonal rhetoric of social science was to be avoided.[36]

The best-known work in the field of early modern Italian studies is Carlo Ginzburg's evocative account of a miller, Menocchio, who lived in Friuli, in northeastern Italy, and who was tried twice, then ultimately put to death for heresy in 1599.[37] The focus was on Menocchio's unorthodox cosmological beliefs, which he had gleaned from a selective, certainly extrainstitutional reading of a number of vernacular texts that were available to him. Ginzburg identified the texts Menocchio probably had consulted, analyzed them carefully, and through meticulous reading of the trial records also (and very significantly), showed much about the act of reading itself, as he brought Menocchio's creative misreadings to the fore. Importantly, as well, Ginzburg situated Menocchio in the small community of fellow hill-town dwellers in which the unusual miller moved. And finally, Ginzburg advanced a theory of cultural reciprocity, or circularity, in thinking about the problem of "high" versus "low" culture, suggestively maintaining that "between the culture of the dominant classes and that of the subordinate classes there existed, in preindustrial Europe, a circular relationship composed of reciprocal influences, which traveled from low to high as well as from high to low."[38]

There have been many practitioners of microhistory, and it is now a dominant current in North American scholarship on early modern Italy, but microhistorical method has not really found its way into the intellectual history of the Italian Renaissance.[39] It is useful for a number of reasons. First, implicitly we are given the reminder that groups of people can wind up marginalized by factors outside their own control; of course, fifteenth-century Latin-writing intellectuals were not marginalized by the mechanisms of capitalism, but by a later cultural essentialism that I have discussed in chapter 1. Still, they exist, but their texts are simply not being read in North America at more than a few institutions. Second, the notion that modes of cultural transmission in premodern Europe are best thought of as circular rather than vertical, and social as well as textual, is important but not current among scholars who work on Renaissance intellectuals. Third, the focus on small communities is essential, if one wants to move toward a fuller picture of Renaissance life than is the norm. There has been no shortage of recent approaches in which intellectual historians have attempted to ask social questions when intellectual history is under discussion. There is room, however, to take some of these approaches further and to suggest some new ones. How can we do this?

I propose that we focus our thoughts both generationally and relationally. In his recent study *A Sociology of Philosophies,* Randall Collins has elaborated a powerful global theory of intellectual change that meshes well with many of the concerns I have already mentioned.[40] While there are any number of specific points that intellectual historians could dispute in his study, his focus on the study of generations is useful and not prevalent in Renaissance intellectual history.[41] He suggests that a typical generation lasts about thirty years, the general period of creativity for a given intellectual. In one generation, there will be from three to six viable competing intellectual positions that develop antagonistically in response to one another. These positions can be passed from one intellectual generation to the next, provided that in a given period there is this limited number of possible positions. The intellectual communities within which these positions develop are of paramount importance.

What constitutes an intellectual community? Presumably, a limited group of people who possess a shared set of interests informed by common material for reflection. It is in the process by which that material changes that we can locate the changing structure of intellectual communities. Integral individual thinkers with individual evolving missions, the members of an intellectual community are also social beings, who evolve their ideas and select their reading materials, the bases of their conversations, in the context of a rich complex of social, political, economic, and cultural factors.[42] If we are thinking about the history of Renaissance intellectual life, one of our tasks is to determine how and why groups of intellectuals chose what to read, and what material came into circulation among them. The historiography of science and the recent sociology of intellectuals can help us formulate the questions. Thomas Kuhn, for obvious reasons, comes to mind. His initial view regarding paradigm shifts and their relation to the transition from "normal" to "revolutionary" science is well known.[43] "Normal" science happens when a group of thinkers shares a method of investigation of a certain problem, informed by consensus on the hypotheses used; the consensus reflects the fact that they share a paradigm. As their work proceeds, the data gathered in general confirm their presumptions. The methods used are standardized, and the results are more or less what is expected— "normal" science. But when enough data amass that do not fit the paradigm, "revolutionary" science occurs. The old paradigm draws attack, and under the powerful personality or personalities of one or more leaders, a new paradigm, or set of shared assumptions, emerges. The move toward normal science recurs; the paradigm has shifted. For our purposes, Kuhn is important because his ideas can help us think about the formation of literary canons in the Renaissance. When certain set texts are not responding adequately to the needs of small communities of intellectuals, new texts are adopted; but new questions must be asked of these new texts, and so the general set of assumptions changes. We can further refine this notion by examining the thought of Gaston Bachelard and Pierre Bourdieu.

In developing his theories, Bachelard (1884–1962) was reacting to the profound changes of his day in the history of physics, specifically to Einsteinian relativity and to new developments in quantum theory.[44] For him, these new developments meant a breakdown in the traditional Cartesian mind-body distinction and suggested the sterility of Kantian universals. Epistemology had to become reflexive and dialectical, reactive to the data nature offered through the continual experimentation of human beings, whose "science" was an on-going rectification of past errors and was quite literally a constructed enter-prise. Bachelard's view of the development of theories was also important, for although it was dialectical, it was not dialectical in the Marxist sense, where one theory is replaced by another that contradicts it. Rather, new theories were seen to evolve which included former ones. In the words of David Swarz, Bachelard's "dialectical reason situates the previous theory in a broader conceptual space that highlights both its strengths and its limitations. This mode of dialectical thought can include several different theories, which at a given level of logic contra-dict each other by virtue of their limits, but, when situated within a broader framework, stand in complementary relationships."[45] When a theory or set of theories emerges that has the capacity to encompass or interrelate those prior to it, Bachelard's "epistemological break" happens.[46] The advantage of considering Bachelard in conjunction with Kuhn is twofold: first, in our quest to formulate generational changes in intellectual interest, it allows us to soften the radical breaks that the normal-revolutionary science distinction sometimes implies. By stressing the notion that new ways of approaching problems are often the result of conscious or unconscious attempts to encapsulate and transcend, rather than simply oppose, previous frameworks, we have the advantages of both synchrony and diachrony. We can begin to think about a shared moment in time among a group of intellectuals, even as we try to account for change over time. Second, considering Bachelard in this way also adds a measure of reflexiveness to our consideration of the process by which ideas are elaborated. It is thus applicable not only to the Renaissance sources themselves but also to the historiography of the Renaissance; hence the attempt in this chapter to find ways to bridge gaps between the synchrony of Kristeller and the diachrony of Garin.

The kind of reflexiveness here implied leads to the thought of Pierre Bour-dieu, for one of the central tenets of his sociological work is the need for the investigator continually to interrogate the history and structure of his disci-pline.[47] This has led him to evolve certain theoretical stances and postulates that all attempt to transcend seemingly fixed categorical hermeneutic differences. The most important aspect of his thought for our purposes is his determination to think relationally and not in terms of ideal categories. This insistence is at the root of most of his key concepts, all of which seek to obviate the traditional and seemingly inescapable divide between subject and object. There are three interconnected concepts that I shall examine here: habitus, capital, and field.

For Bourdieu, the concept of habitus has to do with subconscious structuring dispositions that actors bring with them into their field of activity. In Bourdieu's own words, habitus is "a system of durable, transposable dispositions, . . . principles which generate and organize practices and representations."[48] Or, again, "the habitus is the universalizing mediation which causes an individual agent's practices, without either explicit reason or signifying intent."[49] The habitus, in other words, represents a kind of generative principle that can govern and produce the actor's behavior. For those in medieval and Renaissance studies, it will come as no surprise that the first time Bourdieu used the term *habitus* was in the postface to his translation, published in 1967, of Erwin Panofsky's *Gothic Architecture and Scholasticism*.[50] There Bourdieu highlighted the notion that for Panofsky scholasticism was more than a set of doctrines; it was a set of structuring attitudes—mental habits that could inform an entire approach to the world. Here it is important to note the prereflective nature of the habitus for Bourdieu. The assumptions that bind together those who share the habitus are beneath the level of conscious articulation—they are a *doxa;* they are taken for granted.[51] But when these assumptions are voiced, or when there are attempts to define them, they can produce orthodoxy and heterodoxy, since the formerly undefined limits of the possible are crossed: "Orthodoxy, straight, or rather *straightened* opinion, which aims, without ever entirely succeeding, at restoring the primal state of innocence of doxa, exists only in the objective relationship which opposes it to heterodoxy, that is, by reference to the choice—*hairesis,* heresy— made possible by the existence of competing possibles and to the explicit critique of the sum total of the alternatives not chosen that the established order implies."[52]

To return to habitus, it is worth mentioning that it is a Latin term with a rich medieval history and is in fact the medieval Latin translation of Aristotle's *hexis.* Bourdieu has on occasion claimed some relation to Aristotle's view, though as critics have pointed out, his habitus is unlike Aristotle's in many ways.[53] Some similarities, however, are present. For Aristotle, the hexis is a trained and trainable capacity that one brings from potentiality to actuality by repeated praxis; it is a mean between potency and act.[54] For example, you are born with the hexis of bravery, but you become brave (i.e., bring the hexis from potentiality to actuality) by the repeated performance of brave acts, by practice. If we compare Bourdieu's habitus with Aristotle's hexis, we see immediately that the formalism is absent, since Bourdieu would not admit the kind of actualized state that

Aristotle implies can exist. Still, Bourdieu's focus on practice is a key similarity and is closely tied to the ideas of field and capital.

His concept of capital widens the focus of the term *capital* as normally considered in the Marxist tradition to include "all forms of power . . . material, cultural, social, or symbolic," so that in addition to material capital, an actor can amass cultural, social, and symbolic capital.[55] This broad conception of capital assumes that much of what historical actors do is agonistic and that those who find themselves in a given *field* will be struggling within that field to attain the sorts of capital appropriate to it. But what is a field? Let us take the idea of an intellectual field, which is "that matrix of institutions, organizations, and markets in which symbolic producers, such as artists, writers, and academics, compete for symbolic capital."[56] As Bourdieu wrote, "to think in terms of field is to think *relationally*."[57] A field, in other words, is a network within which we can situate a thinker and her or his intellectual products. That thinker has conscious aims, but the intellectual material she or he produces is also the result of structuring forces, all of which interact continually and relationally with the thinker. There is thus a subjective element, the thinker, and the objective exterior world, the field, with which that thinker interacts on many levels. The danger of this approach, of course, is that the field becomes a kind of explanatory deus ex machina, providing all the answers when one asks why an intellectual did what he or she did. Used reasonably, however, the concept can provide a stimulus to thinking relationally and to considering thinkers not only in relation to the established traditions to which they consciously orient themselves, but also in relation to multiple forces, coactors, and economic and social circumstances that might otherwise escape one's purview.

This book began, in its introduction, with the Renaissance and has wandered far afield, so it will be useful to pause for a moment and recapitulate this chapter's ideas. The most important purely theoretical perspectives are those of Rorty and Bourdieu. Rorty's notion of philosophy as therapeutic and conversational frees us from the tyranny of hierarchical assumptions about the nature of philosophy; and Bourdieu's suggestions about peering beneath the surface of conscious articulation help reveal the nature of those individual-driven conversations, as well as the fact that they cannot be rightly understood without being situated socially. One cannot really comprehend Rorty and Bourdieu in a vacuum, so it was necessary to trace—admittedly with a broad brush—some of the lineaments of twentieth-century thought that lie behind them. Moreover, it was vital to zoom in for a time on history-writing; for microhistorians taught us to refocus our lens when looking at the past, to think about context in a nonteleological way, and to be very careful about where we draw the blurry, ephemeral, and perhaps nonexistent lines between "high" and "low."

So, informed by what has been covered hitherto, I would like to return now to the Renaissance and to see whether the foregoing theoretical considerations make any sense when we try to apply them, practically, to two Renaissance thinkers. As we shall see, it will not be necessary to invoke theory at every turn; the above-sketched ideas should serve instead as background. The two thinkers we shall meet will be treated both alone and in community, both as possessing agency and embedded in structure, in a fashion that employs some of the techniques used by microhistorians but applies them to a different milieu both intellectually and temporally.

CHAPTER FOUR

Orthodoxy

Lorenzo Valla and Marsilio Ficino

AT FIRST GLANCE, Lorenzo Valla (1405–57) and Marsilio Ficino (1433–99) seem to be linked by little more than the fact that they
were intellectuals who lived during a time broadly identified as the Renaissance.
Certainly, if we think in terms of traditional intellectual orientations, each was
decidedly different. Lorenzo Valla, on the one hand, was about as "humanistic" a humanist as one could find: with his pointed focus on problems of language, his cultivated and precisely individual sense of the Latin language, and
his vehement hatred of intellectual dogmatism, he represents much of what Renaissance humanism has come to stand for, especially if one thinks along the
lines of the version of that movement presented by Eugenio Garin. Marsilio
Ficino, on the other hand, was the greatest Renaissance Platonist who was also
well trained in scholastic Aristotelian medieval university traditions, and those
traditions shaped the way he thought. He cared little for cultivating humanistically elegant Latin and believed instead that there was a deeper message to
the history of human intellectual endeavor—a higher truth that lay behind all
wisdom, an "ancient theology" that was Christian in compass but highly inclusive when it came to its ability to adopt other, seemingly separate intellectual
and even religious traditions. Are Valla and Ficino simply best understood as
adherents of different disciplines? Not necessarily. Perhaps, in some way, these
thinkers are linked not by adherence to one or another predefined intellectual
tradition, but rather by the way they tested, refined, pushed, and pulled at the
malleable boundaries of orthodoxies both intellectual and religious. It is this
idea that I explore in this chapter; after some initial considerations of the term

orthodoxy, I move on to a case study of each author, trying to situate him in the fields most appropriate to his circumstances.

Orthodoxy is normally thought of as the condition of being orthodox. The Greek etymological roots of these words, as is well known, signify a combination of "rightness" or "correctness" with "opinion." Someone who is orthodox, in other words, is someone who holds the right opinion. Thus *orthodoxy,* in the words of the *Oxford English Dictionary,* means "belief in or agreement with what is, or is currently held to be, right, especially in religious matters." The word *orthodoxia* in Greek, however, is not a common one, at least in classical Greek; the word first came into its own in late antiquity.[1] Among ancient Latin writers up through the Silver Age, the word is unattested. We find it, however, in some patristic writers. Augustine uses the word *orthodoxus* to signify one who is in adherence with the true Catholic faith, as does Jerome, and forms of the word are used in medieval Latin as well, though not often in connection with heresy.[2]

But etymology can only take us so far. *Orthodoxy* as a word and a phenomenon is essentially reactive. It is intimately tied to the concept of heresy and appears most clearly when heresies are articulated: orthodoxy *fit, non nascitur,* and here, in the subcelestial realm, there is no ultimate source for orthodoxy, no magic book in which orthodoxy's truths clearly repose.[3] Not that this is theoretically a problem in the history of Christianity, for Christianity is a revealed religion in which the process of contestation is essential to revelation. Medieval thinkers in the tradition of Augustine, Aquinas for example, routinely attributed the presence of evil, which includes heresy, to God's providential design, a way to make a larger good come out of a smaller evil. Heretics — and heresies — were put on earth by God as a factor by which faith could be tested, renewed, and then more clearly articulated.[4]

The problem becomes clearer, however, when we consider that what is revealed is God's truth, but the mechanisms of its revelation and articulation are human beings. Who decides when a point of orthodoxy has been reached? Who is left out? What doctrines are endorsed? What written texts are essential to revelation? All are questions capable of endless disputation. But I think the latter question is most relevant, if we are considering Renaissance intellectuals. For oftentimes when Renaissance intellectuals came close to violating, or did violate, the malleable boundaries of religious orthodoxy, it was the final result of an expansion in the canon of acceptable texts.

Since the term *orthodoxy,* as indicated above, is slippery, it is useful to consider canon formation in conjunction with orthodoxy, because it helps shift the focus where it really belongs: away from religion in the abstract and onto small communities of intellectuals and the manner in which they receive and generate new ideas. Both Valla and Ficino, despite their obvious differences, were Renaissance intellectuals interested in applying the ancient past to the present. The continuous unearthing of the past and the reimagining of the present in relation to that past is one of the hallmarks of many of the greatest Renaissance thinkers.[5] Their "classical" past, however, was not the static, beautiful, but crystallized creation of nineteenth-century formalism; instead it was alive, and it was revealed by texts, and therein lie the problems: what texts did one read? How should they be applied to the present? How far did one's intellectual freedom extend? Both Valla and Ficino were wrestling with these questions, sometimes explicitly, sometimes implicitly.

They were also wrestling with what Christianity and, more broadly, monotheism meant in practice.[6] One danger that Renaissance historians face when looking at the orthodoxy of fifteenth-century figures is the temptation to apply post-Tridentine norms of orthodoxy onto pre-Tridentine intellectuals. When one isolates practices or ideas that seem not so easily to fit into a later version of orthodoxy, one assumes that the earlier thinkers under study were somehow aware that they were crossing a boundary and were taking steps to disguise that border crossing. Another danger is that one assumes a kind of medieval stasis leading up to the Renaissance, with the magisterial church and all its rules firmly established. But this was not the world in which Renaissance intellectuals lived.

Many questions concerning the nature of the church and even the nature of the ecclesiastical hierarchy were far from settled in the mid–fifteenth century or had not even been raised. And as Renaissance thinkers appropriated the diverse literary heritage of the ancient world, they were exposed to developments and changes in mentality that in the thousand-year course of antiquity might have taken centuries to achieve, a kind of "cultural compression" that could be explosive in its possibilities.[7] In this sense, the fifteenth century in Italy emerges as a "real" Renaissance, wherein newly discovered, vital intellectual heritages were uncovered *and* wherein thinkers felt relatively free in using those heritages to create the world that they quite literally imagined. The totalitarianizing impulses provoked by the sorts of ideological conflict that would occur later in the sixteenth century were still far off. So when we recover the excitement of newly discovered ancient texts and mentalities in the fifteenth century, it is not only an antiquarian excitement that we find but also a sense of possibility. This sense of possibility, however, did not last long: by the mid–sixteenth century, we find ourselves in a period that one historian of Italy has eloquently termed a *Rinascimento perduto,* a "lost" Renaissance, by which is meant the disappearance of an urbane, literate, and pious ruling class whose members simply assumed a certain amount of intellectual liberty and realized all too late that it was extinguished by the force of ideology.[8] For both Valla and Ficino, despite the different small communities in which they found themselves, many of those later boundaries did not clearly exist, and those that did were much more subtle. In their intellectual pursuits, some of the key textual touchstones were literary products of what we inevitably would consider postclassical antiquity, and this calls for comment.

Renaissance historians inevitably encounter the ancient past, since it was so important to Renaissance thinkers. Classical studies have undergone fundamental evolution in the past thirty to forty years, so it is appropriate that Renaissance historians embrace a vision of the ancient past that is not monolithic but reflective of antiquity's plurality, both temporally and intellectually. First, we should recognize that the eras of the "classical" Greco-Roman past, say fifth-century B.C. Athens, the Roman republic, or the very early Roman Empire, were themselves far from monolithic. When we discuss a Renaissance thinker's creative use of a figure from "classical" antiquity, are we relying on what would now be among classicists an antiquated view of the classical object? If ambivalences are possible even in the realm of "classical" sources, how much more is this the case when dealing with non-"classical" but nonetheless ancient sources? Problems such as these are especially apparent when we think of late ancient studies.

One of the most important points that scholars of late antiquity have touched on recently concerns the evolution of religion and philosophy in late antiquity and the relationship within that context of "paganism" and Christianity. One sometimes assumes that the salient difference between paganism and Christianity was that the former was considered polytheistic, whereas the latter was committed to monotheistic worship of the Christian God, inherited from the Yahweh of the Hebrew Bible. Newer scholarship shows rather convincingly, however, that most educated persons in late antiquity believed in the existence of one supreme being of some sort. The question that divided pagans and Judeo-Christians was one of naming. The Judeo-Christian God is the God who said "I am who am," thereby precluding that he be worshiped by other names or in other ways than orthodoxies eventually proscribed. "Pagan" monotheists were usually more flexible in the issue of just how the supreme being was to be worshiped and whether there were aspects of the supreme being that could be accessed in different ways.[9] And both pagan monotheism and Christianity, despite their superficially vitriolic differences, were undergirded by a set of underlying assumptions that embraced the notion that "monotheism was perfectly compatible with belief in the existence of a plurality of divine beings," to borrow the phraseology of Polymnia Athanassiadi and Michael Frede.[10] The Christian trinity "makes it very difficult to say in precisely what sense Christians believe in one God, . . . and of course there is also the veneration of the saints."[11] This is not to deny that in late antiquity titanic verbal battles were waged to define these matters and—for protagonists on both sides—to make precise exactly what *was* meant by specific concepts and beliefs. At its heart, however, religion, and orthodoxy, was a matter of *construction,* and despite going through discrete and different phases, this constructive process continued to happen. Often, moreover, beneath the surface of apparently divisive intellectual conflict, there can lie a definable set of underlying assumptions that seemingly opposed parties to a debate share. Historians of late ancient religion and philosophy have done a great service by attempting to remove, insofar as they can, the teleology that assumes a "triumph" of Christianity, creating instead a history that tries to recreate life as it was lived, life replete with the excitement of a new doctrine to be understood and perhaps refuted or a new formulation embodied in a text that had to be examined.

In the study of early modern Europe broadly conceived, another, not so dissimilar, set of teleologies is involved. Here the sixteenth century is the key, so that when one looks at the orthodoxy of fifteenth-century thinkers, the temptation is to understand these thinkers in relation to the religious crisis of the sixteenth century: Do they anticipate later positions or conflicts? Can we discern adumbrations in Valla of positions later endorsed by Martin Luther? Questions like these are important and should continue to be asked, but alongside them we should try to evoke the tensions and battles that intellectuals in the fifteenth-century Italian Renaissance lived, from issue to issue and from generation to generation. Scholars long ago dispensed with certain ideas of Jacob Burckhardt regarding the Renaissance, one of the most noteworthy of which was that the Renaissance in a certain way represented a "pagan" revival. But if we reconsider just what *pagan* means, and if we suggest, as I would like to do, that paganism has less to do with a romantically idealized, unfettered polytheism and more to do with a certain fluidity and openness regarding just how one was allowed to worship, then, perhaps, the Italian Renaissance was both more pagan and more Christian than we might previously have imagined.

Lorenzo Valla

Lorenzo Valla's life was itinerant, agonistic, and conditioned by the newness of Renaissance humanism. In chapter 2 of this book, I outlined two major modes of conceptualizing Renaissance humanism, identified with the work of Eugenio Garin and Paul Oskar Kristeller. Kristeller's view was the most comprehensive, we saw, whereas Garin's did a better job of explaining what was distinctive over time. In chapter 3 I suggested that we should try to find ways of conceiving Renaissance intellectual life that encompass the best of both approaches, while attempting to situate thinkers in a larger field than has been the norm. There can be no better person with whom to begin this approach than Lorenzo Valla: his literary production and the course, even the style, of his life are linked and manifested by a dialectical polemicism that suffused everything he did. Indeed, if we can identify a habitus for Valla, an unarticulated but powerfully shaping assumption that underlies his work, it is just that: polemicism. Some of Valla's work is constituted by direct attacks on fellow humanists, but all of his work is adversarial in tone, well reflecting the agonistic world out of which Valla emerged.

Valla lived from 1405 to 1457, and in his day the humanist movement was only beginning to create a permanent institutional place for itself. By the end of the fifteenth century, the *studia humanitatis,* the humanities, would become a standard part of the upbringing of almost every educated European. By then, most universities included the humanities as part of the arts faculty, and most people even at the secondary level would already have had exposure to them, taught in the new, classicizing style. However, in the first half of the century, when Valla was trying to establish himself, individual humanists had to carve out paths for themselves in largely uncharted territory. What was the best way to earn enough money to live, to practice this new and exciting literary craft, and, when possible, to have an effect on the world around you? Humanists sought patronage of all sorts: they worked in political capacities, as secretaries to republics, as parts of princely courts. One of the most prestigious courts was the papal court, the chancery of which was in these years coming to seem apt territory for humanists to practice their trade, even if most of its offices were not in Valla's lifetime exclusively staffed by humanists.[12]

Valla grew up in a family that had close ties to the papal court. His uncle Melchior Scrivani was an official at the court, and Valla at various times in his youth had the distinct advantage of accompanying his uncle during his visits to various literati.[13] His initial education was in Rome, and Valla harbored an ambition to become a papal secretary, which would be fulfilled only decades later. The papal court in the years before 1443 was itself itinerant. After the end in 1417 of the Great Schism—during which there were two, sometimes three contenders for the papal throne—internecine strife in Rome, the eternal city, prevented the papacy from taking up long-term residence there.[14] Not until 1443, when Eugenius IV moved the court back to Rome, would the papacy have its permanent Renaissance base there. In the meantime, the papal court at various periods sojourned in Florence, and it is there where Valla probably first had extended contact with the actual practices of the papal court and the various cultural epiphenomena that trailed it. In his early years and after his initial schooling in Rome, Valla was educated in Florence and had wide exposure to the new culture of humanism, which was fast establishing itself as a cultural ideal in the "Athens on the Arno."[15]

During the first two to three decades of the fifteenth century in Florence, the cultivation of the humanities was accompanied by a social practice that would remain at the heart of the humanist movement and lead to some of the wider sorts of cultural changes that the humanist movement engendered: this was what humanists called *disputatio* (disputation), and its mental operations were embodied in the most significant form of humanist Latin literature, the dialogue.[16]

In the early years of the fifteenth century, Leonardo Bruni (d. 1444), probably the best-selling humanist author of the fifteenth century, wrote a dialogue that captured perfectly the environment and the highest ideals of what disputation meant for humanists, and we can get a taste of the world of the *disputatio* by glancing at this work.[17] At one point, early on, the interlocutors gather at the house of Coluccio Salutati, the humanist movement's elder statesman in the late fourteenth and early fifteenth centuries. Bruni's character Salutati scolds them for having neglected the art of disputation and deprived themselves of a major mode of reasoning: "In the name of the gods, for examining and discussing subtle matters what could be more efficacious than disputation, where the topic is placed as it were stage center and observed by many eyes, so that there is nothing in it which can escape or deceive the view of all?" Salutati recognizes the inherently social nature of group discussions, of conversation: "When the soul is weary and weakened and shrinks from these studies, what could renew and refresh it more than discussions carried on in a gathering, where you are strongly fired to read and learn thoroughly—by glory, if you have overcome others, or by shame if you have been overcome?"[18]

The work in which this briefly quoted passage appears is complex, and scholarly controversy has roiled around it.[19] Bypassing the controversies, we can see that for our purposes the dialogical nature of humanist thought comes to the fore. It is in this sense that rhetoric is inherently philosophical; it is at its heart a Socratic procedure that stimulates the listener or reader to mental action, even while concealing the (perhaps unknowable) intention of the author.[20] In a literary sense, the give and take of conversation is enshrined most easily in the genre of the dialogue, but this give and take constitutes an underlying mentality, a habitus, that pervades rhetorical learning. Three very important aspects of this mentality come to the fore. First, it is inherently antidogmatic; many voices are better than one. Second, it is an agonistic way of thinking in which the public arena decides truth, so that even if a thinker who shares this mentality is writing alone in a study, the dialogical process is inherent to his method of reasoning. Third, ambiguity is not always something to be shunned. The original meaning of the word *philosophy,* coined by Pythagoras, was simply "love of wisdom," not transcendentalist German idealism. Humanists who shared the dialogical rhetorical mentality achieved their wisdom by conversation, sometimes external, sometimes internal.[21] Needless to say, one can easily find thinkers in the Renaissance who were trained in the humanities and who served simply as functionaries or hired pens. But this fact should not obscure what Plato himself had masterfully realized and at times artfully concealed: that rhetoric can itself be philosophical, even if it was not what a later age would term *professionally* philosophical.[22]

Many humanists participated in this culture of the *disputatio,* but none so acutely as Lorenzo Valla. As Valla accompanied his uncle Scrivani on his various peregrinations to the houses of learned men, Valla was exposed to many masterful disputants, to the style in which they thought, and to the elegance with which deep familiarity with classical sources endowed their expression.[23] It was in his late teens and early twenties that he conceived his ambition to become an *orator*, having only an intuition as to what that term really meant.[24] But it had something to do with moving the minds and hearts of people in the right direction and above all with maintaining what Valla would later come to term *liberty of speaking (libertas dicendi).*[25] By this he meant freedom from dogmatism and the ability to discuss topics hitherto seen as out of bounds. Later in life, he would write that an orator "had a knowledge of a great mass of things: the difficult science of moving men's spirits, familiarity with many different affairs, a knowledge of all peoples and every memory of their deeds, and, before all else, sanctity of life, a certain outstanding dignity of spirit, and excellence of body and of voice. Certainly the orator is like a ruler and leader of a people. Because of this, rhetoric is by far most difficult and arduous and not to be grasped by all."[26]

Given these assumptions concerning the true nature of an orator, which Valla refined by careful study of his favorite ancient authority on rhetoric, Quintilian, but developed in his own original way, it is unsurprising that Valla was attracted to the figure of Saint Paul, who after all had himself been a rhetorician.[27] Valla had a deep, if nontraditional, commitment to religion and had strong ideas about contemporary Christianity, ideas that shaped the ever-developing contours of his thought. They informed his contempt for scholastic philosophy, a common target among humanists, for, just as Valla believed that in some important ways modern Christianity would benefit from a return to its apostolic roots, so too did he object to what he saw as scholastic philosophers' abandonment of the very principles of philosophy. "What a great and marvelous praise of modesty" it was, wrote Valla, when Pythagoras, the inventor of the word *philosopher,* replied when questioned that he was not "wise, but a lover of wisdom."[28] It disturbed Valla that, instead of following along in this respected, age-old ethic of humility, modern philosophers, especially dialecticians, had taken the thought of one philosopher, Aristotle, and ossified it, essentially abjuring the freedom of speaking that true philosophy, in Valla's eyes, represented. As much as humanists standardly charged that they felt themselves surrounded by empty pedantry because of the forms modern intellectual life had taken, Valla thought this sort of thing more than most. For him, the culture of the *disputatio* was raised to its highest level, and nothing was exempt from the close scrutiny afforded by the dialectical method that lay behind it.

So if we turn more specifically to the notion of orthodoxy, Valla is an especially interesting example. Looking at his work, we can see what a number of other interpreters have noted: that Valla was living at a time that seemed to many a period of religious crisis.[29] For Valla the period from 1435 to 1448 was crucial, for it was then that he found himself in the service of the great Renaissance king of Naples and Sicily, Alfonso of Aragon, "the Magnanimous."[30] Earlier Valla had attempted to navigate the stormy seas of patronage at the papal court but was undone by rivals. Instead of remaining adrift, he attached himself to Alfonso and gained a great reputation at the court for his learning, though even there he did not avoid provoking the animosity of rival courtiers.[31] It was during this period that Valla wrote or gave final polish to his most important works, and it is in this realm that we see the flexible boundaries of orthodoxy and just what Valla's convictions were.[32] There can be no doubt, of course, that Valla's initial lack of success at the papal court conditioned some of his attitudes toward the present state of organized Christianity and the quality of its rulership; and Valla certainly was not alone among humanists in expressing ambivalence about the moral state of the contemporary clerisy.[33] But it would be foolish to dismiss his contribution as "mere" rhetoric. Rhetoric it is, but in its argumentative power, it takes the philosophical potential of rhetoric to a new level, transforming rhetoric into a philosophical method and changing the paradigm of philosophy from one in which metaphysics stood at the top to one in which life as it is lived takes primacy of place. Moreover, his Pauline view of Christianity is in harmony with the topos of humility that we have already noted and goes beyond other humanistic anticlerical protestations in its conception of the nature of the church broadly conceived. To flesh these themes out, we can glance at four of Valla's works.

"But I am not Paul who could reprimand Peter: yea, I *am* Paul, for I imitate him, and what is more, much more, I am made one in spirit with God when I zealously obey His mandates."[34] This remarkable self-identification with the great evangelist occurs near the beginning of Valla's treatise proving the spuriousness of the Donation of Constantine, undoubtedly his most famous work. The Donation of Constantine itself, the *Constitutum Constantini*, was a forged document written sometime between the middle of the eighth and the middle of the ninth centuries, and it became an important source for the papacy in its emerging medieval struggle to understand, define, and expand the limits of its secular jurisdiction.[35] Purportedly it was authored in the first years of the fourth century by Constantine himself, who, after his baptism by Pope

Sylvester, moved the imperial capital eastward to Byzantium and ceded to the pope all rights over the western territories of the empire. After its forgery, it was by the mid–twelfth century adopted into canon law and was important because, if genuine, it would show that the first Christian Roman Emperor explicitly gave power over western Europe to the popes.

Valla was not the first to question this document. Some had suggested that if the emperor had the power to alienate the western empire, he also had the power to reappropriate it. Others had wondered why there seemed to be no mention of the supposed grant before the ninth century. Still others had made more traditional arguments drawing on the sentiment behind Paul's admonition in his second letter to Timothy, to the effect that no one fighting in the cause of God should mix himself up in worldly affairs.[36] Valla, too, makes arguments along these lines, but his originality comes in another sort of critical method, which he wields with greatest acuity. This is his refined sense of the historicity of language; this sense is manifested in other works of his, where he argues to the effect that meaning in language depends radically on usage, again ringing his own particular changes on themes addressed by Quintilian and, before him, Aristotle.[37] Here, however, Valla's philological precision is apparent in the manner in which he identifies words in the document that could not have existed in the early fourth century. As one example we can note that "Constantine" in the Donation in one place speaks of his grant being made by his own authority together with that of his "satraps." Valla points out that one never finds decrees made in this way in contemporary sources. Another example: Why is the name Constantinople used in the document when at the time of the putative donation it hadn't been renamed and was still known as Byzantium?[38] Valla's criticisms take the form of a passage-by-passage analysis of the text which occupies one-third of the sizable work, carried out with the most minute precision and at times a disturbing abundance of passion.[39] The work is not a dialogue, but it possesses nonetheless the hallmark polemicism that we noted earlier as an underlying characteristic of Valla's work, for it is a treatise that is in part directed at whoever forged the document.

Some of the treatise's vehemence is doubtless due to the fact that when Valla wrote it, his patron Alfonso was having troubles in the form of territorial disputes with the then pope, Eugenius IV.[40] Alfonso wanted to expand his dominions, and Eugenius preferred another claimant as a ruler for a part of the realm. But even when, well after the troubles between the two leaders had passed, Valla wrote a justification of his own work to the pope, he did not back away from any of his treatise's major claims. Moreover, in a 1444 letter to a respected humanist colleague who possessed great facility in Greek and Latin, Giovanni Aurispa, Valla writes concerning his work on the Donation that he has written nothing more *oratorium* (oratorical).[41] Why? First, there is the technical reason that Valla twice refers to the work as an "oration" and that it can even be classified as an example of the genre of rhetoric known as judicial oratory.[42] Beyond the technical features, Valla clearly believes that in writing the work he has demonstrated those idealized, above-noted heroic qualities that a true orator possesses. At the outset he recognizes the bold step he is taking and highlights it: "For someone who knows how to speak well must not be considered a true orator unless he also dares to speak."[43] "I am not doing this," Valla goes on a bit later, "because I want to inveigh against anyone and write what would amount to Phillipics against him (far be that crime from me), but to pluck away error from the minds of men."[44] The "error" Valla refers to is the acceptance as genuine of a spurious work. As he states, "Christian integrity does not need to patronize falsehood."[45] In some fundamental ways, however, Valla is questioning not only the validity of the document but the actual style of the papacy as it was evolving. In so doing he suggests a new and different ecclesiology (though he does not systematically outline one); and more importantly, he is asking what it means to be a Christian.[46]

This sort of query regarding the nature of Christianity is also manifested in another of Valla's works, entitled *On the Profession of the Religious*.[47] Here Valla's basic point is that the *religious*—a term referring to members of religious orders (though Valla contests that meaning in the dialogue)—do not have a special claim to a greater reward for good works than do lay people. In fact they have an easier road to salvation since, although all Christians are bound by certain laws, the religious are artificially separated from the rest of society. As to form, the work is a dialogue, and Valla takes full advantage of the rhetorical possibilities that the genre offers. He says that he is reporting the *disputatio* that took place after a disagreement between two members of a learned circle broke out concerning the status of the life of the religious, and he says he will report the dialogue without interspersing "he said" and other ways of identifying speakers; he will simply give the names, so that the reader feels he is present at a disputation. The style of reporting that Valla uses, however, is occasionally interlarded with narrational comments. This is particularly effective and evocative of the conversational approach that identifies the rhetorical way of thought integral to much of the humanist project.

Conversational, however, should not be construed in any way as "unstructured," for in this work everything has its place. The dialogue is dedicated to Baptista Platamone, who was an important lay member of the court of King Alfonso and, significantly, a judge. The dialogue as a literary form is inherently malleable and antisystematic, but from the beginning Valla sets up subtle strategies to guide the reader's appropriation of the text. The debate begins when a friar has maintained that an advantage of the religious life is that by assuming it one can receive greater rewards for good works, a position that Aquinas himself had endorsed, whereas another disputant had vigorously denied this. The learned men give the debate over to Valla and the friar, so that they can flesh out the important issues. The undercurrents of criticism are as important as the more open points. For example, at the outset, the character Laurentius goes on the offensive. Addressing the friar, he wonders how, if two men lead similar lives, "yet more reward is owed by God to the one who has professed this sect, which you call 'religion' and on account of which you call yourselves the 'religious,' than to the man who has professed no sect at all, either yours or that of the monks or any other, and does not want to profess a sect."[48] So much is contained in this brief opening salvo.

First, there is the fact that Valla refers to the friar as a member of a "sect." As soon becomes clear, the friar is none too happy about this. When the friar takes exception to the term, however, Valla explains what he means. Although admitting that sects have existed among rhetoricians, "'sects' are properly spoken of among philosophers."[49] Among philosophers, there are Stoics, Peripatetics, and so forth; so too is it with the "religious": "You do something similar, not just because some of you are monks, some friars, some eremites, some spiritual friars, but also because there are thousands of types of such individual groups," laughable in their diversity (4.4). Valla then wishes to continue with the analogy to philosophers, who are unbearable because they claim the name of those desirous of wisdom for themselves alone, even as they deny it to men of obvious practical wisdom, like legislators, senators, orators and just monarchs (4.6).[50]

Second, there is Valla's highlighting of the term *religious,* which signals on the surface that Valla thinks it is necessary to focus on precise meanings of words. Just how Valla focuses on these meanings, however, is what we should identify. How has it happened, Valla is asking, that *religious* has come to designate friars alone? Here as elsewhere, Valla wants to recover a deeper, truer meaning of the word, and he locates this in antiquity—Christian antiquity. He suggests that it is arrogant of the friars to appropriate the word for their style of life alone: what could be greater praise for anyone than to be called religious; what greater reproof than to be called irreligious? "After all, what else is being religious than being Christian and, certainly, being truly Christian?" In the rest of the dialogue, Valla uses the most versatile tools that rhetoric can offer and presents critiques of the religious that are traditional—complaints about moral laxity, sexual profligacy, avariciousness, and so on—as well as more involved philological arguments that are carefully organized to expose weaknesses in the position of moral superiority which the friar had maintained.

One should think carefully here and elsewhere about Valla's use of philology. If, on the one hand, he takes the position that words gain their meaning from usage, then how can he arbitrarily decide on the other hand that contemporary usage, which reserves a special meaning for the term *religious,* is untenable? All philology has some sort of ideological substructure. Here, as in other etymological investigations, we can locate the habitus that informs Valla's way of proceeding. It has to do with humility first of all: it is the arrogance of the friars that seems to mean the most to Valla. Moreover, the habitus has to do with the liberty of speaking that we discussed above. The friars are like members of philosophical sects. For Valla, this means that they differentiate themselves in order ultimately to be released from the obligation of thinking freely about various problems: the great peril of any sort of absolute orthodoxy is the loss of intellectual freedom. Valla's critiques are aimed at those who do not have the courage to question why things are the way they are. And when he looks for meanings in antiquity, what he sees there is a freedom of thinking and speaking that medieval thinkers from Boethius (d. 524) onward abjured. Valla, like all humanists, was deeply steeped in non-Christian classical authors, but Christian antiquity had a special valence for him, for the language of the Christian fathers combined the natural elegance of ancient forms of expression with the humility appropriate to a true Christian.[51]

The most elegant humility of all, perhaps, was contained in the Bible, and an important lens through which we can see Valla's relation to orthodoxy is constituted by his *Annotations on the New Testament.* In this work, Valla applies his philological scrutiny to the text of the Latin New Testament—the Vulgate sanctioned by a millennium of use within the Church and believed to have been translated by Saint Jerome, who after having been ordered by Pope Damasus to do the translation, was considered to have been working under divine inspiration. Valla is careful. He never advocates replacing the translation with another, and although his notes are polemical in the vituperation he directs against the "interpres" (the translator), they are not explicitly directed against Saint Jerome, and Valla did not believe that Jerome was the Vulgate's translator.[52] In his preface to the work, dedicated to Pope Nicholas V, he argues that Jerome had been presented with a confused manuscript situation, and Valla goes on to suggest that if the situation Jerome faced was difficult, how much more is this the case now, after one thousand additional years. Valla stresses that he does not intend to replace the translation, just to fix it, as one would fix a leaky roof.[53]

The *Annotations* exists in two versions, the first completed during his tenure at the court of Alfonso, the second during his time at the papal court, probably between 1453 and 1457. The second version is the one discovered by Erasmus in 1504 at the capitular library of the monastery of Parc, outside of Louvain, and which he undertook to publish at the press of Josse Bade in 1505.[54] There are changes in the two redactions. In general the second version is marked by more precision and a reduction of superfluities, and occasionally it reflects greater circumspection on Valla's part, since Valla had in the intervening years been attacked by his formidable rival Poggio Bracciolini on suspicion of impiety. Both redactions, however, constitute the particular marriage of "pure" philology with conviction that distinguishes Valla's oeuvre on the whole. Some of the Annotations are grammatical alone and contain a correction or a different interpretation of a Greek word, some criticize inconsistencies in translation, and others simply offer the reader a guide through possible ambiguities. Throughout, however, one gets the sense that it is this very grammatical precision that gives rise to the larger points Valla often makes.[55]

One such case occurs, for example, when Valla, examining the letter of Paul to the Romans, wishes to elucidate the meaning of a passage in Romans 12:3, in which Paul exhorted his hearers toward humility, writing: "do not know more than is necessary to know, but know up to the point of modesty." In the Greek, "me hyperphronein par'ho dei phronein alla phronein eis to sophronein," the thrust of the exhortation is for the listeners not to think too highly of themselves. The emphasis is on personal humility, and the key verb is *phronein*, which has a connotation of inner, reflective knowledge, rather than syllogistic knowledge. The Vulgate's choice of words on this occasion, "non plus sapere quam oportet sapere sed sapere ad sobrietatem," with the verb *sapere,* to know, being used for *phronein,* could give a misleading impression, perhaps that Paul is saying that listeners should refrain from the kind of knowledge that comes from reason. In the first redaction of his notes, Valla is clear about the meaning of the passage when he writes, "For the Apostle wishes to reduce pride and arrogance of mind and he understands this [pride and arrogance] not as of wisdom or knowledge," but he is not so clear as to what to do about it. In the second redaction, Valla omits the sentence about Paul's intention but suggests a better translation for the key verb in question, the Greek *phronein,* "which ought to be translated as *sentire* rather than *sapere; that is, ne velitis de vobis sentire supra quam oportet sentire de vobis.*"[56] Valla is saying that in this situation, the verb *sentire* much more accurately reflects the somewhat speculative, contemplative import of the Greek *phronein.*

The cited passage, if taken alone, would mean little toward fleshing out the overall contours of Valla's thought. We can step back, however, and set it in the context of the rest of Valla's Annotations and indeed of the rest of the precise grammatical arguments that occur within the larger framework of his literary production. Doing this, we see that, like individual points in a painting by Seurat, these small grammatical arguments are fundamental parts of the whole that demand attention as *both* part and whole. They stimulate the engagement of the perceiver in a way that mediates almost automatically the subject-object dichotomy that seems so often to divide text from reader. Valla's grammatical precision is notable precisely because it is not magisterial. As rhetorical discourse it invites debate, dialogue, and counterclaims and thus helps on some level to liberate textuality from authorial intentionality, while still allowing readers, even centuries later, to discern the larger outlines that informed the whole of Valla's thought. What is this whole? How does one characterize it? We come back to Saint Paul and Valla's paleo-Christian sympathies. In fact, here and elsewhere there are passages in Valla's oeuvre that lead one to think of him as a predecessor to some of the thinkers of the Protestant Reformation. There are quite a number of similarities and some very crucial differences. Valla's Pauline sympathies have to be understood precisely, and there is no better work to use as a touchstone for this examination than his treatise on the freedom of the will, *De libero arbitrio.*[57]

The issue that lay behind the treatise was an old one. Let us posit a supreme being, God, who, precisely by virtue of his being supreme, is necessarily both all-powerful and all-knowing, as well as being the highest sort of good possible. In his omnipotent omniscience he must be able to see all things, and time relative to us must be different from time relative to him. In fact the distinctions we make between past, present, and future must be meaningless to God, who sees all phenomena as if they were occurring within an eternal present. Given these assumptions, dilemmas arise. On the one hand, if God sees everything and therefore knows the future as completely as the present, we can do nothing that God does not know we will do: how can we really be acting freely? On the other, if we do posit the existence of human free will, are we somehow limiting the power of God, in this case his power to know all things? In that case the omnipotent God is no longer omnipotent, God is then not God, and we are faced with an evident absurdity. Moreover, there is clearly evil in the world. People commit evil acts and do things we all acknowledge are wrong; we ourselves sin. If God is fundamentally good, and also all powerful, why doesn't he prevent these evil things from happening? What does Valla say about all this?

As it turns out, Boethius, the "last Roman" or the "first medieval," depending on one's definitional criteria, wrestled with the issue before he died at the hands of the Ostrogothic king Theodoric in 524. In his famous *Consolation of Philosophy,* a beautiful, lyrical work alternating prose and poetry and written when he was imprisoned, Boethius had in fact been the one who outlined the scheme of God knowing all phenomena as if they appeared in an eternal present.[58] Valla was no friend of Boethius. In other works, we see that Valla believed Western thought had taken a turn for the worse with Boethius, who introduced Aristotelian logic into the West and added to the mix neologisms that would become staples of institutional philosophy. For Valla, Boethius was the fount and origin that had unleashed the rancid river of scholastic logic, chopping into the pristine rhetorical forest represented by the mentality and style of thought of the Church fathers.[59] Here, in his *On Free Will,* Valla sees Boethius as someone to transcend, and he proposes a novel way to do it.

Valla and his interlocutor first go through the Boethian arguments, which lead the character Valla finally to say, "It is possible for you to do otherwise than God foreknows, nevertheless you will not do otherwise, nor will you therefore deceive him."[60] Implicitly then, given the presence of mundane evil, it is acknowledged that there are some who will choose inevitably to do evil things. This is essentially the limit to which Boethius had arrived, that is, to assert that divine foreknowledge and causation are not the same thing. One senses, however, that for Valla, ending on this note smacked too much of the sort of assertion, unexplored by rhetorical argument, that he most detested among scholastic philosophers. So Valla goes beyond this position, and ultimately, the answer he proposes is a somewhat disarming one, especially to us who are grappling with the slippery nature of pre-Tridentine orthodoxy: "What cannot be achieved with one god," Valla writes, "can be achieved with two."[61] How does Valla get there?

Valla arrives at this point after a further attempt to clarify the question leads him to draw an example from remotest Roman history, from the transitional moment when kingship was abolished and the early republic established, which had been dealt with memorably by Livy.[62] The character in question is the reprehensible son of Tarquin the Proud, Sextus Tarquinius, whose rape of Lucretia incited the people to overthrow his father and to found the Roman republic. Now let us say, Valla suggests, that Sextus, like many others, went to the oracle of Apollo early on, before committing his most heinous crimes, and asked what his fate would be. The oracle would probably have responded, "An exile and a pauper you will fall, killed by the angry city."[63] What then was Sextus to do? Would it be fair for him to blame the oracle? Could he say to the oracle, Valla asks, "indeed it is your fault, Apollo, who foresee my fate with your wisdom, for, unless you had foreseen it, this would not be about to happen to me?"[64] Of course not. This would be unfair, for Apollo does not cause his behavior, only accurately predicts it. Sextus might be justified in blaming Zeus, or the fates, but not the oracle. In this way, Valla separates God's foreknowledge, obviously represented by the oracle, from God's power of causation . . . but by what is this latter power represented? The question is unanswerable, or rather, the answer is ineffable. In a coda to the dialogue, the interlocutors come upon the obvious problem: why has God inexplicably hardened the hearts of some? The answer: we cannot know. God "has mercy on whom he will have mercy, and whom he will he hardeneth." Continuing in his lengthy citation of Saint Paul's letter to the Romans (9:11–21), Valla queries, does the clay ask the potter why he has formed it in the way he has? "Hath not the potter power over the clay?"[65]

There really is no completely satisfactory way to solve the dilemma intellectually. Either you accept that we do have a free will and that by using it we can contribute to our own salvation (in which case you limit God's power); or, the supremely good being, God, has unfairly (from a human perspective) condemned many to damnation and himself seems somehow, paradoxically, to allow evil. There are ways out of both positions, of course, but all of them boil down to issues of faith, for the essence of this problem is the ability of the human mind to project the notion of a unitary absolute into logical space and the consequences of that projection.

As I mentioned earlier, one of Valla's early ardent desires had been to have a position of prominence at the papal court, especially that of apostolic secretary, a plum job for humanists in midcentury and an office that at that time, as mentioned, was not yet exclusively staffed by humanists. Eventually, he achieved his ambition. Under Pope Nicholas V, Valla became a scriptor, and then under Calixtus III—significantly, a Spanish Pope, a Borgia, who had affection for Valla's patron Alfonso—an apostolic secretary. Still, Valla had questioned the legitimacy of a foundational document of the church, directed criticism against the religious in a way that went beyond standard late medieval anticlerical topoi, publicly critiqued the version of Scripture sanctioned by a millennium of use and hermeneutic, and finally boldly suggested that one can "solve" a problem within the context of Christianity by using "two gods." Political circumstances or no, it is highly significant that he reached one of the highest, most prominent offices of the papal court.

Valla did not do it unopposed, of course. He had rivals, many of them, and his work aroused suspicion. Poggio Bracciolini, clearly a member of the previous generation of humanists, as he himself admits, castigated Valla for writing a "book against Jerome" (Poggio refers to Valla's work on the New Testament), and Valla did have to appear before certain official church offices to defend himself. However, after all of this—after successfully navigating inquiries by the Neapolitan inquisition and the Roman curia, after securing a place for himself within the church hierarchy and obtaining the position he had desired all his life —does Valla change his paleo-Christian opinions or mollify his view of the institutional church? No. In 1457, when he is asked to speak at the main Dominican church in Rome, Santa Maria sopra Minerva, in honor of Saint Thomas Aquinas, the Dominican Order's greatest philosopher, Valla scandalizes the crowd, as he offers so much praise for the eloquent simplicity of the late ancient church fathers, who "had devoted their entire selves to imitating the Apostle Paul," that Aquinas seemed to suffer by comparison.[66]

There is a subtle but underlying conflict present in Valla's thought: on the one hand we have his repeated praise of the *libertas dicendi,* the freedom of speaking necessary to an intellectual life of integrity. On the other, in his treatise on free will Valla recognizes one of the inherent problems of monotheism, later to become a concern in a transmogrified, secularized form of liberal thinkers like Isaiah Berlin: that it is not always easy to reconcile absolute justice with absolute freedom. In his outward personality, Valla was far from an exemplar of personal humility and was probably closer, in Freudian terms at least, to a classic narcissist.[67] But in the ethic, the topos, of humility that pervades his thought and allows the existence of the sorts of contradiction that real life presents, we can see indeed why Valla was proud to define himself *in opposition to* philosophers and institutional philosophy. And, as one might say in Italian, *meno male*— loosely translated, good for him.

And good, perhaps, for us, too. If we return to Valla's two gods, we see that he is not advocating that we worship more than one god or asserting that there is more than one god absolutely speaking. Rather Valla is suggesting that the one God's power can be understood as having different aspects and that we should in our veneration of him understand him accordingly. Not a novel notion, of course, but the way Valla poses it, in a context of literary play, a dialogical back-and-forth with no certain, demonstratively reached conclusion, suggests that he endorses a plurality of opinion rather than unity and is wondering rather openly just how this one God is to be conceived. Important it was to recognize one supreme divinity; not so important perhaps to recognize the supremacy of institutions and magisterial mentalities that men had created. The course of his later career shows quite clearly that this openness, in the intellectual field in which Valla found himself, was allowed. And this notion of possibility rather than nullity, plurality rather than unity, is one of the most important legacies of the humanist movement and something that we should keep in mind when we come, as we soon shall, to Marsilio Ficino.

In Valla's case, we saw that his intellectual field was shaped early on by the culture of disputation, where the many-sided airing out of opinions was preferable to monolithic ex cathedra pronouncements and where truth/victory was decided by the public arena, by consensus rather than syllogism. Doubtless the culture of the disputation, with its inherently conflictual nature, was in the first half of the fifteenth century intimately related to the social conditions under which humanists worked. Although Garin did not quite put it this way, a great merit of his interpretation was that it laid stress on the notion that humanists during this period were essentially outsiders—not always social or economic outsiders, but intellectual outsiders with a fundamentally new orientation.[68] By the second half of the fifteenth century, things had changed. Education in the humanities had become the norm for the Italian cultural elite, and humanists were, institutionally speaking, there to stay. And by the end of the fifteenth century, a basic, fashionably classicizing grounding in the humanities was a Europe-wide ideal.

Marsilio Ficino

When the study of the humanities became a part of elite culture, however, it grew also to serve the needs of the elite and became less incendiary; once avant-garde movements are adopted by the mainstream, they are no longer avant-garde.[69] If the verbally centered culture of the disputation was intimately allied to the progress of humanism, it also contained within it the seeds of its own end. As increasingly sovereign styles of rulership grew in popularity, churches and states all had an interest in restricting the kind of freedom of thought that the true culture of the disputation embodied; and by the late sixteenth century, we can detect a turn on the part of many leading intellectuals away from the verbal and language arts, more easily understandable—and hence, perhaps, repressible—by curious rulers, toward the less easily comprehensible mathe-matical arts, which latter preoccupation tended to insulate one from criticism.[70] Looked at from this larger perspective, the age of Ficino is crucial, and Ficino is a pivotal figure. One of the legacies of the culture of the disputation ideologically had been openness to new texts. While Ficino was unconcerned with "proper" Latin style and was no vigorous critic of traditional institutions, the openness that the culture of the disputation engendered remained, even if Ficino was rarely polemical about his openness; and he, like the later, sixteenth-century thinkers studied by Timothy Reiss, turned, if not to exclusively mathematical, then to increasingly esoteric styles of interpretation and analysis that tended both to insulate him and, moreover, to isolate him.[71] Ficino's approach, like Valla's, was shaped by his intellectual field. If we continue in our look at ortho-doxy, then, we should turn first to the field in which Ficino found himself.

We often forget the tremendous sense of vitality, excitement, and newness that the Renaissance hunt for new texts generated.[72] Part and parcel of the hu-manist movement, this hunt led figures like Giovanni Aurispa (1369–1459), Francesco Filelfo (1398–1481), and others to respond to the humanist convic-tion, as old as Salutati practically and Petrarch theoretically, to include and appropriate the Greek as well as the Latin heritage in their reconstruction of antiquity—an intramental colonial precursor, perhaps, to the voyages of discovery of the sixteenth century. But as the main lines of scholarly inquiry grew clearer—as figures like Leonardo Bruni established chronologies and histories and solidified the basis of their knowledge of classical antiquity—the nature of scholarship changed. As the fifteenth century wore on, it was no longer avant-garde to write, in either ultra-Ciceronian or moderately Ciceronian fashion, a narrative history, in Latin, of your particular region; rather it became routine. Those who were doing it had moved from the pulsing forefront of intellectual life, located often extra-institutionally at the social field's periphery, and had joined the hardened, polished, elite, enfranchised center. Consequently, the front lines of classical literary scholarship changed in nature. We see the rise of the philological commentary in the late fifteenth and early sixteenth centuries, well represented by Poliziano, Beroaldo, and others. Now, the focus was not so much synthetic as particular and precise.[73] In the mid- to late fifteenth century, we also see a deepening of interest in Florence in the Platonic tradition, which was closely related to changing social and political conditions. This fueled the use of texts from late antiquity, which a number of thinkers, especially Marsilio Ficino, wanted to include in the canon of acceptable philosophical and religious works. Debates and controversies, fears and recriminations over orthodoxy eventually ensued.

Marsilio Ficino found himself in this canon-expanding intellectual field in the 1480s, and he was at least partially its architect. He had gained renown in Florence in the early 1460s, when Florence's great patron, Cosimo de' Medici, had entrusted him with the translation of Plato's works. Since then, he had produced a number of his most important works, including his *On the Christian Religion,* his translations and commentaries on Plato, his translations of the *Hermetic Corpus,* and his *Platonic Theology.* He had been sensitive to a dual mission of advancing the frontiers of learning by devoting attention to issues and problems outside the realm of contemporary concerns and communicating to an intellectual public and a public at large. He translated into Tuscan some of his own works (the work *On the Christian Religion*) and wrote some originally in Tuscan, such as his 1478–79 *Counsel against the Plague.* He saw himself as a doctor of souls in Florence, and the initial following that he developed was consequent with that mission. As Arthur Field has shown, after the dramatic and fractious 1450s (among whose many signal events were the peace of Lodi, the ouster of the Medici, and their forceful reascendency in 1458), the time was ripe for an ideology of love, friendship, and harmony, which Marsilio Ficino helped develop.[74] A learned, elite following gathered around Ficino. He advised members of his circle how they might tolerate bad fortune and the sniping of enemies. He stressed that true religion was suffused with love and that the love between friends was religious.[75] After the death of Cosimo, his first patron, he gradually solidified his contacts with the Medici, even if he never established the same sort of relationship he had had with Cosimo. In the early 1470s, Ficino developed an especially close relationship with Lorenzo de' Medici, only to see time and circumstance change its nature.[76]

By the early 1480s, Ficino had amassed a significant amount of social and cultural capital. His On the Christian Religion had established him as a thinker deeply concerned with traditional Christian problems, and his Platonic Theology had made an important statement defending Christianity against some of the by then traditionally heterodox positions, especially those associated with Averroism. He also published his Complete Works of Plato in 1484, thus opening up a new world of Greek philosophy to European intellectuals; for in that work he presented the Latin translations of Plato's dialogues that would be studied, along with Ficino's own commentaries and short interpretations, for centuries thereafter.[77] But by the middle 1480s, Ficino's dual mission was being tested in a number of ways. He was beginning to realize that the frontiers of his own scholarship were located in understanding Plotinus, the later Platonist often taken as the exemplar of Neoplatonism. Yet for Ficino, understanding Plotinus meant interpreting him, and interpreting him meant using every means at his disposal to integrate Plotinus into the prisca theologia (ancient theology), the gradually unfolding but heavily veiled unified wisdom that God had given to mankind and revealed gradually through various interpreters.[78] To do this, Ficino had to turn to increasingly esoteric styles of interpretation that did not have the capacity to communicate as directly as before with Florence's civic leaders; nor were they always as firmly in line with traditional orthodoxies. As to Ficino's social field, he kept his Medici patronage, of course; but he gradually grew to seem one of many artists and intellectuals under that wing of culture, rather than the center of intellectual life, even as his relationship with Lorenzo remained solid and approached, again, its formerly high affective dimension.[79] Given his interpretive concerns and the choices he was making in his scholarship, and given the constitution and evolution of the Florentine sociopolitical field, Ficino lost some cultural capital in the 1480s, as intellectual life began to go in new directions owing to the broadened and multifaceted Florentine intellectual field.

What could one find in the Florentine intellectual world of the 1480s? What was the intellectual field? Thinkers found themselves embedded in a social matrix, to be sure, where patronage in all its dimensions was an essential part of their daily lives. But an individual intellectual's social position was shaped and conditioned as well by the intellectual field, where thinkers advanced competing positions, all of them vying for a specific place in the debate on canonicity and literary legitimacy.

One could find institutionally grounded, university-centered Aristotelianism and professors who engaged actively with Averroist traditions of Aristotelian hermeneutic, even if abjuring Averroist heresies. They were part of the Florentine university, *studium generale* or *Studio,* refounded by Lorenzo in 1473. As Armando Verde and James Hankins have shown, these professors were necessary to keep the university in step with the traditional concerns so important to students of philosophy. As such, Lorenzo offered them patronage and had them brought to the Studio, in which he was so heavily invested.[80] By the late 1480s, these philosophers were well established there.

There was also a growing newer style of philosophical inquiry, which embraced traditional areas of philosophy in a philologically sophisticated manner. This specific type of philological sophistication began, really, with Valla, but in late-fifteenth-century Florence it was exemplified in Angelo Poliziano's miscellanistic style of scholarship. It was becoming clear that philology was a style of thought, so that one sought the highest level of verbal and definitional precision by weighing as many textual examples and testimonies as possible.[81] Poliziano's philological style was most evident in his *Miscellanea,* or *Miscellanies,* which, he wrote, were inspired by the *Attic Nights* of the second-century A.D. Silver Age Latin author Aulus Gellius, which had contained similarly precise and learned discussions.[82] The philological sensibility pervaded almost all of Poliziano's prose work and formed part of his identity as an intellectual; it was also fundamentally at odds with Ficino's style of interpretation. Poliziano's newly evolved philological techniques are strikingly modern, but he developed them in relation to factors in his intellectual environment, in an agonistic social context where the resolution of textual questions was an important means toward the end of amassing cultural capital.[83] This textual style of scholarship even allowed natural philosophy to be seen in a new way, and a certain variety of empiricism began to manifest itself, suggested early on by Lorenzo Buonincontri's approach to Manilius, then refined in Poliziano's own study of Pliny.[84] That Poliziano's approach was opposed to Ficino's must be conceded. When Poliziano, in the 1492 *praelectio* to his university course on Aristotle's *Prior Analytics* (Poliziano's *Lamia*), skewered the figure of Pythagoras and sarcastically sent up the mysterious Pythagorean sayings, the *akousmata,* there can be little doubt that he was taking aim at Ficino.[85]

There were also the traditional social accoutrements of a court society, as the Medici, despite being only the "first among equals" in the republic of Florence, were in step with evolving European trends.[86] Well illustrated in his bawdy Italian poetry, Luigi Pulci's scatological persona forced even Lorenzo de' Medici, his professed friend, to distance himself. Nevertheless, Pulci's presence on the intellectual landscape reminds us of the level of courtly activity, just as Lorenzo's own vernacular poetry serves to point up the same trend; and even Poliziano took part in writing Italian poetry for ceremonial occasions, with his own poems accompanying the courtly jousts.[87] This public style of political life was not the place for Ficino's fundamental interiority and was at least part of the reason for Ficino's seeming distance from Lorenzo through much of the 1480s.

There is the presence of the young Pico della Mirandola to round out the picture. He was part of the intellectual field, though thanks to his private wealth, his relation to Medici patronage was not conditioned by financial concerns. The experience of 1486–87—his abortive Roman *disputatio,* flight to France, and salvation by Lorenzo—was a central transformative one in his experience, for it solidified and gave direction and vigor to the divergent path he would tread vis-à-vis Ficino. In his 1491 *De ente et uno, On Being and the One,* he argued that Plato and Aristotle had agreed on the ontological places of Being and One, Pico averring that the two philosophers had suggested that Being and One were coextensive when most would argue that Plato had placed One above Being. For this latter "misinterpretation" Pico blamed later Platonists, and, as Michael Allen has pointed out, lurking behind these later Platonists was the figure of Marsilio Ficino. Ficino would go on to change his own commentary on the Parmenides to counter Pico's arguments.[88]

Finally, there was in the Florentine intellectual field the rising tide of an anti-speculative fideism represented by Savonarola, a stance to which Pico and Poliziano in the few years remaining to them would adhere. Savonarola's emphasis on faith over reason and his condemnation of "vanities" of all sorts was intimately related to Florentine civic traditions, as was the way in which Savonarola preached and disseminated his message.[89] It was also in step with the evolution of the Florentine sociopolitical field, as the elite who had once surrounded Ficino now gathered around Savonarola. Ficino's scholarly work, growing ever more esoteric in these years, was not a part of Savonarola's style of public piety and controlling orthodoxy. Toward the end of the 1490s, differing versions of orthodoxies were developed, and Savonarola fell victim to the strife in 1498, as his body, having been hanged, was publicly burned in the Piazza della Signoria along with two of his confreres. Ficino never permanently reconciled himself to the Savonarolan trend, though he tried to support it early on—certainly, I think, as a result of the pressures the changing intellectual field was exerting, though that need not make his seeming *voltes-face* less than sincere changes of opinion.[90] In 1494 Ficino played down his devotion to astrology, that most un-Savonarolan practice: Poliziano perceived Ficino to have recanted his views, praising him and suggesting that there was nothing wrong with a philosopher, who learns more every day, changing his opinions; indeed, nothing wrong with a philosopher accommodating his views to the opinion of the crowd, that is, the dominant trend in the intellectual field.[91] The deaths of Pico and Poliziano, his fellow agonists in the Florentine intellectual field, took away from Ficino those who would debate with him concerning astrology, and he returned to his former opinion on astrology and its use. In his bitter *Apologia* after Savonarola's death, Ficino even suggested that Savonarola himself—the "prince of hypocrites, led on by a diabolical spirit"—had been under the influence of poor stars and had been subject to *improbis demonibus*.[92]

In all this Ficino found himself a part of a court society, though not a court intellectual.[93] This is one of the many reasons why Hankins's recent studies concerning the status of the Platonic academy have been so valuable.[94] Ficino, though actively engaged in various forms of didactic activity from the local to the international level, turned into an essentially separatist philosopher, embracing the study of materials and a mode of investigation that fundamentally preserved and isolated him from the center of Florentine intellectual life. Given the above comment on the Florentine intellectual field, we can say that Ficino was extra-institutional.

We should add only one caveat here, and this has to do not so much with the intellectual field, in which intellectuals implicitly or explicitly vie to have their competing positions accepted and understood, but with the social field, the rules of acceptable social behavior in a court society, and the paramount place within those rules of restraint. The need for restraint was documented later by the courtly *sprezzatura* of Castiglione but manifested as well in late-fifteenth-century Florence, which, although technically still a republic, was well in line with European courtly aristocratic norms.[95] When intellectuals who were part of the just-sketched field differed from one another, the forms of their adversarial techniques were conditioned by restraint, whereby ardent advocacy of anything but the traditional virtues was looked down upon. In configuring the Florentine intellectual field and the many different possible antagonistic positions within it, we should keep in mind the subtlety that would compel intellectuals to express their positions in such a way that they would not be seen as violating acceptable boundaries of *amicitia*. Ficino's anger about Savonarola thus says something important about the function Savonarola served. We recall Bourdieu's notion of a *doxa*—a realm of unarticulated assumptions that define the limits of the possible for historical actors. In the 1470s and early 1480s, there had been a doxa of communal love, *amor*, embodied by the diverse sources and mentalities unified in Botticelli's *Primavera* and conditioned by courtly restraint.[96] Then, in the late 1480s and early 1490s, the unspoken boundaries of that doxa were strained if still unnamed, as competing positions developed and coexisted. Finally, in the mid-1490s Savonarola voiced concerns about the very substance of the doxa—multivalent, unspoken, capable of subsuming manifold approaches to current intellectual problems—and in so doing, to echo Sartre, wreaked havoc by finding a name for what had up until then been lived namelessly.[97] The Savonarolan era helped create orthodoxy in late Quattrocento Florence, by defining a field of action as heterodox.

Ficino's treading on the boundaries of orthodoxy comes on the cusp of this transformation in Florentine society and should thus not be seen only as the result of a personal philosophical quest, but also as a social phenomenon, a way to distinguish a position for himself within a complex and changing intellectual field while remaining true to his core convictions. His increasingly esoteric concerns led him to see himself at the frontiers of orthodoxy, even as he was convinced himself of the primarily Christian nature of his mission. In 1489 he published a three-part work, the *De triplici vita*.[98] The first book, which had been written almost a decade earlier, is on caring for the health of scholars, the second on prolonging life, and the third on "making one's life agree with the heavens." Ficino's stated goal is that the *De triplici vita* serve as a manual of health for the learned.[99] In his general assumption that celestial forces and planetary conjunctions had real effects on the substances of remedies as well as on the healing process itself, Ficino was well in line with medieval and early Renaissance tradition. But in his attempt in the third book not only to use but also to manipulate the heavens, Ficino was treading on ground that had been viewed with suspicion throughout the Middle Ages.[100]

In the first two books, one finds a number of medical recipes and recommendations. There is certainly a disjuncture between the first two books and the third, which represents a commentary on a particularly difficult and controversial aspect of Plotinus's oeuvre, his work on the soul. In elaborating Plotinus and attempting to configure the human soul's power, Ficino enters into astral magic and the manipulation of heavenly forces. Despite the seeming differences among the books, there are also commonalities, the most noteworthy of which is Ficino's propensity for holistic inclusiveness. Ficino indicates that human efficacy is the key; remedies of whatever sort that the human operator can employ are part of his purview in all three books.

One of the most arresting sections of the second book comes when Ficino advocates some rather daring treatment for an elderly man in need of medical care. It often happens, Ficino writes, that when one reaches the age of seventy (sometimes sixty-three), the tree of the human body decays, since its moisture has dried up. If this happens, "this human tree must be moistened by a human, youthful liquid in order that it may revive. Therefore choose a young girl who is healthy, beautiful, cheerful, and temperate, and when you are hungry and the moon is waxing, suck her milk; immediately eat a little powder of sweet fennel properly mixed with sugar."[101] This latter step will help integrate the milk into the human body. Rhetorically the bounds of orthodoxy are stretched here, elasticizing the border for what follows immediately:

> Careful physicians strive to cure those whom a long bout of hectic fever has consumed, with the liquid of human blood which has distilled in the fire at the practice of sublimation. What then prevents us from sometimes also refreshing by this drink those who have already been in a way consumed by old age? There is a certain common and ancient opinion that certain wise old women who are popularly called "screech-owls" [*stringes*] suck the blood of infants as a means, in so far as they can, of growing young again. Why shouldn't our old people, namely those who have no [other] recourse, likewise suck the blood of a youth? A youth,

I say, who is willing, healthy, happy, and temperate, whose blood is of the best but perhaps too abundant. They will suck, therefore, like leeches, an ounce or two from a scarcely-opened vein of the left arm; they will immediately take an equal amount of sugar and wine; they will do this when hungry and thirsty and the moon is waxing. If they have difficulty digesting raw blood, let it first be cooked together with sugar.[102]

A number of things must be taken into consideration here. First, there is the sort of argument Ficino will later employ, in the *Apologia* to the *De triplici vita:* if these things exist in nature, why not use them?[103] The way Ficino frames this argument, however, is noteworthy and suggestive of his fluid sense of the boundaries of orthodoxy. For he takes care to mention the "screech-owls" (*stringes* in Latin). In discussing them, Ficino echoes the language of Pliny, when he uses the words "a certain common and ancient opinion"; Pliny was uncertain what bird exactly was meant by the name, though aware that it was used in curses.[104] The most detailed description of the conduct of the screech owls is in Ovid's *Fasti,* where the possibility is raised that the blood-sucking birds are women transformed into birds by enchantment.[105]

Especially noteworthy is the manner in which Ficino connects this bird lore to "certain wise women" (*aniculas quasdam sagas*). For all of these terms had inevitably to evoke the specter of witchcraft, whose stereotypical features were stamped indelibly by a work of which Ficino could not have been ignorant, indeed may even here be echoing: the *Malleus Maleficarum* (the *Hammer of Witches*), published in 1487 by the Dominican inquisitors Krämer and Sprenger, a book prefaced by Innocent VIII's 1484 bull *Summis desiderantes* (he was a pope, incidentally, with strong ties to the Medici).[106] Also, the adjective "saga" used by Ficino connotes, in addition to prophetic ability, one who practices witchcraft,[107] and of course the term "stringes" would have evoked the Italian "striga" (or "strega"), "witch."[108] In addition to the fears about the rising tide of witchcraft that the institutional church was expressing, Ficino published the *De triplici vita* just two years after Innocent VIII condemned Pico della Mirandola's projected disputation at Rome, for "renovating the errors of pagan philosophers" and for endorsing "certain arts, disguising themselves as natural philosophy, harmful to the Catholic faith and humankind, sharply damned by the canons and doctrines of Catholic doctors."[109]

Ficino's stance is noteworthy since, despite all the reasons he would have had for rewriting this position, he does not condemn it, or even qualify it; he often in book 3 will take care to distinguish his reporting the efficacy of a certain practice from his appearing to advocate it.[110] A few short chapters later, Ficino winds up a discussion of the manner in which the elderly can receive benefits from the planets, saying that one must have inner faith in these things and believe that "faith is the life of medicines that conduce to life" and that "God will favor you when you supplicate him, and that the things created by him, especially the celestial things, have without a doubt a marvelous power to lengthen or preserve life" (*DV* 2.13). The nourishing powers of human milk and blood are perhaps not celestial but are part of God's created world nonetheless, and hence suitable for medical use.

Ficino's medical suggestion that it is licit to ingest human blood is also part of a folkloric tradition in premodern Italy that condones the uses of products such as human cranial powder, urine, milk, excrement, and blood for the curing of various ailments.[111] This blood-drinking passage in Ficino's oeuvre is helpful to us precisely because it makes explicit a fact that is always implicitly true: the boundaries between "high" and "low" culture in premodern Europe were malleable and not always located where we might expect them. Ficino the philosopher-physician is also Ficino the magus, folk-healer, and teller of tales, and borders that we create between those aspects of his personality impose later assumptions about culture on a time to which they would have been alien.[112]

Ficino's *De triplici vita* as a whole is permeated by the notion of an animate cosmos, which divinity has endowed with life. This cosmos is distinct from God but nonetheless divinely alive. In book 3 these notions are brought to the fore in a more complex way, for Ficino here discusses how human beings can access nature's divine power. The point of departure for book 3 is Plotinus, Ficino tells us, though he is reading Plotinus through post-Plotinian lenses.[113]

Throughout book 3, he fears transcending orthodoxy, even as he obviously recognizes its malleability: "Let us by no means ever attempt anything forbidden by holy religion" (*DV* 3.8: 280–81). He stresses throughout that he does not *affirm* any practices contrary to the faith; but he does not deny their possibility, and he cannot resist adjoining an ancient testimony of a practice's efficacy to one of these "non-affirmations." Some, he writes, himself included, doubt that images have celestial power: "were it not that all antiquity and all astrologers think they have a wonderful power, I would deny it. . . . In order to interpret Plotinus [*ad Plotinum interpretandum*]," he avers, "I will then briefly adduce what can be alleged from the opinions of magicians and astrologers in favor of images . . . provided I will have warned you here at the outset that you must not think I approve the use of images, only recount it. For as for me, I use medicines tempered in accordance with the heavens" (*DV* 3.15: 320–21). Ficino is truly "interpreting," or even "translating" Plotinus, so that Plotinus becomes who Ficino needs him to be: not the Plotinus of the late nineteenth and early twentieth centuries—an island of post-Kantian rationality in a sea of late antique decadence—but rather a *priscus theologus* in whose work lay buried much of the ancient theology's power. A bit later, Ficino writes: "It would be unduly curious and perhaps harmful to recite what images they fashioned and how, for the mutual meeting of minds or their alienation, for bringing felicity or inflicting calamity, either to some individual, or to a household, or to a city. I do not affirm that such things can be done. Astrologers, however, think such things can be done, and they teach the method, but I dare not tell it. Porphyry in the book where he sketches the life of his master Plotinus confirms that such can be done" (*DV* 3.18: 340–41). Ficino reads Porphyry and Plotinus through Iamblichan eyes, since Porphyry's point in his life of Plotinus, to which Ficino here alludes, was not to show the efficacy of magic but to show his master's great-souled nature in resisting it.[114] Ficino goes on to recount the incident, but his intentions are clear: to draw Plotinus and Porphyry into the orbit of the affirmation of magic, though they would have denigrated it, at least in the philosophical life. Later, Ficino discusses the power of images over spirit and spirit over images, as well as the emotional state of the user and operator. He denies that images have long-range effects, thinking rather that they have effects only on the wearer and that what force "they do have is caused by the material rather than the figure, and as I said I prefer medicines to images by far. Yet the Arabs and the Egyptians ascribe so much power to statues and images fashioned by astronomical and magical art that they believe the spirits of the stars are enclosed in them" (*DV* 3.20: 351).[115]

The divine has implanted in the cosmos things we can use, things inaccessible to reason, or at least to reason unaided: "At the same time we do not say that our spirit is prepared for the celestials only through qualities of things known to the senses, but also and much more through certain properties engrafted in things from the heavens and hidden from our senses, and hence only with difficulty known to our reason" (*DV* 3.12: 298–301).[116] He recognizes that Albert the Great and Thomas Aquinas disagreed about images. Albert went so far as to describe the images that could be used for evil ends, in order to distinguish between what was licit and what was not (*DV* 3.18: 340–43).[117] But Aquinas attributed such things to deceiving demons; thus Ficino writes, "insofar as he [Aquinas] requires it, I give them [i.e., images] no credit at all" (ibid., 340–41).[118] Yet even here it is worthwhile to note that the days of Aquinas were the days when diabolology as a science was being born, with Aquinas himself as one of its principal architects. Formal means for prosecuting heresies had only been around for a very short time, so Aquinas was necessarily very cautious in his affirmations.[119] Aquinas's caution, one can see, is something Ficino accepts, but his acceptance is not permeated with the same sort of enthusiasm we find in other parts of the *De triplici vita*.

For Ficino as for Iamblichus, the use of various theurgic means is part of a larger system, one not to be abused for personal advantage. It is important for the practitioner not to be deceived by maleficent demons along the way; so the use of images is an especially dangerous and worrisome topic. Ficino's interpretation of Porphyry on a certain, image-related point, makes his motivation clear:

> Porphyry also in his *Letter to Anebo* testifies that images are efficacious; and he adds that by certain vapors arising from fumigations proper to them, aerial daemons would instantly be insinuated into them.[120] Iamblichus confirms that in materials which are naturally akin to the things above and have been both collected from their various places and compounded at the right time and in the proper manner, you can receive forces and effects which are not only celestial, but even daemonic and divine. Proclus and Synesius absolutely agree. (*DV* 3.13: 306–7)

Here Ficino's interest is apparent, so much so that he does not focus on the difference of opinion between Porphyry and Iamblichus. Porphyry had granted various theurgic means a certain efficacy but had ultimately, especially in the *Letter to Anebo,* denied their worthiness for the true philosopher; Iamblichus had insisted on their necessity, even in the philosophical life, always advising caution and insisting that lower theurgic techniques be used in preparation for higher ones, whose final goal was *henosis*—unification with the One. Ficino, however, chooses to emphasize the similarity, reading Porphyry through Iamblichan eyes.

Later, Ficino goes on: "For Iamblichus too says that those who place their trust in images alone, caring less about the highest religion and holiness, and who hope for divine gifts from them, are very often deceived in this matter by evil daemons encountering them under the pretense of being good divinities.

Iamblichus does not deny however that certain natural goods come to pass from images constructed according to a legitimate astrological plan" (*DV* 3.18: 342–43). In fact, continues Ficino, it is safer to trust oneself to the use of material means, in this case medicine. Images, however, possess power not because of the figure imposed on them; rather, their efficacy is due to the natural disposition of the material of which they are crafted.[121] Moreover, "we ought not rashly to allow even the shadow of idolatry" (ibid.).

The specter of heterodoxy haunts Ficino throughout the *De triplici vita,* and it is something he must combat. When he does, two things are apparent: first, the notion that it is possible to discuss these dangerous matters and debate them. This is not a closed system, and we can see that, in a sense, Ficino is thinking about how to form a canon and what its boundaries were, even if he was far from using those terms. Second, also apparent are his post-Plotinian tendencies.[122] While denying vigorously anything not approved by the church, Ficino employs what is really a topos of humility to defend his notion of life in the cosmos, life given to it by the divine and, also by divine gift, accessible to us. Ficino too reflects Iamblichus's opening of the traditional canon. Just as Iamblichus had been the first Platonist in late antiquity to adopt the *Hermetic Corpus* into philosophical Platonism, Ficino introduced a wide, new range of esoteric material into the mainstream of European intellectual life, material that was often regarded with suspicion. One of his defenses concerns the possible charge that he is a priest, one who should not be busying himself with medicine and astrology. But it is necessary to note, stresses Ficino, that ancient priests, those of the Chaldeans, the Persians, and the Egyptians, were doctors and astronomers (*DV, Apologia:* 396–97). To help effect a sound mind in a sound body, it is necessary to join medicine with the priesthood. Even Christ enjoined his disciples to cure the sick and, in Ficino's view, would himself advocate using herbs and stones to effect cures, if words alone were inefficacious.

In answer to another hypothetical objection, Ficino states that he is not advocating magic, just recounting it in his interpretation of Plotinus. "Nor," he writes, "do I affirm here a single word about profane magic which depends upon the worship of daemons, but I mention natural magic, which, by natural things, seeks to obtain the services of the celestials for the prosperous health of our bodies. This power, it seems, must be granted to minds which use it legitimately, as medicine and agriculture are justly granted, and all the more so as that activity which joins heavenly things to earthly is more perfect" (*DV, Apologia:* 396–97).

The magus is like a farmer, practicing an art as natural, patterned, subject to the seasons, sometimes as arcane, as that of farming. How could people be so arrogant as to deny life to the heavens? How could people who see life in even the lowest animals and the vilest grasses not see life in heaven and in the world?[123] Perhaps the world does not possess a soul, but must we not grant the world at least some sort of life, a life that God, not being greedy, granted to us to use? In the final analysis, one is struck by the humility with which Ficino attempts to reimagine the world and the place of humankind within it. His post-Plotinian tendencies accord us a certain power in manipulating the world, even as he recognizes humanity's radical dependence on divine aid, a dependence that is truly, intimately psychological and which recognizes the melancholy truth that our soul, with all its natural desires to reach the divine, is fated in this life not to do so.

Ficino's tendency to stretch the boundaries of orthodoxy is closely tied to his style of discourse in the *De triplici vita*. For there, unlike in his earlier, more systematic *Platonic Theology,* his stance is that of the prophetic revealer of truth, and not the scholastic expositor. His apparently disordered approach has been cited as being "unphilosophical," and it must reflect at the very least Ficino's own fears and ambivalences regarding what he was writing about.[124] But perhaps, in an intellectual field such as the Florentine one of the late 1480s and early 1490s, the concept of *philosopher,* infused as it is with post-Enlightenment implications regarding the necessity of external coherence and consistency in a thinker's work, is not useful in analyzing Ficino. His work does not display a remarkable consistency in this regard.[125] But there is an internal coherence in his style of thought and in the relationality in which his thought unfolds. Ficino quietly pushed and pulled at the borders of orthodoxies intellectual and religious, expanding the canon of Platonic–Christian philosophy. In so doing, he staked out his own individual position in the Florentine intellectual field, even as the choices he made in his own enterprise of cultural translation moved him from the center to the periphery of the city's social field.

✧

LIKE VALLA, Ficino reimagined religion and its practice and used a lost wisdom to do so. Both thinkers had an interest in what we would term post-classical antiquity, though they were of course unconcerned with our varieties of periodization. For Valla, what was lost was twofold: first, the humility of paleo-Christian days, as this was represented by the elegant simplicity of Paul, a rhetorician who had used the power of persuasion to alter the lives of real-life people not cloistered in a study; second, a kind of eloquence that could be refined along the lines suggested by Quintilian, whose panoramic view of the function of rhetoric and the place of the rhetorician offered, Valla believed, a full-fledged cultural system. For Ficino on the other hand, the lost wisdom was a matter of continuous revelation that the modern interpreter had to be proactively involved in revealing, and the interpreter had to use all the textual artifacts necessary to do so, while recognizing humbly that divinity had endowed the world with powers yet to be discovered. Both men, too, were situated in social environments. These environments were not so structurally rigid or deterministic as to preclude Valla and Ficino from staking out interesting and independent positions regarding religion. But their social context was important in giving us a fuller sense of their work and of their individual intellectual evolutions. In the chapter that follows, I shall turn to certain early-fifteenth-century humanists who were acutely conscious of their own social place and who left behind intriguing observations regarding the society in which they found themselves.

CHAPTER FIVE

Honor

The Humanists of the Classic Era on Social Place

I don't deny that the scholastic definitions and descriptions
composed by learned men in their sheltered leisure are useful as a
kind of preparation, like jousting for the use of arms. You have to
live in the world, however, and deal with the actual ways and
habits of men. . . . Let us, therefore, in everything we do, serve
the public eye.

LEON BATTISTA ALBERTI, *I libri della famiglia*

IN THE PRECEDING CHAPTER I attempted to show one
way in which certain categories and conceptual strategies drawn from
contemporary critical theory and philosophy can illuminate "traditional" Renaissance intellectual history. In this chapter I argue for the wider relevance
of Renaissance intellectual history and maintain that much of the "lost literature" we have been discussing can help illuminate issues of contemporary relevance. One such issue concerns the intersection of gender and honor. Gender
studies constitute a major recent theoretical area that has almost completely
passed Renaissance intellectual history by. Theoretical trends come and go, of
course, and when they are highly prized, there tends for a relatively short time
to be a concentration of publications in those fields. To some, the very volume
of new studies and their varied quality are irksome. However, this seeming tran-
sitoriness of trends has led many Renaissance intellectual historians to ignore

completely most recent ones, including gender studies; yet most styles of intellectual exchange were at least at one time trends, and most trends have at root
something to recommend them.[1] In the case of gender studies, the advantage is
that the field can help us to understand more deeply how Renaissance thinkers
understood their social identities by focusing on how they conceived of honor.
Toward this end, I consider the work of two different scholars and then suggest how the concepts they fostered and applied to the past can illuminate the
intellectual culture of early-fifteenth-century humanism, especially insofar as
humanism had a connection to the papal court.

In a well-known study that first appeared in the mid-1980s, Joan Wallach
Scott proposed that it would help historians if they learned to treat gender as
an analytical category of thought.[2] She argued that gender was a fundamental
fact of the creation of people's identities and that the biological fact of gender
as a simple category of difference also meant that "gendered" sources of differ-
entiation would be found in almost all corners of life: "[G]ender is a constitutive element of social relationships based on perceived differences between
the sexes, and gender is a primary way of signifying power."[3] Binary systems
of representation, culturally available symbols (such as Eve, the Virgin Mary,
Christ), and the "social institutions and organizations" that help define them,
as well as the subjective identities of individuals, all came under the purview of
gender. Men constructed their identities as men, with underlying, sometimes
unarticulated categories of maleness undergirding their behavior and choices,
and the same was true for women and femaleness. The task became not to write
the histories of men and women as separate stories but rather integratively, to
see how, why, and in what contexts those gendered, behavior-structuring categories arose, and to find, in our terms, the gendered habitus that underlay their
behavior.

Scott's work was highly influential for at least three reasons: it was a concise
summing up of the best work in the theory of gender, a powerful stimulus to
further work, and a truly synthetic new statement that helped define a field.
One could find, of course, numerous past thinkers who had suggested that gender was a historically articulated construct: one thinks of Christine de Pizan
in the early fifteenth century; or Henricus Cornelius Agrippa in the early sixteenth century; or John Stuart Mill, who in his *Subjection of Women* wrote that
"what is now called the nature of women is an eminently artificial thing."[4] And
one could cite numerous instances in the Western past when a *querelle des femmes*

broke out. Despite this, as Scott contended, "gender as a way of talking about systems of social or sexual relations did not appear" before the late twentieth century.[5] She was right. To see where this can get us in the study of Renaissance intellectuals, we can turn to an area relatively close in time to the Renaissance, the High Middle Ages, and to the work of a scholar whose work came into prominence in the early 1980s.

In her *Jesus as Mother,* Caroline Walker Bynum epitomized the best of what can happen when gender theory is brought to bear on areas of intellectual culture that have not hitherto benefited from its application.[6] The assumption of gender as a category allowed Bynum first to observe, then to describe, certain phenomena particular to twelfth-century Cistercian writers who were male. Her point of departure was a common rhetorical topos in a group of twelfth-century Cistercian texts: maternal imagery employed to describe Jesus. Setting her study within the twelfth-century context of a rise of affective spirituality and a gradual feminization of religious language, Bynum suggested that the Mother-Jesus topos fulfilled a need for a language to speak about authority, which had traditionally been understood, especially among abbots (in the long wake of Benedict's *Rule*) as fatherly. Given the nature of their communities and the rise in affective spirituality, the writers Bynum examined seemed to want to soften the traditional paternal image somewhat; conventional "fatherly" behavioral typologies no longer sufficed, and Cistercians in positions of authority adopted feminine language in their writings in three distinctive ways. There was (1) a persistent pairing of *mater* with *pater, dominus,* and *magister;* (2) a consistency of sexual stereotypes, wherein characteristics like gentleness, compassion, tenderness, nurturing, and security were associated with the "female" or "maternal," while authority, command, and judgment were "male" or "paternal" and instruction, fertility, and engendering were associated with both sexes; and (3) a literary tendency wherein breasts and nurturing were more frequent images than conceiving and giving birth. This language helped the writers both to define their own relation to divinity and to fashion behavioral patterns adequate to their new calling.

The point is that Bynum was able to understand an intellectual community and the textual artifacts they produced in a way that was deeper and more persuasive than would have been possible with a "purely" theological or philosophical reading. She did not neglect texts, however. Instead they, along with an innovative and informed social sensibility, were the basis of her analysis.

And that is precisely the problem in Renaissance studies. If intellectual historians have been neglectful of social factors including gender when conceiving of communities of Renaissance intellectuals, scholars interested in gender very rarely include lengthy readings of Renaissance Latin texts in their work. So it is difficult for innovative work like Bynum's to appear in Renaissance studies. What can we do about this?

The first imperative is to realize the flexibility that thinking about gender requires and widen our purview to ask what were the gendered categories of difference that various small communities of Renaissance intellectuals shared. Honor and reputation were important and were often connected, as we shall see, to issues of masculinity. But we need precision: what communities are we talking about, where, when? Here I want to focus on the "classic" phase of Italian humanism, roughly coterminous with the first half of the fifteenth century. The term *classic* calls for some explanations, given the earlier considerations, especially in chapter 2, on the historiography of humanism, and so I would like to recall the discussion introducing Lorenzo Valla in chapter 4 of this book. There I stressed, as had Eugenio Garin, that during Valla's lifetime, which ended in 1457, the cultivation of the *studia humanitatis* had not yet established firm institutional roots in higher education, nor had it really gained a Europe-wide foothold as the basis for the education of the European elite. It is precisely this absence of strongly felt institutional links that makes the humanism of the first half of the fifteenth century so exciting, distinctive, and unique.[7] At that time it was a movement analogous perhaps to the era of the young Hegelians in the early nineteenth century, the type of environment where intellectuals are conscious of sharing a métier that makes them, to evoke the military sense of the term, *avant-garde,* in the front line, gaining ground but unsure of the final outcome.

One of the most important attempts to transcend the divide between social and intellectual history in the study of humanism was made by Lauro Martines in his *Social World of the Florentine Humanists,* which appeared in 1963. Having studied the economic and social place of a number of leading fifteenth-century Florentine humanists in greater detail than anyone before or since, he dismissed the notion that they were disfranchised intellectuals and concluded instead that humanists were anything but alienated.[8] Most tended to be associated with wealth and power, and if they were not, they tried to affiliate themselves to those who were. It was a brilliant study that came at the problem in an entirely new way. Still, there seem to be ways in which one might modify the assessment concerning the humanists' enfranchisement without taking anything away from Martines's remarkable achievement. One freely acknowledges that the way the humanists measured their own prestige, their honor, was dependent in one sense on the professional positions they achieved: if you are a chancellor of the city of Florence, you are pleased that the city's oligarchs hold you in high esteem, and a part of your own honor rests in the honor of your city and the form of its politics. When in the first years of the fifteenth century Coluccio Salutati, the first great humanist chancellor of the city of Florence, writes an invective against Antonio Loschi of Vicenza, he reflects his own link to Florentine republican traditions and his intimate ties to the world of the Florentine merchant elite.[9]

However, a deeper, more intimate means of measuring honor came from the opinions of fellow humanists.[10] It is only fair when considering humanists to take into account not only their social place but their social practices as well, which include, first, their own Latin writings and, second, the epiphenomena of writing, especially before the widespread dissemination of printing with movable type. By "epiphenomena of writing" I mean the way they circulated their works and the processes of evaluation that the works were subjected to by contemporaries. Although Martines presented a wealth of information about the economic circumstances of leading humanists, there was no extended close reading of their actual works. The more one gets into their writings, the clearer it becomes that their communities were bounded not only or even primarily by geography or local politics, but also by the blurry, sometimes ephemeral borders of the republic of letters.[11] Esteem and honor depended mostly on what their fellow intellectuals thought of their literary effort. As Hanna Gray pointed out long ago, humanists wanted to be known as men of eloquence,[12] and the best judges of eloquence were not, in the final analysis, the cloth merchants and bankers who were paying the bills but rather their fellows in the new literary movement, who were all over Italy. In a sense, asking about "Florentine" humanism is a *question mal posée*. In the late fourteenth and early fifteenth centuries, a distinctive intellectual moment occurred in Florence, but from about 1420 to about 1460, before the humanist movement became firmly rooted in Italian, then European institutional culture, there was a scattered but noteworthy community of voices whose members mattered to each other, even if they did not yet matter definitively to European institutions.[13]

An environment such as this was inherently unstable and not linked to existing institutions. It was unavoidable that questions of honor and reputation were even more important than they might have been for practitioners of an intellectual discipline that had firm institutional roots, where individual success could be measured by comparing one's progress and career with those of well-known figures in whose footsteps one could follow. This is why gendered categories are important, for when one is talking about honor, it is inevitable—in these predominantly male, small intellectual communities—that the construction of masculinity is called into play. Even the acquisition of the Latin language, the instrument with which humanists plied their trade, was predominantly though not exclusively male. Latin was a second language, acquired outside the home in a relatively organized, more or less public fashion, and was expected to be used in public situations. When Leonardo Bruni in the 1420s wrote a treatise on education to lady Battista Malatesta, he suggested that even a woman who desires to be quite learned should shy away from rhetoric, a discipline that was, needless to say, a central concern of humanists. Should a woman gesticulate the way an orator sometimes has to do, "she would probably be thought mad and put under restraint," for "the contests of the forum," he went on, "like those of warfare and battle, are the sphere of men."[14]

The exceptional achievements of Renaissance-era women have received much attention in the last thirty years, owing to the work of many outstanding scholars. By now, however, it should be no heresy to remark that these achievements of Renaissance women were exceptional in both senses of the word. The world of the now almost forgotten Latin texts of the Italian Renaissance was predominantly a world of men. For better and for worse, it should be taken seriously as such. Indeed, certain assumptions of most male humanists were well in step with what seems—in five centuries of (Western) hindsight— to be a fundamentally misogynistic era. Women's virtues were the essentially private, traditionally maternal ones of modesty, humility, obedience to men, and so forth: in short, their experience included and embodied all those factors which, for millennia before the Renaissance and for centuries thereafter, denied women an active, public, participatory role in political society.[15] Women in the Renaissance era had "agency," of course, in the strict sense that they did things, at times in public contexts, which can be studied today by scholars and indeed deserve attention.[16] But they did not possess the kind of efficacious political agency and power that most people in the Western world today assume is normative for living in a civil society.[17] In any case, because of the public nature of the way Latin was used, women were often left out, and humanist communities as such were predominantly male. And the world of the Renaissance, to borrow the much more recent statement of Lauro Martines, "was not an eighteenth-century drawing room."[18] The men who wrote this literature were intellectuals, but like all intellectuals they were social creatures, affected inevitably by the habits and customs of their time.

So sometimes, as we shall see, humanists use gendered categories in an oppositional way, so that a thinker, in order to emphasize the right kind of behavior or action, will deploy its opposite in vilifying an opponent. And as we observe their struggles, intrigues, and intellectual conflicts, we are reminded of a salient social phenomenon of long duration: when it comes to masculinity and honor, as David Gilmore has suggested, "[a] man's effectiveness is measured as others see him in action, where they can evaluate his performance."[19] Masculinity is performative, though it cannot be reduced only to acts of performance; it is a quest for experience that must be validated in community; and it is embodied in a culture of seeing and hearing. Is it a surprise that humanists loved the dialogue form, which transposes private learning to an imagined public venue, where interlocutors dispute and their character is on display? Can we be astonished to find that humanists from Petrarch onward wrote and collected their own letters with the purpose of publicly circulating them? Or that oratory, whose public aspect needs no elaboration, was yet another favored genre? More specifically, is it any wonder that one of the humanists we shall meet in this chapter will marvel at the prospects for advancement at the papal court, explicitly likening it to an esteemed theater, where one's acts are always on view?

For Italian Renaissance humanists of the early fifteenth century, the central defining issue of their social lives was how to find a practical way to engage in the newly articulated and now avant-garde art of Renaissance humanism and not go broke in the bargain. This tradition reached back to the fourteenth century, to the career of Petrarch (1304–74). His convictions were anchored not in the bedrock of any one political tradition but in his own, deeper psychological roots, nourished by his upbringing in southern France, roots that needed to issue forth in a self-expression at once profoundly religious and deeply humane.[20] Although his family origins were Florentine (his father had been a Florentine notary, ejected from the city in the same series of political purges that exiled Dante Alighieri), Petrarch found patronage alternately with a wealthy Roman cardinal, the Visconti despots of Milan, the republic of Venice, and the ruling dynasty of Padua, the Carrara. In other words, Petrarch was willing to work for extremely diverse patrons with widely varying political concerns.

Petrarch was seeking a deeper consistency in the development of his own thought. The underlying theoretical coherence we see in him was not civic or political primarily; it reflected his interest in reorienting toward religion an already existing culture of classicism in Italy. Petrarch wanted to create a cultural model that could harmonize the eloquent humanity of the ancients with the late medieval religious concerns so important to many thinkers of the era.[21] To effect this turn toward a religious humanism, he needed patronage first of all. Where it came from was less important than that it was there. For the humanists of the next two intellectual generations, this need to find patronage from diverse sources remained. Later in the fifteenth century, things were different as the study of the humanities became so well diffused that the institutional possibilities for humanists were greater. But in the first half of the fifteenth century, there were a number of small environments, not necessarily bounded by spatial geography, where we see institutional, social, and intellectual history intersect.

The papal court, especially before the early 1440s, is a good place to look for these intersections, for it functioned as a kind of clearinghouse for European intellectuals.[22] It was an institution in flux and was a place that certain humanists, whose literary métier was still coming into focus, saw as a good locus of possible employment. While the papal bureaucracy itself did not offer unlimited possibilities to humanists in the first decades of the Quattrocento, the general curial environment offered enough opportunities that humanists often saw it as a place to find employment.[23] The first half of the fifteenth century was a time of transformation in the papal court. First, the papacy itself was rebounding from a dramatic loss in international authority and prestige: for the first three-quarters of the fourteenth century, the papacy was in Avignon, not Rome, its historic seat, and then, from 1378 to 1417, the years of the Great Schism, there were two, and after 1409 three, contenders for the papal tiara, with support for each individual determined more often than not by political loyalties. Next, when Martin V was elected pope at the Council of Constance in November 1417 (signaling the end of the Schism), he returned to a fractious Rome, divided by the internecine war and clannishness characteristic of the city in the later Middle Ages but especially intense in the early fifteenth century.[24] As a result, Martin, who was pope from 1417 to 1431, and his successor Eugenius IV, pope from 1431 to 1447, were not always safe in Rome. It was not until 1443 that

Eugenius returned the papal court to Rome decisively, and of course, no one living then could know that the return would in fact be definitive. The point is that the court itself was in flux and was thus just the right kind of institution for the culturally avant-garde humanists to try to graft themselves onto. The question was how.

In the papal court, there were positions that humanists could staff.[25] At the top of the court's administrative branch were the apostolic secretaries, below them the papal scriptors, and then the abbreviators; and we do know of occasional instances of vertical mobility in the first half of the fifteenth century. Much more important, however, was the lateral mobility that was possible.[26] There were usually around twenty-four cardinals in the first half of the fifteenth century, and each of them had a *familia,* which we might think of as a loosely shifting network of support staff based residentially, some of whom would travel with the cardinal. These *familiae* were microcosmically like the papal court, so that a humanist might find himself taken in by a cardinal as a private secretary, or perhaps as an in-house tutor to the cardinal's nephews. Alliances often shifted, and a humanist interested in finding a patron had to keep open as many options as possible. Humanists occasionally thought about the conditions of court life and recorded their ideas in elegantly ambiguous, carefully constructed dialogues. The nature of court life was a subject of fascination for humanists, both those who were insiders and those who were outsiders.[27] Many were tied to various sorts of curial life, and not just at the papal court; they sought and gave advice, they shared their anxieties with one another, and they were deeply concerned with their own honor.

As an exemplar of this concern for honor, we can turn to a humanist whose work is certainly a part of the "lost" literature I have been discussing in this book. His name was Lapo da Castiglionchio the Younger, and his life was marked by cruel blows of fortune until his early death in his thirty-third year.[28] From an old Florentine family—a member of that caste of untitled merchant-aristocrats who had pride of name but little wealth—Lapo found himself in his late twenties an adept of the avant-garde art of humanism and, like most of his compatriots, in need of employment suitable to allow him to continue his literary labors. Lapo is especially noteworthy because, until his early death, he was something of an outsider when it came to patronage. We glance at him now, and he seems always on the verge of breaking in and having an important position: when a patron dies, such as his great patron Cardinal Giordano Orsini; or when Lapo himself becomes ill at a critical moment, as he did just before he was to take up a teaching position in rhetoric and moral philosophy; or, finally, in 1438 and perhaps on the verge of a permanent appointment at the court, when Lapo succumbs to an outbreak of plague, which in his day was still pandemically active even if its most destructive period had passed by the mid–fourteenth century.[29]

In his own day, Lapo's reputation was high despite his youth, and he was well known among his fellow humanists as an expert translator from Greek to Latin. An ancient Greek or Roman writer of equivalent importance in his own day (whose work survived) would by now have been edited, reedited, and translated numerous times. There are many other little-known Renaissance thinkers like Lapo, their voices echoing sometimes vainly in the abandoned palaces of nineteenth-century intellectual neoclassicism and telling us much about their lives and times. Lapo left behind a lot of work, much of it valuable precisely because of the ambiguous social position he held. Lapo was a closely placed outsider looking in on privileged environments, and his anxieties, desires, and opinions concerning social life give us a remarkable window into the shifting culture of early-fifteenth-century humanism.

One of the underlying motifs of Lapo's work in general is a resolute focus on matters pertaining to honor and honorable behavior. Lapo translates Plutarchan works that treat of the lives of great men of the past, ancient exemplars of honor.[30] Lapo wrote numerous letters, and in them we will sometimes see Lapo's sense of honor violated if, say, a correspondent does not respond promptly enough. In lengthier works, he outlines sometimes bitterly, sometimes humorously the behavior of people in a group context, acutely sensitive to the way some uphold an ideal of honor while others violate it. When Lapo zooms in and explicitly considers honor and honorable behavior, he returns persistently to a few key masculinizing ideas. First, there is the notion of opposites. In this sense, Lapo describes nonhonorable behavior as effeminate, associating the two in a gendered way. In an early epistolary treatise, still unedited, Lapo discusses the relative merits of the military versus the scholarly life. The letter is directed to a friend who has just given up the military life and is wondering whether he has made the right choice. Lapo takes the position that the scholarly life is superior, and part of his argument consists in questioning the moral status of contemporary military leaders, who can never rise to the level achieved by the ancients. Their practices are scandalous and dishonorable; "they act effeminately."[31]

The last major work Lapo wrote before his early death was a dialogue on the papal court, ostensibly praising the court; in reality, though, it was a brilliant short work containing many ambiguities.[32] Lapo reveals much about the texture of life at the papal court in his work and along the way offers implicit and explicit criticisms of certain of its denizens. He accuses them often of luxury, as they spend too much time organizing and indulging in banquets. The worst must be characterized, again, by a gendered opposite. These curialists, many of whom, we must remember, are clerics, not only look for the rarest and finest of foods, but they "squander their fortunes pointlessly; they consider not what is becoming to themselves but rather what pleases them at the moment. They make their lewd desire the limit to their expenditures," and they even "zealously seek out beautiful servant boys to serve the meals, as well as catamites and men whose hair is done a little too finely."[33] Some, in their dealings with young boys, employ a "strange and unheard-of teaching" method by which the boys are transformed into men; but this method reminds Lapo of Tiresias and Caeneus—two ancient mythological figures who changed genders completely.[34]

Lapo is not alone among fellow humanists in this feminizing antityping. In a number of the fierce outward polemics in which humanists engaged, it was a standard strategy to heap reprobation on the sexual morality of one's adversary. Nor is he alone in recognizing the particular nature of court life, especially life at the papal court. In May of 1452, George of Trebizond, for example, has a physical altercation in the environs of the papal court with Poggio Bracciolini, spurred on by an old literary grudge. During their fight, George would later write bitterly to Poggio, "Rightly I could have bitten off the fingers you stuck in my mouth; I did not. . . . I thought of squeezing your testicles with both hands. . . . I did not do it." George requests a sword from a bystander to scare Poggio away, and it does the trick: Poggio, "like a Florentine woman" *(ut florentina femina)* flees in fright.[35] But Poggio was well established at the papal court, and later he demands of a highly placed cardinal that George be ejected. George does not wait around, knowing that Poggio (in our terms) has accumulated enough social capital. So only a short while later, George has left the papal court to seek his fortune at the Aragonese court of Naples. Even still, he believes he is being stalked by assassins sent by Poggio and writes the pope to this effect.[36]

To return to Lapo: he is far from straightforwardly negative about the morality present at the papal court. Rather he is wistful, lamenting the poor moral state of the papal court even as he believes strongly in the inherent goodness of the institution and its capacity to realize its potential—if only it could find leaders who could actualize that potential. If only the curia could recover its *honestas,* its honorable integrity. If only Lapo's ideas would reach the ears of the pope himself: "Certainly," Lapo writes, "it would be better for him [the pope] to think about his own interests, his own worth, the reputation of the curia, as well as the safety and success of the curialists who desire to live honorably."[37] Out with the disgraceful men! They "should retreat, retreat I say, from the curia, retreat from the magistracies, retreat from their dignified status, retreat from the company and concourse of such widely accomplished and illustrious men, which [company] they have almost completely defiled with their most wicked crimes." Then "the good might at last catch their breath, and raise themselves up by their own merits. They would take possession of honors and bring home rewards worthy of their own works." As a final result of this hoped-for purging, "virtue and honorable dealing would have their honor."[38]

Just as the institution has its honor, so too do individuals, and Lapo is always at pains to outline positive models of honorable behavior among the princes of the Church. They are people who behave moderately and courteously, grave men who understand that their public comportment matters, that it is in fact the very basis of their honor. Although they are powerful, they do not spurn those of a lesser station. If they are greeted publicly, they will always return the greeting. When they engage in public functions necessary to the proper performance of their office, say, by sponsoring a banquet, these upright curialists always act appropriately. They "would come by nothing at all in a dishonorable fashion. As a result of their conduct, it is not so much with wealth as with virtue that they look after their own honor as well as the generosity of the Pope. With themselves these men are sparing, and only with others who are worthy are they generous; and they measure their desires with probity." Importantly, "they do and think nothing weak or shameful." Finally, these good men "prepare splendid and refined foods in relation to the rank of their guests; yet the banquets themselves—the costs, the servants, and the rest of the refinement and pomp—are calculated not in relation to pleasure, but rather to their own honor and greatness and to that of the whole curia."[39]

The public nature of the curialist's life was metonymic for the public and agonistic nature of humanist life in general during this, humanism's classic phase. One's reputation was all one had, and most of the discernible anxieties in the "lost literature" have to do with public perception. This problem of anxieties is a particularly important one and is often intimately bound to notions of honor. We glimpse humanist anxieties at the interstices of intellectual life, at the time when manners and courtliness run out and give way to polemic, insecurity, and frustration. Focusing on humanist anxieties can help us understand the concerns that made up the habitus in which many humanists found themselves enmeshed. Beyond classic, exaggerated polemics, there are times when the humanists' patience runs thin. They appear hyperconcerned with reputation, on the edge of politesse and collapse, so much so that an unanswered letter yields obsessive complaints desperately intertwined with fears concerning career advancement. In the middle 1430s, for example, Lapo had written to a friend who, Lapo hoped, would serve as a mediator in the give-and-take world of curial patronage. Upon receiving no response, he writes again, angrily: "I even wrote you a letter that was especially short, so you would think it would be easier to write back. And you haven't responded, not even to this day."[40] "And so," he goes on, "since you can have no excuse left, you had better take care that your letters get to me as quickly and rapidly as possible, so that with them you can purge yourself of this crime and satisfy my desire, or else get ready to be cursed! What else can I do other than inveigh against you as I might against a man who is idle, neglectful, proud, disrespectful, and a hater of friendship? Or I could just be forever silent with you. Now it is up to you that neither of the two options happens."[41] Lapo's teacher Francesco Filelfo exhibits many of the same traits, building a reputation by carefully cultivated, shifting networks of support.[42]

Curial humanists competed; their lives were agonistic. A well-known early-fifteenth-century example concerns the famous Florentine chancellor Leonardo Bruni, who won a letter-writing contest to earn the post of papal secretary in 1403. He and his competitor for the position wrote letters on an assigned topic. The letters were read out loud, and Bruni won, by the acclaim of the audience. Later, even those few who had arrogantly preferred the other contestant (he tells us somewhat immodestly), lamented and admitted they had been led astray; and in any case, the pope, after rejecting the other candidate, congratulated Bruni straightaway and awarded him the position, which Bruni terms an *officium* and a *dignitas*, an "honor."[43]

At the papal court itself, as at other courts, one was forever on display. It was a public style of life and a place that offered, in the words, again, of Lapo, "a field of play to those who want splendor and the propagation of their name." The curia was "the greatest and most esteemed of theaters, [where] many peoples have come . . . to watch. Nothing admirable can be done here that does not draw everyone's notice and is not illuminated by everyone's praises."[44] For the humanists themselves, it was the small community that was important. Especially in the preprinting era, but for some time after printing as well, reputations were made and lost in these microcommunities, these face-to-face cultures whose texture will be familiar to anyone who has studied premodern European urban life. The paradigm was in fact urban, and the courts, papal and otherwise, functioned as microcosms of urban life. All the pressures, pleasures, and possible rewards of the city were available in a concentrated fashion, and one is reminded of the beautiful phrase of Johan Huizinga, discussing the alterity of life in the later Middle Ages: "In short, all things in life had something about them glitteringly and cruelly public."[45]

The emerging republic of letters was a public place, and there were standards of intimacy and honor in humanists' relationships with one another, especially in an environment like the papal court. Anthony Grafton has recently pointed out Lapo's relationship to one curial humanist, Biondo Flavio, who was preoccupied with the history of Italy from its earliest days.[46] Having heard of Lapo's reputation as a stylist, Biondo sent Lapo a draft of his work to correct and interpret. Lapo was touched and felt honored, "for," he wrote back to Biondo in a letter, "we normally do not share such of our most cherished and personal efforts except with our intimates, with whom we enjoy a long established friendship and on whom we know we can rely."[47] Lapo, hungering for status and social place, saw this gesture as a "pledge and testimony of your sentiments toward me, so that I may hope that the friendship between us, which has begun in this way, will last forever, or at least a long time."[48] Lapo perceives here a newly created intimate bond precisely because of the public nature of the curia. It was dangerous for one's reputation to send a draft of a newly written Latin work to an unknown critic. What if you had made an embarrassing mistake in your Latin, turned a phrase unclassically, or made a statement in ignorance of some newly rediscovered ancient text that would have changed your argument? As Grafton again points out, if you could not trust the person to whom you sent your draft, in place of a generous *emendatio*—a kind of Renaissance "reader's report" that charitably corrected your mistakes without ruining you—you received instead an excruciatingly public airing of the flaws in your text.[49] Since the inherent instability of a highly public marketplace of ideas was always before you, it could be ruinous.

It could even be dangerous. There was a legendary animosity between our polemical friend Lorenzo Valla and the equally contentious Poggio Bracciolini, the papal secretary whose testicles George of Trebizond chose not to grab. It all came to a head in 1451, but their argument had a history. By the early 1440s, Poggio had rightly or wrongly got the notion in his head that Valla had criticized Poggio's Latinity. Valla had written a lengthy tract against another curial humanist (Bartolomeo Fazio, a curialist at the Aragonese court of Naples), and Poggio in revenge had taken up the pen against Valla to defend Fazio. Their quarrel was public and literary, or at least it started that way. Valla retorts to Poggio's attacks and finds numerous expressions in Poggio's prose that are insufficiently elegant or classical: Poggio uses the verb *taedet* incorrectly, employing it with (horrors!) "a nominative subject and accusative object, instead of the proper genitive and accusative"; he uses language that a cook or a stable boy would use; and like a cook who clumsily breaks pots in the kitchen, so too does Poggio fracture the Latin language.[50] Between the two men, there is a series of battles and counterbattles, and Valla's line of attack is relatively consistent. In crafting our Latin—the most important of cultural imperatives—we should try to express ourselves not *grammatice* but *latine,* that is, not according to rigid grammatical norms, even if those norms are drawn from ancient sources, but rather according to the *consuetudo eruditorum atque elegantium*—according to the custom of the learned, elegant writers of antiquity. And we should be able to determine their custom rhetorically and *exemplis,* by means of examples, by means of what Erasmus would later call a *copia* of examples, which we draw from the best writers. But even as we do so, we must realize that we have to be flexible, because the world is historical; it evolves, and language, even the Latin language, cannot remain frozen.[51]

Faced with criticism of this intellectual depth, what could Poggio do? He recognized that there was a gap between his generation of humanists and Valla: in a letter of this period, he writes that *philosophiae ars a me abest* (I lack the art of philosophy).[52] He meant not only philosophy but also the advanced sort of philology that Valla represented, a philology that, in fact, was well poised to challenge contemporary philosophy on its own ground. So Poggio often resorts to the most banal sort of establishment-style critique: Valla is a coward and a heretic; he has no standing among the mighty; he is not of a distinguished family; he does not hold high office; everyone hates him, especially renowned papal curialists like Leonardo Bruni, Francesco Barbaro, and Lauro Quirini.[53] And this from Poggio, an author who had suggested that true nobility be based on merit, not birth![54]

Even later in life, in 1454, when a friend, Pietro Tommasi, tries to effect a reconciliation between Valla and Poggio, Poggio writes that there is no chance, and he recapitulates all his earlier criticisms. His disgust is palpably, bodily physical as he tries to tell his friend just how awful Valla really is: "If he were a friend of mine, I would reject not only the friendship of a such a monster, but even the everyday intercourse of life, and I would cut off of myself any part of my body that persuaded me of his goodwill. Really, what good man could be a friend to Valla, that fanatic, that idler, slanderer, boaster, heretic, that abusive belittler of the learning of all of the most famous men, present and past?"[55] He goes on: "This loathsome beast, out of his mind and insane, has inveighed against not only ancient pagan authors but even against Augustine, Jerome, Lactantius, and on top of that against all the philosophers."[56] Valla is such a perverse animal by his very nature and stubborn stupidity that he mustn't be admonished with words; no, he would have to be restrained by prison and whips.[57] Poggio wants his friend to avoid Valla. For Poggio, Valla, and other Renaissance men, disputes that involved matters of honor often seemed a zero-sum game: your motives are entirely honorable, the enemy's entirely dishonorable.[58] We cannot properly understand these seemingly exaggerated, immensely vitriolic Renaissance polemics between cultivated intellectuals as anything but frivolities of merely antiquarian interest unless we situate the debates where they belong: in the social, public context of the acquisition, protection, and maintenance of masculine honor.

To return to Lapo, elsewhere he says that anyone at the papal court "sees many things, hears many things, learns many things. . . . He takes advantage of the talk, conversation, and social interaction of many men."[59] The wisest will profit from this, for:

It is, after all, characteristic of the cunning, skillful, crafty, and tricky—as well as of the knavish—intelligence to know the natures of those whom they desire especially to win over. They perceive the deepest recesses of their spirits and minds, all of their intentions, their plans, longings, and desires. They know their routine, the food they eat, their domestic habits, whom they have in their homes as managers of property, as servants, as valets; they know to whom they entrust their secrets, their money, whom they associate with as friends, close associates, and companions; they know how much they trust each one, and to what employment and business each one of these devotes his time and energy. And having thought about these things, they apply what amount to stratagems in order to capture them by storm, to be in their company, to flatter them; they try to take some of them in by feigned friendship, others by personal appearance, others by pandering, and still others with presents. Now the ones who can do all these things—they are certainly not upright men. Nevertheless, they must be considered savvy, very clever, and very diligent, nor are they to be cheated out of their share of a little glory, since they do try to raise themselves up through work and industriousness, and become equal to those who are higher.[60]

As a courtier one often had to compromise one's values. Again we sense the anxieties that humanists must often have experienced. Along these lines Lapo also tells us, when enumerating the "pleasures" to be had at the court, that among them is the auditory pleasure, meaning that you hear many varied things, given the constant circulation of news both true and false. You hear about everyone's adventures and foibles, "for a great liberty and license is allowed in the Roman curia for reproaching and abusing," and you realize after a while that this serves not only the obvious function of amusing your fellows. You come to understand that "no one can escape you when the whole curia is like this. And so," Lapo goes on, "if you ever need a favor from these people, the result is that, almost like a learned doctor, you have your medications ready and prepared. You can apply them as if to some kind of illness, so that, if you know how to use your medications correctly, you are never turned away by anyone." He concludes: "I do not know if there can be any place better or more desirable than the curia for one who wishes to live opportunely among men."[61] Some short years later, Poggio would characterize the curia and its propensity for circulating and discussing almost any type of news as a *bugiale,* a "shop of lies."[62] Castiglione's early-sixteenth-century discussions about the value of deception at court become more resonant, and Machiavelli seems less a bolt from the blue when we realize that by their day there was a century-old tradition of historically *real* unvarnished speculation on the motivations of men and the way those motivations have to be studied, sifted, and utilized in a public environment.

And it was a tradition: Lapo, again, was not alone. One of his good friends, the much better-known Leon Battista Alberti, was an indefatigable dissector of his own personality and motivations, even as his work on art and architecture, family life and household management reflected his omnivorous intellect and wide-ranging interests.[63] Although born to privilege, after his father's death and through the machinations of relatives, he received (by his own account) no substantial inheritance. He bitterly resented his lost social standing, enviously describing the conduct of the rich as they vaunted their status, accompanied by proud retinues.[64] He dissected the life of the scholar, complaining about the way such a life removed one from the world in an unhealthy way.[65] He knew, like Lapo and Poggio, that the public marketplace was the only way to win acclaim, however distasteful and dangerous it might be.

In one of his short Latin works, most of which were written in the 1430s, he engages a complex and elegant metaphor for the manner in which he and his contemporaries in many fields must reuse antiquity. One takes pebbles from a sacred fount, cleans and polishes them. Even still, the crowd appreciates the cleaned-up pebbles less than they might. Severe judges abound, and they all come from different, sometimes mutually exclusive perspectives. Despite this, there is no solution but to go public with one's pebbles: "you possess many rare and worthy things. If only you show that you have them, they will be valued more than you think by men who desire them. . . . Whatever their quality, you must display them publicly."[66] In a number of his other short Latin works, Alberti satirizes one of the most respected and feared judges of literary worth, the antiquarian taste-maker Niccolò Niccoli, who could make and break literary reputations, but who, tellingly, published no major work of his own. In one dialogue, Alberti introduces Niccoli as a character named Libripeta, the "bookseeker."[67] One character, Lepidus (a stand-in for Alberti himself), is seeking advice on a career as a writer and has been "busy," he says, "with [his] books, striving to sow seeds of fame by writing." Libripeta responds: "You should abandon your vain and useless toils. I strongly advise you against publishing your research, for our vigilant and severely censorious masses are quick to condemn. And you should especially fear me. For by disparaging everyone publicly, I command more authority than if I were to praise many."[68] Here and elsewhere, Alberti engages in a complex dance of resistance and acquiescence vis-à-vis the literary establishment.

In one of Alberti's most famous works, *On the Family,* written in the Tuscan vernacular, he fully embraces and understands the public quality of life, and he advocates explicitly that honor and reputation be based on the public opinion of the wise: "Let us therefore, in everything we do, serve the public eye [agli occhi della moltitudine], for it is our task to please the public if we hope to draw an abundance of friends to ourselves, whom we shall choose from the public." Later he writes: "When we compete for such prizes as the favor and grace the people can bestow, I think it is hardly right once engaged in the contest to think our own judgment less fallible than public opinion. If we have taken the position that those who confer the dignity are competent and are guided by reason and thought, it is a matter of honor and a sign of self-discipline to accept their judgement."[69]

Alberti—and Lapo—codified what was common, if often unarticulated, knowledge among humanists of the first half of the fifteenth century: honor and reputation were singularly important, public commodities that could be acquired only in small communities of like-minded individuals. Humanists in this classic period did something new and different: with an innovative sense of how ancient texts and history informed their worldview, they turned that acutely refined sensibility on their own world, recognizing its public and ago-nistic quality and documenting it for their own age and beyond.

CHAPTER SIX

What Is Really There?

THE PREVIOUS TWO CHAPTERS were limited case studies, addressing specific problems in the Renaissance, orthodoxy and honor, as these were reflected in the work of a few Renaissance intellectuals. Even among Renaissance specialists, some of the works discussed are little known, but I hope to have shown that they are important in helping us understand the contours of Italian Renaissance life. The relative obscurity of the works highlights another pressing concern, one that has run like Ariadne's thread throughout this book: the problem of Renaissance Latin sources in general — their relative importance, their availability, and their relevance. In the first two chapters I attempted to show why they were absent from the great collective efforts of the nineteenth century and how this problem was handled in the twentieth, and in the third chapter I offered a flexible theoretical framework to understand these very particular, important, but little-studied texts. In this chapter we need to consider how these sources are distinctive, what it is we will find in the end (in other words, is the lost Latin literature worth studying?), and the chronological limits of the period I have been discussing.

To understand the unique nature of our source material, we have to focus on the differences between "classical" philology and Renaissance philology, what we can learn from them, and what we can "do" with Renaissance philology that we cannot do with classical sources. So it is best to begin with a discussion of what *classical philology* is. For the longest time, classical philology, and specifically text editing, has been defined by a procedure termed the *Lachmann method,* named after Karl Konrad Friedrich Wilhelm Lachmann (1793–1851), the Berlin-based philologist who in his lifetime did fundamental editorial work on texts as varied as the New Testament, Lucretius, and medieval German literature.[1] The idealized form of this method, also called the genealogical method, has been best and most succinctly defined by P. L. Schmidt: "The genealogical method, applied to Latin texts of antiquity," he writes, is "the constitution of manuscript groups or families by means of shared errors of transmission."[2] He goes on: "These families may lead back to an archetype, standing somewhere between the original and the medieval copies. Their historical relationship may then be illustrated by a stemmatic reconstruction of the historical process."[3] The reconstruction of the family relationships among manuscripts was essential, for, once that was accomplished, one could discard lesser variants; one could perform an *eliminatio codicum descriptorum,* an "elimination of codices that had been copied [from the leading member of the 'family']," which would make the formidable work of editing a text with many witnesses possible while still remaining "scientific." The first phase (the gathering of evidence, the comparing, the elimination) is known as *recensio,* and the second phase (the creation of an edition based on these pared-down remains) is known as *emendatio.*

Schmidt shows both that many in Lachmann's generation shared this general "scientific" aim and that, paradoxically—something that Sebastiano Timpanaro had also emphasized—Lachmann himself often did not follow this method but rather turned to one that is often opposed to it. In practicing this other method, the editor selects the "best" manuscript and uses it as a base, emending the text when necessary and providing copious notes in the text's critical apparatus which reflect the texts of other manuscript witnesses. Coincidentally, many of the "best" manuscripts for the editions Lachmann worked on happened to be found in libraries close to home; and Lachmann was not as thorough as legend would have it about reporting the other manuscript readings, implying rather than demonstrating, often with great sententiousness, that a thorough stemmatic analysis had been done before he "eliminated" the other witnesses. One can pass over the fact that, in all probability, the reason Lachmann's work made such an impression on his contemporaries rested with his personal qualities and the seeming certainty with which he issued his philological proclamations—he was, to use a German academic colloquialism, *professoral.*[4]

For our purposes, what comes into relief is this: faced with the impossibility of ever encountering an autograph manuscript, classical text editors attempt to reconstruct an *Urtext,* an original text that, were it possible, its author would sanction as authoritative. The editor, in other words, creates a "critical" edition of a text, a text that is not attested in any one single manuscript but rather represents the editor's intramental synthesis of all the available textual witnesses, which, guided by his own trained and trainable instincts, he has grouped into families. Once the families are adequately ascertained, he eliminates all but the best representatives of each family. From these best representatives, he can reconstruct the *lectio tradita,* the "transmitted reading," as opposed to the *lectio recepta,* or the "received reading," which has depended, so the argument goes, on standard but hitherto uncritically examined sources.

At least four observations are in order. First, there is the established fact that this method is an ideal that is in reality almost impossible to achieve, a Platonic form in which we can only participate imperfectly and limitedly.[5] Second, by the late nineteenth and early twentieth centuries, the conviction grew—as it had in other areas of the humanities—that this "method" was reliable enough to approximate the natural sciences in efficacy. Third, we should remember simply that, when it came finally to editing *Renaissance* Latin texts, precisely because the language was Latin, the methods used were those imported from classical studies, for good or for ill. Unsurprisingly, it was not classicists but medievalists who launched useful early-twentieth-century criticism of the Lachmann method, though they were for the most part dealing in their editorial work with vernacular literatures.[6] Fourth, as Martin West has written, "once the basic principles have been apprehended, what is needed is observation and practice, not research into the further ramifications of theory."[7] In short, we should remember that despite the technical terms that tend to accrue among philologists, good editorial practice involves, above all, extended common sense.

In our case, common sense demands the very strong articulation of the following notion: Renaissance Latin philology is different from classical philology, for the obvious reason that we are much closer in time to the period and can thus encounter autograph manuscripts. And even if the manuscripts we possess are not autograph, they are much more valuable than mere "witnesses" to support the Urtext. Even *codices descripti,* manuscripts that clearly depend on another, better version, are living witnesses to the reception of the author in question, showing where, when, and by whom his work was read in a way unimaginable for ancient texts in their time.[8]

In the case of autograph manuscripts, there is a wide variety of illuminating possibilities. For example, occasionally one will encounter a final copy-book, of the sort that an author might give to a scribe for final copying or, when appropriate, to a printer. These sorts of sources allow us to see an author at work, as the changes he makes—scratching passages out, changing formulations, and so forth—document his changing approach to the subject he is treating. We recall Lapo, treated in chapter 5 of this book, casting about the papal court for patronage in the late 1430s and seemingly unable in his short life to find a niche. By looking at the two autograph manuscripts that we are fortunate enough to possess (one of which contains the dialogue *On the Benefits of the Curia*), we can deepen our sense of the texture of Lapo's work and thereby enter more deeply into Lapo's own mental world.[9]

The physical structure of the manuscripts often points to Lapo's search for patronage. Like others on the lookout for potential sponsors, Lapo would often translate a relatively short Greek work into Latin in the hopes of dedicating it to a prominent churchman, a civic leader, or some other wealthy patron. When we look at the manuscripts themselves, we see that Lapo would translate a work first, then decide to whom he might dedicate it. In his copy-book, it is clear that he left himself blank space to write a dedication after he had mulled over to whom it would be most appropriate to dedicate the work; sometimes he filled the full space and sometimes not.[10] Lapo himself corroborates this practice, when he writes in a dedication to a cardinal: "After I had translated into Latin Plutarch's account of the peacetime affairs and military deeds of the most famous leader Aratus the Syconian and had determined—in line with my customary practice—to send it to some prince, I found myself in doubt and deliberation concerning the man among our leaders to whom I might dedicate this little work of mine."[11] If we can trust the dating in the manuscript, we see that Lapo was in doubt for quite a while and waited approximately a year to choose a dedicatee.[12] During that time he must have been waiting, watching, and calculating, as he turned his critical eye on his surroundings and wondered to whom he might appeal for support.

Also apparent from the autographs is Lapo's philological fastidiousness, which he undoubtedly inherited from his mentor, the controversial thinker Francesco Filelfo. When Lapo translates Greek, he often includes snippets of the Greek in the margins, and there we see how attentive he is to an often complex Greek diacritical system, very rarely erring in the marks of accentuation that appear above Greek words.[13] He also paid special attention to Greek verse embedded in a lengthier prose text, noting those passages with special care in the margins and occasionally leaving them out and leaving blank spaces in the copy-book, so that he might attend to these important matters later, an ambition frustrated by his early demise.[14]

Finally, to stay with Lapo, perusing his autographs can even give us a sense of the emotion of writing and the way his anger and frustration sometimes broke through the mask of sober melancholy that his contemporaries noticed about him.[15] We recall that his dialogue on the papal court, written in the last year of his life, showed his implicit consciousness of his own marginal status in the environment of the court, and although he structured the work as a praise of the papal court, it was riven with ambiguities. When we look at the final autograph on which the modern critical edition is based, Lapo's additions and changes to the text (noted in the margins and adopted by the other surviving manuscript witnesses to the text), admit us into the turmoil of his mind. Two examples will suffice.

In the first, the dialogue's two interlocutors, Lapo and Angelo, are discussing one of the chief benefits of the curia, which is that it is a concentrated seat of religion. The complex, back-and-forth-style reasoning of the interlocutors reveals that there are two sides to the same coin and that to some the curia seemed to be remarkably far from religion. One senses that Lapo felt himself on shaky ground when he was writing this section, wondering just how far he might go in revealing his critiques of the curia, even if they were many times implicit. In the particular passage I have in mind, the interlocutor Lapo is trying to persuade Angelo of the religious importance of the curia, but Angelo refuses to be convinced, realizing only at this very moment that his fellow interlocutor is trying to persuade him.[16] As we can see from the autograph manuscript, the first version of Angelo's response was as follows: "But if I had understood this earlier, then you never would have carried it through, and certainly now you won't make me admit it with any argument." Lapo revises the text to read: "But if I had understood this earlier, then you never would have carried it through, and certainly now you won't make me admit it with any argument. *For what can be more alien to the curia than religion?*"[17] The passage, we see, is the same, but Lapo endows it with an even more critical, and perhaps radical, aspect by his short addition, a rhetorical inversion that dissociates the curia from what it is supposed to be most intimately connected to.

Further along, the interlocutors are discussing another merit of the curia, which is that one can experience a number of sensory pleasures there, one of which is the pleasure of taste. This advantage too is double-sided, for one can experience this pleasure most effectively at the lavish banquets thrown by the curia's ecclesiastical princes. Some of them behave virtuously, in Lapo's view, and he admires them tremendously. Others however, "as if they were on constant holiday" (the interlocutor Angelo is speaking), "think of nothing else but that they should have in their houses the most precious and valuable wines and the most sumptuous food, as well as the most sophisticated chefs."[18] The interlocutor Lapo responds, mollifying this judgment and stressing the virtuous curialists who "measure their desires with probity," who "prepare splendid and refined foods in relation to the rank of their guests," and who "invite into their homes . . . foreign guests, legates, and princes, curialists as well as pilgrims—most honorable and magnificent men."[19] In other words, the interlocutor Lapo points to those who take the weighty responsibility of being a prince of the church seriously, for "in this way, among all foreign peoples the name of the curia is made famous."[20]

Then he goes on, in a passage that the autograph manuscript reveals to be an addition: "In addition, when the princes of the curia themselves throw banquets of this sort—well, fear deters me from saying with what pomp, variety, and abundance they are carried out, lest I seem to approve the extravagance of these affairs or seem myself to take excessive pleasure in this kind of thing."[21] In the dialogue, Lapo the interlocutor is often assigned the role of moderating the harshest critiques leveled against the curia, but Lapo the author can almost never resist adding one more critique, sometimes explicit, sometimes, as in this case, implicit. From a literary perspective, we see that by passing over the "pomp, variety, and abundance" and the "extravagance of these affairs," Lapo brings them into starker relief. But it is only by looking at the manuscript itself that we can see the complex, visceral, and sometimes tormented process of mental back-and-forth that led our young, almost-but-not-quite enfranchised author to conceive of his milieu in the way he did. Direct inspection of the manuscript shows us the emotional dimension of the compositional process, and it allows us into the dialogical procedure of humanism in a way inconceivable for classical studies.

Even when we do not have an autograph manuscript, the manuscript environment tells a lot about the way works were read and understood in their own time. One more example from Lapo's literary corpus will suffice. We saw in chapter 5 that Lapo and the Renaissance's first "universal man," Leon Battista Alberti, were friends, sharing a sense of disfranchisement and, in the 1430s, writing often on similar topics in similar styles. It is illustrative, and it helps to deepen our sense of their interrelation, that at least in one case, their works were bound together. In a manuscript in the Florentine National Library, we find a copy of works whose frontispiece lists, in a later but not a modern hand, works by Alberti. On closer inspection we see—something noticed by Kristeller— that one of those works is in fact Lapo's dialogue on the papal court.[22] Contemporaries, in other words, saw Alberti and Lapo as pieces of the same puzzle who were worthy of being anthologized together. We can see that, from the point of view of their audience, Lapo and Alberti were speaking to similar concerns.

Many other complexities regarding the manuscript heritage could be brought into relief. The relative abundance of Renaissance material (relative to classical sources, that is), presents editors with particular problems. Sometimes, for example, we know that an author in his own lifetime will have "published" more than one redaction of a work. Especially before, and for a time during, the era of printing with movable type, publishing meant coming up with a respectable, final version of one's text that was suitable to be circulated among targeted intellectual communities. Naturally, people often revise their work, and there are cases when, from contemporary testimonies in other sources, an author's own account, and the manuscript history of a text, one can identify discrete, different redactions, each overseen by the author himself. One of Lorenzo Valla's works not treated extensively in chapter 4, his work on logic, went through different redactions, and its editor, Gianni Zippel, prepared critical editions of them and published them together.[23] Recently Maria Grazia Blasio published a brilliant critical edition that contains the texts of two separate known redactions of a work, *On the False and True Good,* by the papal curialist and first prefect of the Vatican library, Bartolomeo Platina.[24] The blessing of Renaissance manuscript material, that there is a lot of it, is also a curse that demands an increased amount of discrimination, critical judgment, and simple labor on the part of Renaissance scholars. Moreover, the world of early printed texts (a topic to which we shall shortly return) was more fluid than is often acknowledged. While modern critical editions of early printed texts tend to concentrate on the last edition an author could have seen in his or her lifetime, these final editions are quite often not the ones Renaissance thinkers were reading.[25] A specific audience might have had a first or second edition in hand and simply not have had access to the last edition. Instead of seeking an Urtext and thus implicitly eliminating important sources of historical insight, Renaissance philologists must learn to move in the manuscript and early print world with more sensitivity to the conditions under which intellectual life was actually conducted—to attend to the *practice* of intellectual life as well as to the written remains.

Faced with these seemingly Herculean labors, we need to ask the most important question of all: what will we really find among the many little-known Latin works of the Renaissance? Keeping in mind that we will encounter our share of pedantry and unoriginality, as we do in any era, I believe we will confront at least two, perhaps three important facets of western European intellectual life that have not received the attention they deserve. First, we will encounter a limited number of thinkers who deserve a place in any canon of readings from the period and without whom our literary and philosophical heritage is diminished. In cultural history overall, there are plenty of examples of thinkers and artists who took some time to be rightly appreciated: Thomas Aquinas did not become Catholicism's official philosopher until the Council of Trent, Bach needed to be rehabilitated by Mendelssohn, Van Gogh was unappreciated in his lifetime, and so on. Among the lost Renaissance thinkers of enduring power, we will find intellectuals who were profoundly important in their own day, like Leonardo Bruni, whose contemporary popularity we can gauge by the high number of surviving manuscripts and early printed editions containing his works.[26] Or we will find thinkers some of whose works did not travel so widely in their own day (perhaps because what they then wrote was too radical or too forward-looking to be properly received) but who might prove very important for present-day concerns; one example of this latter type is Lorenzo Valla, whom I addressed in chapter 4. All of these Renaissance thinkers have been written out of history because an age later than theirs deemed some of their fundamental assumptions about culture inappropriate.

Second, and more commonly, we will find *missing links*. By this phrase I mean that, as I say in chapter 5, a thinker like Machiavelli makes a lot more sense when we realize the depth of the tradition out of which he emerged, a tradition in which certain thinkers routinely offered real, unvarnished evaluations of human motivations.[27] Also, thinking about the real humanist innovation— their embracing the dialogical mentality highlighted in chapter 4—we will find links to the sixteenth-century culture of conversation, well reflected in Castiglione's *Courtier* and beyond. The emergence and transformation of this culture of conversation has been the subject of a number of recent good books, but the depth of the Italian humanist contribution to later, sixteenth-century intellectual developments might have been more fully integrated into those studies, had the earlier sources been more easily available.[28] And third, perhaps we will even discover—and this of course reflects my own bias—an antecedent to the conversational culture of consensus that Richard Rorty has made a centerpiece of his work, which I highlighted in chapter 3. But we won't find out any of these things about Renaissance thought until we listen to what the thinkers have to tell us.

A moment ago a reference to printing with movable type found its way into the discussion. This development should be amplified and discussed, for the large-scale acceptance of printing as a viable medium of communication coincides with the end of the Renaissance period with which I am primarily concerned. On occasion I have alluded to the early sixteenth century as an ending point for the "long fifteenth century," whose Latin literature is this book's point of departure. Every decade within that period and every locality had its own specific conditions under which, within which, sometimes against which intellectuals worked. But there is a definable end that has sometimes been lost sight of. Printing is a part of this endgame, as are language and politics. Let us look at each of these three elements in turn.

Printing was introduced into Italy by the German printers Sweynheym and Pannartz in the 1460s and spread quickly. By the 1480s and 1490s we see a generation of Renaissance intellectuals—one thinks especially of Ficino, Filippo Beroaldo, and Angelo Poliziano—who worked directly with printers, leaving fewer manuscript remains than the previous generation had.[29] By the end of the fifteenth century in Italy, there were viable print shops in every major city, and in fact Italy, and specifically Venice, would take the Europe-wide lead in the new "art of writing artificially," as it was called early on. And over the long haul, Italy, like the rest of Europe, experienced the truly revolutionary changes that printing was a part of: new forms of intellectual communication on a broader level, new standardization of texts, the gradual emergence of "critical" editions of texts, new collaborations of authors and publishers, the possibility of intellectual superstardom, and so forth.[30]

Like many revolutions, the move to printing possessed continuities with past practices on many different levels, and for the first fifty years or so, print culture was more similar to manuscript culture than it would later be.[31] The first printed books were made to look like manuscripts; early printers, like scribes, identified themselves only at the end of the work, in its colophon, instead of placing themselves stage center on the title page; there was no concerted attempt to standardize Latin spelling in early editions; and even the process of textual editing was sometimes actually retrogressive, as an early printer might simply print the closest manuscript he had at hand of a text that might have better witnesses elsewhere, thereby diffusing immeasurably an observably inferior text. We have seen that one of the sources of vitality for humanists in the first half of the fifteenth century was the instability of their institutional environment and that this crucial lack of fixed institutional places was a contributing factor in the themes they chose to address, the creativity with which they did so, and the subtle acumen that they brought to their intellectual labors. By the second half of the fifteenth century, as we have also seen, this institutional situation had changed, as the papal court became predominantly humanist, as humanist education came to seem desirable for Italian elites, and as humanists made their way into university faculties. The gradual effacement of the instability and newness of print culture in the late fifteenth century constituted one of the final pieces in the puzzle of the ultimate enfranchisement—and consequent loss of a biting edge—of Italian humanism.

Another piece in this puzzle, completed by the third decade or so of the sixteenth century, is represented by the way attitudes toward language changed. First, we must foreground the fact that Latin was an acquired language for all who learned it Renaissance Italy, from Petrarch to Pietro Bembo, and that in a certain sense Italian Renaissance intellectuals, like medieval intellectuals, were bilingual. Because of the different disciplinary tracks from which scholars studying the Renaissance have come, however, there has at times been a tendency to separate the Latin from the Italian production of Renaissance thinkers and thereby to contribute to a long-standing, though now crumbling, distinction between "high" and "low" culture which does not always help evoke the reality in which most Renaissance thinkers lived.

Let us take the case, for example, of late-fifteenth-century Florence, which came under discussion in chapter 4, in a discussion of orthodoxy. We have seen that, far from being only a cultural environment of an ethereal, disinterested Platonism, the period was characterized, especially before the Savonarolan era, by a plurality of intellectual and cultural interests, from the rich vernacularity of the Medici jousts and the scatological witticism of Luigi Pulci, to Poliziano's dual participation as both vernacular poet and classicist commentator, to Ficino's medical and Christian vernacular writings, the *Counsel against the Plague* and the *On Christian Religion* (this latter he wrote first in Latin but translated immediately after into Tuscan), to his speculations about the nature of the soul in the *Platonic Theology*, for which only Latin could have been appropriate. Our thinkers' dual identities as both Latinate and vernacular should be brought into relief, because scholarship that has come from separate disciplinary tracks has often separated the two strands. Thus, for example, we might have a Ficino who is *either* an idealist, metaphysically inclined Platonist *or* an alien, premodern magus, venturing dangerously into forbidden areas of occult practice, but rarely *both* at the same time—which, in fact, he was. He was a thinker who, as we have seen in our examination of the strange blood-drinking passage, was close to and influenced by folk wisdom and, likely, street magic. Ficino was also in contact with the artisanal community, with the clock-maker Lorenzo della Volpaia, with whom he collaborated in designing a mechanical mechanism to represent the motion of the planets in harmony with the zodiac.[32] Yet, Ficino was the best Platonic scholar of his day, a tireless translator and interpreter of Plato, Plotinus, Iamblichus, Proclus, and the Hermetic texts, a Christian apologist, a fighter against then-traditional heresies. The one side shows us Ficino the esoteric hermetist, linking theory and practice, for whom the performative aspects of life were as important as the textual. The other is Ficino the dedicated, brilliant, indefatigable scholar, engaged with the Platonic tradition and doing his best to pass his version of it on to future generations. One sees that the unique nature of our source material in the long fifteenth century, Latin and Italian, "high" and "low," can be best understood not in the context of separate disciplines foreign to the Renaissance era itself, but as differently shimmering facets of the same unique jewel.

When it comes to language, there is another commonsense point that needs to be highlighted, which carries with it a set of particular problems. Italian Renaissance intellectuals from Petrarch onward consciously changed the way they wrote Latin—long an institutionally standard means of communication among intellectuals—to make it conform to their perception of appropriate ancient standards.[33] Education is an inherently conservative enterprise, so it is unsurprising both that many medieval Latin grammar manuals remained in use throughout the fifteenth century and that most of the actual educational methods used by humanist pedagogues were tried and true medieval classroom techniques.[34] Overemphasizing this inherently synchronic point, however, can lead to a flattening of the period and can blind one to the real advances that the leading Italian humanists' approach to language brought with it, primary among which is what Garin, Thomas Greene, Riccardo Fubini, Ronald G. Witt, and many other eminent scholars have emphasized: by focusing so intensely on ancient Latin, humanists evolved the historicizing ability to look at texts in a way that we now recognize as modern.[35] This style of reading among humanists—which by no means reached all levels of even the educated population—has achieved such a taken-for-granted status that one sometimes forgets that they did it first.

There was lively discussion throughout the period on the appropriate sphere of Latin. This realm of cultural debate is part of the *questione della lingua,* the language question, in which thinkers from Dante to Bembo and beyond pondered the relative places of Latin and the vernacular, asking which was superior, which was natural, what was the nature of the vernacular, what was the proper use of Latin, whom among the ancients one should imitate and to what extent, and the like.[36] By the early sixteenth century, the set of intellectual tools that the humanists developed, generation by generation throughout the long fifteenth century, were applied to this interlocking set of questions. Latin would continue to thrive as a specialized means of communication in early modern Europe, and indeed in modern Europe, for centuries.[37] But something changed when theorists began patrolling and regulating European vernaculars.[38] This set of intellectual moves occurred in Italy in the early sixteenth century, and by about 1525, the year of the first edition of the *Prose della volgar lingua,* Pietro Bembo's canon-making treatise on vernacular prose, the real debate was effectively ended.[39] At the beginning of book 2 of that work, Bembo articulated what would become the dominant notion: that the Italian vernacular represented a natural continuation of Latin, a succession so felicitous that a number of poets could already be found who wrote in that language.[40] All that remained—and this was the task to which Bembo set himself—was to regulate the vernacular, to create out of many local and temporal variants one language that was suitable for high literature. For Bembo, the proper model was represented by the variety of Tuscan created and employed by Petrarch in his poetry, which was now to be employed as well by prose writers of high aspirations.[41] And Bembo was no *deus ex machina.* Rather, he was the culminating expression of a final phase in the humanism of the long fifteenth century, lasting from Paolo Cortesi to Giulio Camillo Delminio, from the 1480s to 1530, when a number of thinkers began to reflect systematically on the progress of ancient Latin. Humanists from Valla onward, and especially Angelo Poliziano, had realized that to be truly creative, one's Latin had to be somewhat eclectic, a personal, individual creation sensitive to the changing vagaries of history while still remaining rooted in ancient norms of usage. But this newer generation insisted instead, with a historical acumen, quite ironically, developed by their earlier humanist forebears, that ancient Latin had gone through phases and reached a period of perfection in the time of Cicero. Since Latin was no longer in everyday use but still had its (limited) function for the learned, if one were to write in Latin, it was best to do it in the style of Cicero. Doing otherwise, Delminio maintained in 1530, would be like going to France today and coining new words—foolishness.[42] Thereafter, as Martin McLaughlin has written, "the key question of Latin versus vernacular had been settled in favour of the *volgare:* after this point no Italian writer considered Latin an appropriate medium for major works, and humanism became detached from creative Italian literature and largely confined to the academies and universities."[43]

So by the early sixteenth century, the desire of many humanists since Petrarch—to be able to establish and use Latin as a language of high philosophical and literary import—had ended. With hindsight we see that the dream was doomed to be unfulfilled. But how unrealistic, in its own day, was this hope? The perceptive Latinist Terence Tunberg has recently remarked that "to a person of our own age, when language and culture are so often considered an inseparable aspect of nationhood, the result of this evolution [toward the vernacular] may perhaps seem inevitable, but to many thinkers of the Renaissance this would not have been apparent at all."[44] Latin seemed more stable than the vernaculars, since they were always evolving; Latin enabled one to communicate to an international audience; and Latin had a long tradition, one linking it to Italy's greatest period of ancient Roman glory.[45]

Finally, if we think a bit outside our chosen temporal parameters, we can highlight the case of modern Hebrew and its use from the late nineteenth century onward in Palestine. With the strenuous efforts of Eliezer Ben-Yehudah (1858–1922) and his associates, Hebrew—a language that had not been used by any "native" speakers for centuries—became a school language and, within about two generations, a "native" language, even a "mother" tongue, once again.[46] For that matter, Italian itself was not really consolidated as a uniform national language until the twentieth century, despite the vehement exertion of sixteenth-century thinkers, the tip of which iceberg we have briefly touched on above in our discussion of Bembo. From his day on, regional dialects persisted in the lives of everyday Italians, and it was really not until the age of radio and television that a modified Tuscan became the standard "high" Italian, taught in a relatively uniform fashion in Italian schools.[47] In sum, if we remove the inherited prism of nineteenth-century nationalistic attitudes, we can see that, from their own perspective, the humanists' position on the Latin language was anything but unrealistic; rather, it was an open question whose answer only generations of cultural practice would decide. As mentioned, however, by about 1530 the language question, at least with respect to the use and appropriate sphere of Latin, was settled, and the "first" Renaissance was over, even if the intellectual habits fostered by the humanist dialogical mentality continued to exist, to be creatively transformed in every European locality where they found a home.

It will not have escaped specialists that my use of the term *the long fifteenth century* is a bit deliberately provocative, since in recent years one has become accustomed to speak of the long sixteenth century. This latter designation takes its point of departure from the ideas, discussed in chapter 3, of Fernand Braudel, which were then systematically augmented and transformed by Immanuel Wallerstein in his well-known *Modern World-System*.[48] For Wallerstein, the long sixteenth century saw the full-fledged emergence of global capitalism in its broadest perspective, from about 1450 to 1650. During this period, in western Europe and the Atlantic world, the large-scale desire to accumulate capital became a primary mechanism of social life. Global markets were created, which were best promoted by large territorial states that became their most effective protectors. This latter factor meant that Italy, which lacked a cohesive political unity, turned into a grouping of client-states. There have been many critiques of this perspective.[49] Here I wish only to point out that the primary object of this historical approach is economic and seeks to understand the emergence of capitalism on a global level, as opposed to a relatively local one; the favored political framework—the sovereign state—is favored precisely because its development is linked to the economic transformations. However, if we are focusing on early modern Italy, and especially if we seek to foreground Renaissance intellectuals and their achievements, then the concept of a long fifteenth century is an equally appropriate and useful analytical instrument.

Recently, a number of thinkers have begun to rethink the question of sover-

eignty, with its connotations of enormous territories unified by massive institutional apparatuses.[50] Scholars have noted that even if Italy did not follow the
broader developmental courses along the more familiar Spanish, English, and
French lines, the Italian city-states and their political traditions contributed to
emerging notions of sovereignty in other ways. Pierangelo Schiera notes, for
example, that "the origin of the modern state was not merely institutional, that
is, centered on the construction of an apparatus, but also cultural, that is, connected with legitimacy, and behavioral, that is, connected with doctrine and
discipline."[51] In other words, the fifteenth-century Italian heritage, whose hallmark was the 1454 Peace of Lodi engineered by Cosimo de' Medici and Francesco Sforza, was not just an ephemeral political legacy.[52] Both the concept of
active political citizenship within the republics and the notion of legitimacy
assumed and furthered by citizens within the despotisms provided important
European background for the larger, essentially sociological question of what
sort of political arrangement people will assume is legitimate.

We can also highlight the fact that, if we look at the historiography of Italy
as a whole in the last fifty years, one of the most noteworthy developments has
been the inclination to question established interpretive categories, divisions,
and teleologies.[53] This tendency has been welcome, for a number of reasons. It
has enabled scholars to work outside the bounds of a history nourished on self-
serving regionalist Italian mythologies—such as, for example, Florence as the
perfect "republic," Venice as the "most serene," seaborne city, fostering only con-
cord, or the premodern Italian rural south as barbaric, somehow fundamentally
different from premodern Europe as a whole.[54] Indeed, the danger in conceiving
of the long fifteenth century is that, if one uses the concept unreflectively, one
can fall into the trap of some of the older traditional positions that I outlined
in chapter 1: fifteenth-century Italy becomes only a transitional phase whose
thinkers planted seeds that were destined never really to flower on native soil.
With this caveat in mind, however, it is useful to highlight one commonsense
political point. Contemporaries like Machiavelli and Guicciardini noticed that
after 1494 there was a decisive change in Italy's cultural climate.[55] The invasion
that year by the French king Charles VIII signaled a real change: in an age of developing sovereign states, Italy's greatest strength—that it was a place of powerful, vigorously independent city-states with a nevertheless undeniable unity, an
"Italianness"—became its greatest political weakness. In an era of centralizing,

bureaucratizing power politics, Spain, France, and England came to the fore as the sixteenth century wore on, and Italy's proud little city-states were reduced to dependencies, even if, as has been pointed out, much of the ideologically political legacy remained. Nor would the Italian states follow the slightly later Low Countries model and turn themselves into a united group of city-states: Italy would have no William of Orange (1533–84), no Union of Utrecht (1579). And in any case, after 1527, the Sack of Rome by the Spanish Habsburg Emperor Charles V, the process of loss of international *political* prestige was complete. This is not to deny that after that time there were periods and movements of outstanding creativity in Italy, indeed a kind of "second" Renaissance.[56] But by 1530 the "lost" Renaissance was over, and Italy's long fifteenth century had come to an end.

So when these three pieces of the puzzle—the settling of the media of communication, the language issues, and the politics—all fall into place in the early sixteenth century, does this moment signal the end of the Italian Renaissance? Yes and no. It is certainly the end of the "lost" Renaissance that this book has been at pains to identify. This is the lost Renaissance whose voices are not nearly as available as equivalently important ones from other periods; the Renaissance that could have been better integrated into a number of fine recent studies that have dealt with the sixteenth and seventeenth centuries; and that, at the very least, can fill the artificial intellectual gap that, beyond an ever-diminishing number of specialists, exists for the period between Dante and Machiavelli. In another sense, however—one that I find quite congenial and to which Peter Burke has given the most eloquent recent statement—this early sixteenth-century moment was a beginning.[57] In this regard the lost Renaissance was not lost at all but is best thought of as a movement or set of interlocking attitudes and intellectual habits that made their way throughout Europe. This Renaissance was cultural, not political; nor was it simply a re-evocation of a lost, ossified classical Greek and Roman world; and it was not accomplished only by heroic individuals or the emergence of an immanent spirit of humanity, but rather by distinctive thinkers working in intellectual communities. The mental habits that the thinkers of the lost Renaissance fostered would later serve, at times, as a means for intellectuals to maintain at least some measure of independence in the face of the increasing power of emerging sovereign states. And the lost Renaissance was behind the adoption of a dialogical thought world whose traces we see in Machiavelli and Castiglione, Erasmus and Melancthon, Montaigne and Bacon, Galileo and Vico, and—dare one say it?—in the enlightened thinkers of the eighteenth century, who used critical habits of mind to rethink what it meant to be a human being. This is the Renaissance that is waiting to be uncovered.

Appendix
The State of the Field in North America

HAVING EXAMINED THE QUESTION of the "lost" Renaissance and its literature, we recall the primary reason that scholars in other fields, like medieval and classical studies, were able to transcend the divide between social and intellectual history: they had at their disposal reasonably good sets of sources that had already been gathered in the nineteenth and early twentieth centuries. Without the results of the gathering work done in classical and medieval studies, can Renaissance studies realistically hope to catch up? I believe it can, and in this brief appendix I offer some thoughts on how this can be accomplished. My thoughts can be summarized under the headings "editions and translations" and "electronic resources." Needless to say, this selective epilogue intends to open doors, not to close them, so I offer these suggestions and *pensées* as points of departure, rather than the only solutions to the problem.

At present, there is quite a bit of momentum in the international scholarly world for creating reliable critical editions of Renaissance Latin texts. There is less momentum, however, for translations. If Renaissance intellectual history has any hope of surviving, especially in the United States, I suggest that translations need to be as accessible as editions. The various editorial projects and text series presently under way which aim to create reliable editions of key Renaissance Latin texts are innumerable and are especially well represented in Italy, Germany, France, and the Netherlands. Indeed, I have not wished to sound pessimistic or naive, or to give the impression that Renaissance Latin has gone ignored in recent years. Presently, there are at least three major publishing entities planning editions of Renaissance authors. *Belles Lettres* is publishing, with critical text and *en face* translations, certain works of Ficino in their series Les classiques de l'humanisme. There is a new Italian series, the Edizione nazionale dei testi umanistici, in which certain excellent volumes have already appeared.[1] The Renaissance Society of America has sponsored a series devoted to making texts available. And Harvard University Press in cooperation with Villa I Tatti, the Harvard University Center for Italian Renaissance Studies, has begun a series of Renaissance texts with *en face* translations, entitled the I Tatti Renaissance Library. Moreover, the Istituto Nazionale di studi sul Rinascimento in Florence has been publishing critical editions of texts for years, as has the Humanistische Bibliothek series of texts, based in Munich, under the direction of Eckhard Kessler. The Belgian journal *Humanistica lovaniensia* has since its inception been without doubt the strongest supporter of neo-Latin studies, and the late Joseph IJsewijn, from that same context, served as the initial impetus for an ongoing series of worldwide conferences that have done much to facilitate contact among scholars interested in neo-Latin. The Warburg Institute in London has sponsored numerous projects dealing with postmedieval Latin, as well as publishing its esteemed journal, *The Journal of the Warburg and Courtauld Institutes,* which often highlights the Renaissance Latin heritage. One could go on. In general research on neo-Latin and more specifically on Renaissance Latin has been vigorous.[2] Perhaps we have now arrived at a point—now that Kristeller's *Iter Italicum* has been completed and is even available electronically, and now that electronic resources make the gathering of information a bit easier—where we can begin to think more systematically, comprehensively, and internationally about the sorts of texts that need to be edited and, frankly, translated.

Translation is the key problem confronting the field in the United States. The above-mentioned initiative of Harvard University Press, the I Tatti Renaissance Library, is a brilliant and necessary step; still, the format of publication makes it unfeasible to assign more than one or two volumes as textbooks in most universities. Although there has been no shortage of initiatives in the United States, the field has never entirely confronted the shape of the problem as manifested in American terms. Quite simply, translations are as necessary as editions of texts, perhaps even more so. Classical studies in the United States, on the verge of extinction as a field in the 1970s, saved itself as a discipline in that decade by finally deciding to teach ancient literature in translation.[3] Courses on ancient literature and myth proliferated and, despite some recent doomsaying,[4] classics is in relatively good health as a discipline—or it is at least as healthy as possible in the current American environment, where permanent academic positions in the humanities have been in short supply overall since the 1970s.[5] Classics saved itself, in other words, by recognizing reality. Renaissance historians must make an analogous leap. Editions must continue to flourish, but so, especially in the United States, must translations in affordable, accessible formats.

It is simply not possible to expose university students to the breadth of thought found in Renaissance texts, when there are so few available for classroom use. One of the most widely used (and readily available for teaching) collections of texts, *The Renaissance Philosophy of Man*, which has full texts from Petrarch, Valla, Ficino, Pico della Mirandola, the Aristotelian Pietro Pomponazzi, and the Spanish humanist Vives, was put together in the 1940s.[6] The language of the translations now seems antiquated, and the introductions are somewhat out of date. Because of these two factors, it is difficult for students to appreciate the richness of the material presented. The other most widely used collection, *The Earthly Republic,* is much more recent and accessible and presents lively translations of works by Petrarch, Coluccio Salutati, Leonardo Bruni, Francesco Barbaro, Poggio Bracciolini, and Angelo Poliziano.[7] These latter texts focus on Renaissance ideas of public activism and an emerging secularism. One can see in the principles of selection the clear importance of the debates related to the ideas of Hans Baron and his "civic humanism" thesis, which I discussed in chapter 2. Beyond these two collections, there are few accessible (and easily available for student purchase), sets of sources to use in teaching, or at least that go beyond presenting very short excerpts. The latter, that is, collections of very short excerpts of texts, are sometimes worse than nothing at all, since in practice one sees that real-life, everyday students often confuse the excerpts with one another and come away from the texts without a sense of authorship.

There are many more translated Renaissance Latin texts available, of course, but they are usually reprints of old translations whose language does not connect with today's students, or they are published by presses that quite frankly have trouble meeting the book orders. It is a delicious irony and a comment on the politics of "post-1968" scholarship in the United States that the only recent series of early modern texts in translation published by a major university press is titled The Other Voice in Early Modern Europe. This deservedly well-esteemed series, published by the University of Chicago Press, aimed from its outset to make texts from the period 1300–1700 available that dealt with the "other voice": these were texts in both Latin and the vernacular, written by both women and men, that raised a voice of protest against the predominantly male, misogynist (from a post-1968 perspective), majority culture of the Renaissance. From its inception in the mid-1990s, the series has published works primarily by women writers, like the poems of the learned courtesan Veronica Franco or the letters and orations of the noblewoman Cassandra Fedele. The irony is that while we can, from antiquity through the Middle Ages, hear very clearly—to use the series' editors' own terms—that "first voice," which they define as "the voice of the educated men who created western culture," we cannot hear the voice of the majority culture of the Renaissance itself.[8]

Let us take a different approach (because this one is starting to get a little dangerous). If one looks in a major world library catalog (like OCLC, which is available online) and finds, as I did, six separate English language publications *since 1990* containing new or updated versions of the work of Menander—the sitcom author of the ancient world—one fast comprehends the problem: for any subject area related to Greco-Roman antiquity up through about 200 A.D., even authors who are recognizably less important as "literature" have been worked over numerous times and are available in relative profusion, whereas Italian Renaissance authors are comparatively unknown. The problem comes into special relief when we realize that some works of a thinker like Marsilio Ficino, whose influence in his own era can be compared to that of Freud in ours, must be sought out in their original Latin *in manuscript* in the Vatican Library and that many of his other major works are still only available in a sometimes faulty sixteenth-century compendium.[9] Needless to say, most who encounter Plato, including classicists, first encountered him in their own language, not in Attic Greek. And most whose native tongue is not German and who read Freud will turn to any number of reliable translations before turning eventually to the well-edited German texts. Of course it is best, especially when dealing with specifics, to approach any text in its original language. But is a pious fraud to suggest that this is the only way that ideas expressed in other languages can be understood, especially when there are many levels in various interpretive communities.

To put it still another way: imagine if you wanted to read a certain work by Freud, but there were not only no English translations available; there was not even a reliable original-language edition of the work in question and, before you could read the work, you had to reconstruct it from three different manuscripts that often disagreed with one another. Unimaginable, of course, but precisely the case in Italian Renaissance intellectual history for many texts of many important thinkers between Petrarch and Machiavelli. We need translations so that the initial enthusiasm for confronting this difficult situation can be stirred up among younger students and scholars in different but related fields. But it is hard to translate without even a preliminary edition to work from, and it is even harder in many cases to assess what is actually out there. So we also need to play catch-up, and this is where new technologies will inevitably come into play.

Electronic resources make large-scale, collaborative international projects more feasible than ever before. At present, however, electronic media are unstable: not fully accepted by all scholars as viable means of assessing scholarly merit, they are in a state of flux. It is inevitable that they will grow in importance, though, especially in an age of declining resources for academic publishing. And the needs felt in Renaissance studies are precisely those that electronic technologies are best suited to address, for one of the main problems the field faces now is not knowing exactly what is available. What we currently possess is a congeries of valuable information, all of which either is already online or could rather easily be put online. We can examine the benefits of using new technologies by looking at a specific case, that of Paul Oskar Kristeller's *Iter Italicum*, mentioned in chapter 2 of this book. As noted, the *Iter* represents a lifelong effort on Kristeller's part to single out Latin manuscript sources relevant for Renaissance intellectual history in primarily European libraries. His collection was, of course, shaped by his own tastes and interests, but those interests were fortunately so wide that a tremendous amount of material found its way into the *Iter.* The publisher of the collection, Brill, has recently issued an electronic version of the *Iter Italicum* on CD-ROM, and it is now available online, enabling one to search immeasurably more quickly and efficiently than before through the dense collection of more than six thousand pages in small type, two columns per page.[10] One might type in the name of a humanist and find all the manuscripts in which the humanist is mentioned, one can cross-list various terms, and so forth.

One realizes quickly that the possibilities are seemingly endless if we focus our consideration on the flexibility that publication on the World Wide Web offers. It is a different form of publication from print or CD-ROM in that it is inherently impermanent and updatable. It is thus perfectly suited to projects such as catalogs and inventories, since new discoveries are always being made. Think, for example, of an archaeological dig. A director conducts a dig for ten seasons in a row, finally having enough material to present a seemingly comprehensive and complete site report, which will be published by a major university press, heavily subsidized and extravagantly illustrated. A year after publication, someone finds a new set of pot shards; then a supplement has to be issued, then another supplement, and on and on. The world of manuscripts is a lot like this, as we can illustrate with two types of examples. Occasionally, for instance, an important individual Renaissance text will be in a miscellany, and a catalog will have reported only the author of one of the texts in the miscellany as the author of the entire manuscript. Only after a scholar has examined the manuscript in detail can an identification of the individual work be made. Another type of example has to do with uncertain authorship. At times a manuscript may contain a short work but no attribution of authorship, so even the *Iter Italicum* might list it as anonymous or omit the listing of an author. One example comes from a fifteenth-century Latin manuscript in the Florentine National Library, which includes among a number of other works a very short treatise, "On the Sects of the Philosophers," a topic of interest among Renaissance intellectuals concerned to trace the genealogies of ancient thought.[11] The little work begins with the words "Philosophers are called by a Greek name which translates into Latin as 'lovers of wisdom.'"[12] The *Iter* lists the work but without offering attribution. On further scrutiny, one finds that the treatise is simply a Renaissance-era excerpt from Isidore, bishop of Seville (c. 560–636), the early medieval etymologist and cultural synthesizer.[13]

In either type of case, if the original were online and easily able to be updated, all that would be entailed is a quick correction and a credit to the scholar who contributed it, perhaps by listing him or her in a growing international list of contributors. One can envision eventually linking bio-bibliographies to the individual manuscript notices of a Renaissance author and the creation of a worldwide, evolving library: a powerful, searchable set of research instruments that will by no means replace careful scholarship, with its combination of trained intuitions and detailed reading of sources, but that will instead serve as a new form of reference. By now these sorts of speculations are old hat in the scholarly world, and Renaissance studies are just beginning to take advantage of them. Electronic sources are out there, worthwhile, and with every passing year progressively easier to use.[14] However, for the study of the lost literature, these commonsense ideas will have to be united to considerations specific to Italian Renaissance intellectual life, the unique conditions under which its literary products were articulated, and the reasons why these texts should be studied today. Without a vision of why the field is important, Italian Renaissance intellectual history will continue to be little represented in North American universities.

Introduction

1. On the restoration of the notion of *objectivity* among American historians after World War II, see P. Novick, *That Noble Dream: The "Objectivity Question" and the American Historical Profession* (Cambridge: Cambridge University Press, 1988), 281–319.

2. For the majority status of social history, see ibid., 440.

3. One or two representative works from each: W. Burkert, *Homo Necans: The Anthropology of Ancient Greek Sacrificial Ritual and Myth,* trans. P. Bing (Berkeley: University of California Press, 1983); P. Brown, *Augustine of Hippo: A Biography* (1967; reprint, Berkeley: University of California Press, 2000); C. W. Bynum, *Jesus as Mother: Studies in the Spirituality of the High Middle Ages* (Berkeley: University of California Press, 1982); H. A. Oberman, *The Harvest of Medieval Theology: Gabriel Biel and Late Medieval Nominalism* (Cambridge, Mass.: Harvard University Press, 1963); idem, *Luther: Man between God and the Devil,* trans. E. Walliser-Schwarzbart (New Haven, Conn.: Yale University Press, 1989); L. A. Hunt, *Politics, Culture, and Class in the French Revolution* (Berkeley: University of California Press, 1984).

4. One could push back to the world of the early modern antiquary; see P. N. Miller, *Peiresc's Europe: Learning and Virtue in the Seventeenth Century* (New Haven, Conn.: Yale University Press, 2000), 83–84. A bit later, one thinks of Friedrich August Wolf and his all-encompassing approach to classical philology; see A. Grafton, "Prolegomena to Friedrich August Wolf," *Journal of the Warburg and Courtauld Institutes* 44 (1981); or Friedrich Gottlieb Welcker (1784–1868) (whose most famous student was Karl Marx), doing much to advance the so-called *Totalitätsideal* (see the literature cited in William M. Calder III and D. J. Kramer, *An Introductory Bibliography to the History of Classical Scholarship Chiefly in the XIXth and XXth Centuries* (Hildesheim: Olms, 1992), 312–13 and 382–83; and W. M. Calder III, *Men in Their Books: Studies in the Modern History of Classical Scholarship* (Zürich: Olms, 1998), 55–80. And of course there was the *Annales* movement; see chapter 3.

5. For three recent contributions to this effort in Renaissance studies that come at the problem from different perspectives, see A. Grafton and N. Siraisi, introduction to *Natural Particulars: Nature and the Disciplines in Renaissance Europe,* ed. A. Grafton and N. Siraisi (Cambridge, Mass.: MIT Press, 1999); G. Ruggiero, "The Strange Death of Margarita Marcellini: *Male,* Signs, and the Everyday World of Pre-Modern Medicine," *American Historical Review* 106 (2001): 1141–58; and the monumental synthesis of R. G. Witt, *In the Footsteps of the Ancients: The Origins of Humanism from Lovato to Bruni* (Leiden: Brill, 2000).

6. Some representative publications: J. E. Sandys (1844–1922), *A History of Classical Scholarship,* 3 vols. (Cambridge: Cambridge University Press, 1903–8); U. von Wilamo-

witz-Moellendorff (1848–1931), *Geschichte der Philologie,* ed. with intro. by Albert Hein-richs (1921; reprint, Stuttgart: Teubner, 1998), Eng. trans.: U. von Wilamowitz-Moellen-dorff, *History of Classical Scholarship,* trans. A. Harris, ed. with intro. by H. Lloyd-Jones (London: Duckworth, 1982); R. Pfeiffer, *History of Classical Scholarship from 1300 to 1850* (Oxford: Clarendon, 1976); M. Beard, *The Invention of Jane Ellen Harrison* (Cambridge, Mass.: Harvard University Press, 2000); L. Canfora, *Ideologie del classicismo* (Turin: Einaudi, 1980); and idem, *Intelletuali in Germania: Tra reazione e rivoluzione* (Bari: De Donato, 1979); A. Momigliano, *Contributo alla storia degli studi classici,* 7 vols. in 9 (Rome: Edizioni di Storia e Letteratura, 1955–84); and idem, *Studies on Modern Scholarship,* ed. G. W. Bowersock and T. J. Cornell (Berkeley: University of California Press, 1994); H. Flashar, K. Grunder, and A. Horstmann, eds., *Philologie und Hermeneutik im 19. Jahrhundert: Zur Geschichte und Methodologie der Geisteswissenschaften* (Göttingen: Vandenhoeck und Ruprecht, 1979); M. Gigante, *Classico e mediazione: Contributi alla storia della filologia antica* (Rome: Nuova Italia Scientifica, 1989); G. W. Most, ed., *Historicization: Historizierung* (Göttingen: Vandenhoeck und Ruprecht, 2001); A. Robinson, *The Life and Work of Jane Ellen Harrison* (Oxford: Oxford University Press, 2002); and Calder, *Men in Their Books.*

7. See R. H. Bloch, *God's Plagiarist: Being an Account of the Fabulous Industry and Irregular Commerce of the Abbé Migne* (Chicago: University of Chicago Press, 1994); N. Cantor, *Inventing the Middle Ages: The Lives, Works, and Ideas of the Great Medievalists of the Twentieth Century* (New York: Morrow, 1991); G. Spiegel, *The Past as Text: The Theory and Practice of Medieval Historiography* (Baltimore: Johns Hopkins University Press, 1997); M. S. Brownlee, K. Brownlee, and S. G. Nichols, eds., *The New Medievalism* (Baltimore: Johns Hopkins University Press, 1991); J. Van Engen, ed., *The Past and Future of Medieval Studies* (Notre Dame, Ind.: University of Notre Dame Press, 1994); K. Biddick, *The Shock of Medievalism* (Durham, N.C.: Duke University Press, 1998); P. Geary, *The Myth of Nations: The Medieval Origins of Europe* (Princeton, N.J.: Princeton University Press, 2002); C. Gerrard, *Medieval Archaeology: Understanding Traditions and Contemporary Approaches* (London: Routledge, 2003); R. Morrissey, *Charlemagne and France: A Thousand Years of Mythology,* trans. C. Tihanyi (Notre Dame, Ind.: University of Notre Dame Press, 2003).

8. See the classic biography of Burckhardt by W. Kaegi, *Jacob Burckhardt: Eine Biographie* (Basel: Schwabe, 1947–82). Most recently, see the excellent study of L. Gossman, *Basel in the Age of Burckhardt: A Study in Unseasonable Ideas* (Chicago: University of Chicago Press, 2000).

9. W. K. Ferguson, *The Renaissance in Historical Thought: Five Centuries of Interpretation* (New York: Houghton Mifflin, 1948).

10. See J. B. Bullen, *The Myth of the Renaissance in Nineteenth-Century Writing* (Oxford: Oxford University Press, 1994). Ferguson and Bullen offer admirably broad surveys, Ferguson in his temporal sweep and the more recent Bullen in his critical sagacity. My approach is different from both in its emphasis, as will be seen.

11. E. Muir, "The Italian Renaissance in America," *American Historical Review* 100 (1995): 1095–118; K. Gouwens, "Perceiving the Past: Renaissance Humanism after the 'Cognitive Turn,'" *American Historical Review* 103 (1998): 55–82; see also J. Martin's suggestive study "Inventing Sincerity, Refashioning Prudence: The Discovery of the Individual in Renaissance Europe," *American Historical Review* 102 (1997): 1309–42; A. Molho, "The Renaissance: Made in the USA," in *Imagined Histories: American Historians Inter-*

pret the Past, ed. A. Molho and G. Wood (Princeton, N.J.: Princeton University Press, 1998); and J. Hankins, "Two Twentieth Century Interpreters of Renaissance Humanism: Eugenio Garin and Paul Oskar Kristeller," *Comparative Criticism* 23 (2001): 3–19. See also W. Bouwsma, "The Renaissance and the Drama of Western History," *American Historical Review* 84 (1979): 1–15 (now in his book *A Usable Past: Essays in European Cultural History* [Berkeley: University of California Press, 1990], 348–65; see also in that volume his "From History of Ideas to History of Meaning," 336–47); as he noted, intellectual history was not so much disappearing as changing, moving from the "disinterested" study of the history of ideas to the more complex but no less interesting history of the way groups in the past constituted meaning among themselves; and he suggested usefully that Renaissance history could and should be part of that new set of narrative possibilities. But that process of reconfiguration has not really happened (with respect to the fifteenth-century Italian Renaissance) to the extent that it has in other fields. For a later period, see J. W. O'Malley, *Trent and All That: Renaming Catholicism in the Early Modern Era* (Cambridge, Mass.: Harvard University Press, 2000); and related to the concerns in this book, see R. Fubini, *L'umanesimo italiano e suoi storici: Origini rinascimentali—critica moderna* (Milan, 2001).

12. P. Burke, *The European Renaissance: Centres and Peripheries* (Oxford: Blackwell, 1998).

13. One noteworthy exception to the divide has been the work of Lauro Martines, but in some sense it is an exception that proves the rule; in his landmark book *The Social World of the Florentine Humanists, 1390–1460* (Princeton, N.J.: Princeton University Press, 1963), he studied a number of leading fifteenth-century Florentine intellectuals. However, although his work elucidated the social conditions in which the humanists operated, there was very little attention given to their texts themselves. The same goes for his most recent, again excellent and highly interdisciplinary, study, *Strong Words: Writing and Social Strain in the Italian Renaissance* (Baltimore: Johns Hopkins University Press, 2000); here Martines is concerned to explore the way literature in the Italian Renaissance at all levels (he even includes doggerel and street poetry) interacts with society; but again, there is no extensive treatment of the period's Latin literature.

14. For some representative works, see F. Lane, *Venice: A Maritime Republic* (Baltimore: Johns Hopkins University Press, 1973); R. De Roover, *Business, Banking, and Economic Thought in Late Medieval and Renaissance Italy,* ed. J. Kirshner (Chicago: University of Chicago Press, 1974); M. Becker, *Florence in Transition,* 2 vols. (Baltimore: Johns Hopkins University Press, 1967–68); R. A. Goldthwaite, *Wealth and the Demand for Art in Italy, 1300–1600* (Baltimore: Johns Hopkins University Press, 1993); G. Brucker, *The Civic World of Early Renaissance Florence* (Princeton, N.J.: Princeton University Press, 1977); S. Cohn, *Creating the Florentine State: Peasants and Rebellion, 1348–1434* (Cambridge: Cambridge University Press, 1999); in addition to the works cited above by L. Martines, see at least his *Lawyers and Statecraft in Renaissance Florence* (Princeton, N.J.: Princeton University Press, 1968); and his *Power and Imagination: City-States in Renaissance Italy* (New York: Knopf, 1979); A. Molho, *Marriage Alliance in Late Medieval Florence* (Cambridge, Mass.: Harvard University Press, 1994); D. Herlihy, *Medieval and Renaissance Pistoia: The Social History of an Italian Town, 1200–1430* (New Haven, Conn.: Yale University Press, 1967); N. Rubinstein, *The Government of Florence under the Medici (1434–1494),* 2d ed. (Oxford: Oxford Univer-

sity Press, 1997); R. Trexler, *Public Life in Renaissance Florence* (New York: Academic Press, 1980).

15. For surveys of works of this type, see the articles of Muir and Molho, mentioned above.

ONE   ✧   *An Undiscovered Star*

EPIGRAPH : J. Burckhardt, *Die Cultur der Renaissance in Italien: Ein Versuch* (1860), ed. H. Günther (Frankfurt am Main: Deutscher Klassiker Verlag, 1989), 202; Eng. trans.: *The Civilization of the Renaissance in Italy,* trans. S. C. G. Middlemore, intro. by P. Burke (London: Penguin, 1990), 136.

1. L. Gossman, *Basel in the Age of Burckhardt: A Study in Unseasonable Ideas* (Chicago: University of Chicago Press, 2000), 251–95.

2. Meine Herrn, Völker sind Gedanken Gottes! See J. Burckhardt, *Briefe: Vollständige und kritisch bearb. Ausg. mit Benützung des handschriftlichen Nachlasses,* ed. M. Burckhardt, 6 vols. (Basel: Schwabe, 1949–86), 1:160–61; cited in F. Gilbert, "Jacob Burckhardt's Student Years: The Road to Cultural History," *Journal of the History of Ideas* 47 (1986): 249–74, at 256.

3. See A. Momigliano, *Studies in Historiography* (New York: Harper and Row, 1966), 105; H. White, *Metahistory: The Historical Imagination in Nineteenth Century Europe* (Baltimore: Johns Hopkins University Press, 1973), 164; White also notes (172–73) that for Ranke the idea of the nation—the fullest development of a people—was reified, "timeless and eternal." Cf. S. Milner, "Partial Readings: Addressing a Renaissance Archive," *History of the Human Sciences* 12 (1999): 89–105, at 92. For Böckh's opposition to Hegel, see J. Whitman, "Nietzsche in the Magisterial Tradition of German Philology," *Journal of the History of Ideas* 47 (1986): 453–68, at 459; for Ranke's opposition to Hegel, see F. Gilbert, *History: Politics or Culture? Reflections on Ranke and Burckhardt* (Princeton, N.J.: Princeton University Press, 1990), 23–25. Droysen: A. Momigliano, "Per il centenario dell'Alessandro Magno' di J.G. Droysen: Un contributo," in his *Contributo alla storia degli studi classici* (Rome: Edizioni di Storia e Letteratura, 1955), [1]:263–73, esp. 264–65.

4. Cf. P. Bahners, "National Unification and Narrative Unity: The Case of Ranke's German History," in *Writing National Histories: Western Europe since 1800,* ed. S. Berger, M. Donovan, and K. Passmore (London: Routledge, 1999), 57–68, at 58–59; Burckhardt: Gilbert, "Jacob Burckhardt's Student Years," 269.

5. Cf. Gilbert, *History,* 17–18.

6. Cf. D. Kelley, *Faces of History: Historical Inquiry from Herodotus to Herder* (New Haven, Conn.: Yale University Press, 1998), 250–72; Momigliano, *Studies in Historiography,* 107; idem, "Two Types of Universal History: E. A. Freeman and M. Weber," in his *Ottavo contributo alla storia degli studi classici e del mondo antico* (Rome: Edizioni di Storia e Letteratura, 1987), 121–34, at 122; and Gilbert, *History,* 25–30.

7. The quotation is from A. Grafton, "Polyhistor into Philolog: Notes on the Transformation of German Classical Scholarship, 1780–1850," *History of Universities* 3 (1983): 159–92, at 161; specialization in scholarly fields: Gilbert, *History,* 22–23. In the elevation of philology to a secular religion, perhaps no figure from the nineteenth century was

more important than Ernest Renan; see E. Said, *Orientalism* (New York: Pantheon, 1978; Vintage, 1979), 132–48.

8. On the *Encyclopédie,* see R. Darnton, *The Business of Enlightenment: A Publishing History of the* Encyclopédie, *1775–1800* (Cambridge, Mass.: Harvard University Press, 1979); D. H. Gordon and N. L. Torrey, *The Censoring of Diderot's* Encyclopédie *and the Re-Established Text* (New York: Columbia University Press, 1947); J. Lough, *The Encyclopédie* (London: Longman, 1971); and idem, *Essays on the* Encyclopédie *of Diderot and D'Alembert* (Oxford: Oxford University Press, 1968); and in general, see P. Gay, *The Enlightenment: The Birth of Modern Paganism* (New York: Norton, 1966); and J. G. A. Pocock, *Barbarism and Religion,* 2 vols. to date (Cambridge: Cambridge University Press, 1999).

9. *Encyclopédie ou Dictionnnaire Raisonné des sciences, des arts, et des métiers,* (Neufchastel, 1765), 9:243 (s.v. "langage"):

> Mais la différence des climats, des moeurs et des tempéraments fait que tous les habitants de la terre ne sont pas également sensibles ni également affectés. . . . Puisque du différent génie des peuples naissent les différens idiomes, on peut d'abord décider qu'il n'y en aura jamais d'universel. Pourroit-on donner à toutes les nations les mêmes moeurs, les mêmes sentimens, les mêmes idées de vertu et de vice, et le même plaisir dans les mêmes images, tandis que cette différence procede de celle des climats que ces nations habitent, de l'éducation qu'elles reçoivent, et de la forme de leur gouvernement?

D'Alembert damned the modern use of Latin in his *Sur l'harmonie des langues et sur la latinité des modernes;* cf. J. IJsewijn, *Companion to Neo-Latin Studies,* 2 vols. (Louvain: Louvain University Press, 1990 and 1998), 1:47. All translations from non-English sources are my own, unless otherwise indicated.

10. Cf. U. Eco, *The Search for the Perfect Language,* trans. J. Fentress (London: Blackwell, 1995), 111; see also M. Olender, *Les langues du paradis: Aryens et sémites, un couple providentiel* (Paris: Gallimard, 1989). On Humboldt, see P. Sweet, *Wilhelm von Humboldt: A Biography,* 2 vols. (Columbus: Ohio State University Press, 1978–80). Humboldt founding the University: O. Vossler, "Humboldts Idee der Universität," *Historische Zeitschrift* 178 (1954): 251–68.

11. Cf. Kelley, *Faces,* 261. Friedrich Meinecke recognized this evolutionary paradigm in the writing of history itself and the evolution of *Historismus;* cf. his *Historism: The Rise of a New Historical Outlook,* trans. J. E. Anderson (London: Routledge, 1972). He also believed that the heart of historicism was German and constituted the application to history of principles discovered by Leibniz and Goethe; cf. *Historism,* lv; and D. Womersley, *The Transformation of* The Decline and Fall of the Roman Empire (Cambridge: Cambridge University Press, 1988), 4.

12. See J. J. Winckelmann, *Gedanken über die Nachahmung der griechischen Werke in der Malerei und Bildhauerkunst* (Stuttgart, 1755), in J. J. Winckelmann, *Kleine Schriften, Vorreden, Entwürfe,* ed. W. Rehm (Berlin: de Gruyter, 1968), 27–59, at 29–30; cf. D. Sweet, "The Birth of *The Birth of Tragedy,*" *Journal of the History of Ideas* 60 (1999): 345–59, at 347–48.

13. On *historicism,* see G. G. Iggers, "Historicism: The History and Meaning of the Term," *Journal of the History of Ideas* 56 (1995): 129–52.

14. On which, see G. G. Iggers, *The German Conception of History: The National Tradition of Historical Thought from Herder to the Present* (Middletown, Conn.: Wesleyan University Press, 1968; rev. ed., 1983); and F. M. Barnard, *Herder's Social and Political Thought: From Enlightenment to Nationalism* (Oxford: Clarendon, 1965). On the recognition of cultural pluralism in Herder, see I. Berlin, *Vico and Herder: Two Studies in the History of Ideas* (New York: Viking, 1976).

15. Gilbert, *History*, 83–84, with n. 4.

16. See A. Momigliano, *Studies on Modern Scholarship*, ed. G. W. Bowersock and T. J. Cornell (Berkeley: University of California Press, 1994), 46.

17. Cf. F. Paulsen, with R. Lehmann, *Geschichte des gelehrten Unterrichts auf den deutschen Schulen und Universitäten vom Ausgang des Mittelalters bis zur Gegenwart*, 2 vols., 3d ed. (Berlin: de Gruyter, 1921), 2:210–47.

18. Ibid., 2:251–52.

19. Cf. O. Ribbeck, *Friedrich Wilhelm Ritschl: Ein Beitrag zur Geschichte der Philologie* (Leipzig, 1879–81), 1:131; cited in Grafton, "Polyhistor," at 185 n. 5; the latter article shows well why, from the perspective of actual practice, philology by midcentury had become somewhat lackluster in its appeal. For Ritschl in general, see F. Ritschl, *Kleine Philologische Schriften*, 5 vols. (Leipzig: Tenbro, 1866–79); W. M. Calder III and D. J. Kramer, *An Introductory Bibliography to the History of Classical Scholarship Chiefly in the XIXth and XXth Centuries* (Hildesheim: Olms, 1992), 273.

20. Calder and Kramer, *Introductory Bibliography*, 312–13 and 382–83.

21. See W. M. Calder III, *Men in their Books: Studies in the Modern History of Classical Scholarship* (Zürich: Olms, 1998), 173 and 175 with n. 35.

22. See A. Böckh, *Enzyklopädie und Methodenlehre der philologischen Wissenschaften*, ed. E. Bratuschek (Darmstadt: Wissenschaftliche Buchgesellschaft, 1966), 25; Eng. trans.: A. Böckh, *On Interpretation and Criticism*, ed. and trans. J. P. Pritchard (Norman: University of Oklahoma Press, 1968), 22; both cited in Calder, *Men in their Books*, 170 n. 15.

23. L. Bruni, *Humanistisch-philosophische Schriften mit einer Chronologie seiner Werke und Briefe*, ed. H. Baron, Quellen zur Geistesgeschichte des Mittelalters und der Renaissance, 1 (Leipzig: Teubner, 1928; reprint, Wiesbaden: Sändig, 1969), 81–96; with L. Bertalot, *Studien zum italienischen und deutschen Humanismus*, 2 vols., ed. P. O. Kristeller, Storia e letteratura, Raccolta di studi e testi, voll. 129–30 (Rome: Edizioni di Storia e Letteratura, 1975), 2:378–79; for an English translation, see that of Hankins in L. Bruni, *The Humanism of Leonardo Bruni*, ed. G. Griffiths, J. Hankins, and D. Thompson (Binghamton, N.Y.: Medieval and Renaissance Texts, 1987), "On the Correct Way to Translate," 217–29, at 220.

24. F. A. Wolf, *Prolegomena ad Homerum*, 3d ed. (Halle, 1884; reprint, Hildesheim: Olms, 1963); for a translation with notes, see F. A. Wolf, *Prolegomena to Homer 1795*, trans. A. Grafton, G. W. Most, and J. E. Zetzel (Princeton, N.J.: Princeton University Press, 1985); see also S. Reiter, *Friedrich August Wolf: Ein Leben in Briefen*, 3 vols. (Stuttgart: J. B. Metzlersche Verlagsbuchhandlung, 1935); idem, *Friedrich August Wolf: Ein Leben in Briefen: Ergänzungsband 1 Die Texte* (Halle, 1956; reprint, Opladen: Westdeutscher Verlag, 1990); and idem, *Ergänzungsband 2 Erläuterungen*, ed. R. Sellheim and R. Kassel (Opladen: Westdeutscher Verlag, 1990); the studies in J. Ebert and H.-D. Zimmerman, eds., *Konferenz zur 200. Wiederkehr der Gründung des Seminarium Philologicum Halense durch Friedrich Au-*

gust Wolf am 15.10.1787 (Halle, 1989); Calder and Kramer, *Introductory Bibliography*, 321–22; S. Cerasuolo, ed., *Friedrich August Wolf e la scienza dell'antichità: Atti del convegno internazionale (Napoli 24–26 maggio 1995)*, Pubblicazioni del Dipartimento di Filologia Classica dell' Università degli Studi di Napoli Federico II, 14 (Naples, 1997); and Sweet, "The Birth of *The Birth of Tragedy*," 350.

25. Cf. Grafton, "Polyhistor"; and G. Most, "One Hundred Years of Fractiousness: Disciplining Polemics in Nineteenth-Century German Classical Scholarship," *Transactions of the American Philological Association* 127 (1997): 349–61.

26. *Sitzungsberichte der Königlich Preußischen Akademie der Wissenschaften zu Berlin* (Berlin, 1890), 792; cited in R. Vom Bruch, "A Slow Farewell to Humboldt? Stages in the History of German Universities, 1810–1945," in M. G. Ash, *German Universities Past and Future: Crisis or Renewal?* (Providence, R.I.: Berghahn, 1997), 3–27, at 14, from whom the quotation is taken.

27. Ferguson, *Renaissance*, 196. There was also a long-term process at work, in which many thinkers since Descartes took "flight from ambiguity," in Donald Levine's words, employing ever-more-precise, seemingly exact, mathematically influenced uses of language, a tendency that manifested itself not just among philosophers but also among many connected with a number of the "human sciences." See D. N. Levine, *The Flight from Ambiguity: Essays in Social and Cultural Theory* (Chicago: University of Chicago Press, 1985).

28. The work first appeared in 1872. The edition I have used is F. Nietzsche, *Die Geburt der Tragödie, oder Griechenthum und Pessimismus*, in *Nietzsche-Werke, Kritische Gesamtausgabe*, ed. G. Colli and M. Montinari, vol. 3.1 (Berlin: De Gruyter, 1972), 1–152.

29. For Nietzsche the "Wesen des ästhetischen Sokratismus" is "alles muss verständig sein, um schön zu sein" (ibid., 81). Therein lay the problem. The point is made more strongly in Nietzsche's *Twilight of the Idols*, where he points especially to Socrates' use of dialectic as a sign of a changing mentality; the notion is that Socrates was awkward, without good taste, and out of step with his fellow Greeks: "Was sich erst beweisen lassen muss, ist wenig werth." See F. Nietzsche, *Götzen-Dämmerung, oder Wie man mit dem Hammer philosophirt*, in *Nietzsche- Werke, Kritische Gesamtausgabe*, ed. G. Colli and M. Montinari, vol. 6.3 (Berlin: De Gruyter, 1969), 49–154, at 64. After Socrates things went even more downhill, in a sense: "Der Moralismus der griechischen Philosophen von Plato ab ist pathologisch bedingt; ebenso ihre Schätzung der Dialektik. Vernunft = Tugend = Glück heisst bloss. . . . Die Instinkte bekämpfen müssen—das ist die Formel für *décadence*: so lange das Leben aufsteigt, ist Glück gleich Instinkt" (66).

30. Cf. Whitman, "Nietzsche in the Magisterial Tradition." Though see Gilbert, *History*, 74–75, who shows that Burckhardt cited *Geburt* with approval four times in his own *Griechische Kulturgeschichte* and that Burckhardt too emphasized aspects about the ancient Greeks that were in marked contrast to the Winckelmann-Schiller view.

31. Alles wahrhaft Religiöse ist dem Christentum verwandt. Cited in Grafton, "Polyhistor," 183. Schoemann was making the case that the Zeus of Aeschylus's *Oresteia* was to be seen as a beneficent god.

32. H. Cancik, "'Mongols, Semites, and the Pure-Bred Greeks': Nietzsche's Handling of the Racial Doctrines of His Time," in *Nietzsche and Jewish Culture*, ed. J. Golomb (London: Routledge, 1997), 55–75.

33. Cf. H. Lloyd-Jones, introduction to U. von Wilamowitz-Moellendorff, *History of Classical Scholarship*, trans. A. Harris (London: Duckworth, 1982), v–xxxii. For Wilamo-witz's early response, *Zukunftsphilologie! Eine Erwiderung auf Friedrich Nietzsches "Geburt der Tragödie,"* which he could not place in a scholarly journal and had to have privately printed in 1872, see Whitman, "Nietzsche in the Magisterial Tradition," 456–58. Despite the reaction of silence, however, one should not underemphasize the "countercultural" nature of the *Birth of Tragedy*. Even if it was in fact a work within a solidly reconstructible magisterial tradition, Nietzsche was nevertheless sincerely dissatisfied with the institu-tional development of philology as it was beginning to be practiced in German univer-sities. Wilamowitz's response is important, not so much for its immediate value, that is, when it was published, but because it represents seeds of the approach that would later be responsible for the place Wilamowitz would hold, as he revived philology by combining, as Calder has put it, the "*Wortphilologie* of Hermann with the *Totalitätsideal* of Welcker." See Calder, *Men in their Books,* 171.

34. See Gossman, *Basel in the Age of Burckhardt,* 271; and O. Murray, editor's intro-duction to *The Greeks and Greek Civilization,* by J. Burckhardt, trans. S. Stern (New York: St. Martin's Griffin, 1999), xi–xliv, at xxv–xxxii.

35. More on this in chapter 2.

36. Lloyd-Jones, introduction to Wilamowitz-Moellendorff, *History of Classical Schol-arship,* esp. x–xi.

37. On the *Biblioteca teubneriana,* see F. Schulze, *B.G. Teubner, 1811–1911: Geschichte der Firma in deren Auftrag* (Leipzig: Teubner, 1911); and R. Merkelbach, "Die Altertumswissen-schaft bei Teubner," in *Wechselwirkungen: Der wissenschaftliche Verlag als Mittler: 175 Jahre B.G. Teubner, 1811–1986* (Stuttgart: Teubner, 1986), 13–26, esp. 16. I thank Dr. Elisabeth Schumann for referring me to these works.

38. See P. Sutcliffe, *The Oxford University Press: An Informal History* (Oxford: Oxford University Press, 1978); I thank Dr. Martin Maw, archivist, Oxford University Press, for this reference; "The Loeb Classical Library: A History," at www.hup.harvard.edu, last accessed 12 May 2003; E. Malcovati, "Nel cinquantenario della morte di Carlo Pascal," *Athenaeum* 64 (1976): 3–18; cf. I. Lana, "Italia: La filologia latina nel secolo XX," in *La filo-logia greca e latina nel secolo XX: Atti del congresso internazionale, Roma, 17–21 settembre 1984,* ed. G. Arrighetti et al., 3 vols. (Pisa: Giardini, 1989), 2:1141–67, at 1152; and M. Desgranges, ed., *Les Belles Lettres, 75e Anniversaire* (Paris, 1994), 9–19. I thank Dr. M. Dubois of *Belles Lettres* for sending me this publication.

39. Cf. J. P. Migne, ed., *Patrologiae cursus completus, Series graeca,* 161 vols. (Paris, 1857–66); and idem, ed., *Patrologiae cursus completus, Series latina,* 221 vols. (Paris, 1844–64). On Migne, see R. Howard Bloch, *God's Plagiarist: Being an Account of the Fabulous Industry and Irregular Commerce of the Abbé Migne* (Chicago: University of Chicago Press, 1994); and A.-G. Hamman, *Jacques-Paul Migne: Le retour aux Pères de l'Eglise* (Paris: Beauchesne, 1975). Medieval studies: cf. the *Corpus Christianorum, Series Latina* and *Corpus Christianorum, Series Latina, Continuatio Medievalis* (both published by Brepols).

40. For an introduction to the field of neo-Latin studies, see J. IJsewijn, *Companion to Neo-Latin studies;* and W. Ludwig, *Litterae neolatinae: Schriften zur neulateinischen Literatur* (Munich: Fink, 1989).

41. Cf. P. O. Kristeller, "The Origin and Development of the Language of Italian Prose," in his *Studies in Renaissance Thought and Letters* (Rome: Edizioni di Storia e Letteratura, 1956), 473–93. *Loci classici* for this position include V. Rossi, *Il Quattrocento* (Milan: Vallardi, 1933), now available with updates by R. Bessi (Padua: Piccin Nuova Libraria, 1992); here cf. esp. 7–9; and G. Fioretto, *Gli umanisti* (Verona: Kayser, 1881), 121 et seq., both cited in Kristeller, "The Origin," 483 n. 27. As Kristeller points out (cf. 484), in this case the essentializing view was anachronistically applied to a largely imagined fourteenth-century prose style, theorized for the first time in the sixteenth century by stylists like Lionardo Salviati (cf. his *Degli avvertimenti della lingua sopra 'l Decamerone* [Venice, 1584], cited in Kristeller, "The Origin," 475 n. 7) and then adopted with vigor in the later nineteenth and early twentieth centuries. On the problem of language in the Quattrocento, see chapter 6.

42. E. Gibbon, *The Decline and Fall of the Roman Empire*, ed. J. Bury, 6 vols. (1776–88; New York: Heritage, 1946), 6:391 in the 1946 ed., chap. 66 in the original.

43. Ibid., 6:392.

44. F. Schlegel, *Geschichte der alten und neuen Literatur, Vorlesungen gehalten zu Wien im Jahre 1812* (Vienna, 1815), in his *Werke*, 1–2, 2:14; cited in W. K. Ferguson, *The Renaissance in Historical Thought: Five Centuries of Interpretation* (New York: Houghton Mifflin, 1948), 151.

45. Ferguson, *Renaissance*, 152.

46. J. C. L. Simonde de Sismondi, *Histoire de la Renaissance de la liberté en Italie*, 2 vols. (Paris: Treuttel et Würtz, 1832), 1:247. Moreover, in his *Historical View of the Literature of the South of Europe* (1813), trans. T. Roscoe, 4th ed., 2 vols. (London: George Bell and Sons, 1888), 1:309, Sismondi wrote that "the men who flourished at this period [the humanists], and to whom we owe the revival of Greek and Latin literature . . . do not properly belong to Italian literature"; thus he excludes extended description of their work from his account. Cf. Ferguson, *Renaissance*, 168.

47. L. von Ranke, *Die Geschichte der Päpste*, ed. W. Andreas (Wiesbaden: Emil Vollmer, 1957), 35–40; the work originally appeared in three volumes, from 1834 to 1836 (cf. Andreas, Einleitung, viii). My quotations are from L. von Ranke, *The Ecclesiastical and Political History of the Popes of Rome during the Sixteenth and Seventeenth Centuries*, 3 vols., trans. S. Austin (London: Murray, 1840), 1:63–64.

48. Ranke, *Geschichte der Päpste*, 36. Compare Burckhardt's later opinion of Bembo; after discussing the perfection of a Latin epistolary style in the letters of Poliziano and Bembo, he goes on: "Together with these there appeared in the sixteenth century the classical style of Italian correspondence, at the head of which stands Bembo again. Its form is wholly modern, and deliberately kept free from Latin influence, and yet its spirit is thoroughly penetrated and possessed by the ideas of antiquity." Burckhardt, *Die Cultur der Renaissance in Italien;* Eng. trans.: *The Civilization of the Renaissance in Italy*, 153.

49. Ranke, *Geschichte der Päpste*, 37; in *History of the Popes*, 1:66.

50. G. Voigt, *Die Wiederbelebung des classischen Althertums, oder das erste Jahrhundert des Humanismus* (Berlin: Reimer, 1859), 445; cited in Ferguson, *Renaissance*, 160.

51. G. Voigt, *Die Wiederbelebung des classischen Althertums, oder das erste Jahrhundert des Humanismus*, 2 vols., 4th ed. (Berlin: Walter de Gruyter, 1960), 2:364.

52. Cf. Gossman, *Basel in the Age of Burckhardt*, 73.

53. Voigt, *Die Wiederbelebung* (1960), 2:365.

54. Ibid., 2:372–94.

55. Ibid., 2:369: ". . . So war denn in diesen schöngeistigen Kreisen die Sittlichkeit dem einfachen Gewissen völlig entrückt und in eine Welt des Scheines versetzt."

56. The work first appeared in 1858. Quotation from Burckhardt, *The Civilization of the Renaissance in Italy*, 136. For Burckhardt's view of the use of Latin in the writing of contemporary history among humanists, see 160: "Contemporary history, no doubt, was written far better in the language of the day than when forced into Latin." For Burckhardt's time in Berlin (1839–42), where he followed Ranke's lectures, see Gilbert, "Jacob Burckhardt's Student Years"; F. Meinecke, "Ranke and Burckhardt," in *German History: Some New German Views*, ed. H. Kohn (Boston: Beacon, 1954), 142–56; W. Kaegi, *Jacob Burckhardt: Eine Biographie* (Basel: Schwabe, 1947–82), 2:54–75; O. Markwart, *Jacob Burckhardt: Persönlichkeit und Jugendjahre* (Basel: Schwabe, 1920). Burckhardt remained faithful to a number of Ranke's central ideas; cf. Gilbert, *History*, 93–105; R. Fubini, "Rinascimento riscoperto? Studi recenti su Jacob Burckhardt," *Società e storia* 61 (1993): 583–607, esp. 598; and N. Hammerstein, "Leopold von Ranke und die Renaissance," in *Il Rinascimento nell'Ottocento in Italia e Germania / Die Renaissance im 19. Jahrhundert in Italien und Deutschland*, ed. A. Buck and C. Vasoli (Bologna: Il Mulino, 1989), 45–64.

57. Burckhardt, *The Civilization of the Renaissance in Italy*, 176. He treats Renaissance Latin poetry on 167–77.

58. Ibid., 98. Here he highlights the importance of small aristocratic states in the formation of Renaissance Italians.

59. Gossman, *Basel in the Age of Burckhardt*. See also C. E. Schorske, *Thinking with History: Explorations in the Passage to Modernism* (Princeton, N.J.: Princeton University Press, 1998), 56–70; and F. Meinecke, *Zur Geschichte der Geschichtsschreibung*, ed. E. Kessel (Munich: Oldenbourg, 1968), 93–110.

60. J. A. Symonds, *Renaissance in Italy*, 7 vols. (London, 1875–86), 2:40; Ferguson, *Renaissance*, 202. For a similar, later opinion, cf. F. A. Wright and T. A. Sinclair, *A History of Later Latin Literature* (London: Routledge, 1931), 335. Some, like Thorndike, would be even less charitable, reverting to the Rankean view; see L. Thorndike, *A History of Magic and Experimental Science*, 8 vols. (New York: Columbia University Press, 1923–58), 5:9: "Partly perhaps because of the emphasis upon eloquence, humanism and the classics, the sixteenth century in general was not an age of scientific specialization but marked by a somewhat amateurish literary interest."

61. Peter Brown suggests that for Momigliano English became a more precise and finely honed instrument than was his native Italian; see Brown's "Arnaldo Dante Momigliano" in *Proceedings of the British Academy* 74 (1988): 405–42, at 415; and cf. O. Murray, "Arnaldo Momigliano in England," in *The Presence of the Historian: Essays in Memory of Arnaldo Momigliano*, History and Theory, Beiheft 30, ed. M. P. Steinberg (Middletown: Wesleyan University Press, 1991), 49–64, at 62. Panofsky: see E. Panofsky, *Meaning in the Visual Arts* (Garden City, N.Y.: Doubleday, 1955), 321–46, at 329–30.

62. See P. Bourdieu, *Outline of a Theory of Practice*, trans. R. Nice (Cambridge: Cambridge University Press, 1977); and idem, *In Other Words: Essays towards a Reflexive Soci-*

ology, trans. M. Adamson (Stanford, Calif.: Stanford University Press, 1990); F. Ringer, *Fields of Knowledge: French Academic Culture in Comparative Perspective, 1890–1920* (Cambridge: Cambridge University Press, 1992), 1–25; and the discussion in chapter 3 of the present book.

63. Muratori: L. A. Muratori, *Rerum italicarum scriptores*, 25 vols. in 28 (Milan, 1723–51); some of his works are conveniently edited in L. A. Muratori, *Opere*, ed. G. Falco and F. Forti, 2 vols. (Milan: Ricciardi, 1964); see, there, 2:1324–27, at 1325, for his respect for the learning of the humanists (taken from his *Annali d'Italia*, preface to the fifteenth century); see also on this point a letter defending the Italian contribution to science and philosophy, highlighting Pico and Ficino for their renewed study of Plato and Zabarella and Francesco Piccolomini for their sagacious use of late ancient Greek commentators on Aristotle to "purge Aristotle's system from the ineptnesses of the Arabs" (by which he means the legacy of Averroes and other medieval Arabic Aristotelian commentators). The letter is partially cited in A. Andreoli, *Nel mondo di Lodovico Antonio Muratori* (Bologna: Il Mulino, 1972), 219–20. In general on Muratori, see also S. Bertelli, *Erudizione e storia in Ludovico Antonio Muratori* (Naples: Istituto Storico, 1960); for Muratori and his effect on British historical enterprises, see D. Hay, "Muratori and British Historians," in *L.A. Muratori storiografo: Atti del convegno internazionale di studi muratoriani* (Modena, 1975), 323–39. Muratori's general interests, often with more specific focus on the fifteenth century, were carried on later by, e.g., L. Mehus, *Historia litteraria florentina* (Florence, 1769; reprint, with intro. by E. Kessler, Munich: Fink, 1968); or A. M. Bandini, *Catalogus codicum manuscriptorum bibliothecae mediceae laurentianae*, 8 vols. (Florence, 1764–78); or Saverio Bettinelli, *Risorgimento d'Italia negli Studj, nelle Arti, e ne' Costumi dopo il Mille* (1780; 2d ed. in 2 vols., 1786), cited in E. Garin, *La cultura del Rinascimento* (Milan: Saggiatore, 1988), 9. Cf. G. W. Most, "Classical Scholarship and Literary Criticism," in *The Cambridge History of Literary Criticism*, vol. 4, *The Eighteenth Century* (Cambridge: Cambridge University Press, 1997), 742–57.

64. In *The Varieties of History*, ed. F. Stern (New York: Vintage, 1973), 59–60; for the German, see L. von Ranke, *Aus Werk und Nachlass*, 4 vols., ed. W. P. Fuchs and T. Schieder, *Vorlesungseinleitungen* (Munich: Bayerische Akademie der Wissenschaften, 1964–75), 4:88; cited in Gilbert, *History*, 29.

T W O   ⟋   *Italian Renaissance Humanism in the Twentieth Century*

E P I G R A P H : B. Croce, *La teoria della libertà* (Bari: Laterza, 1945), 10; cited and trans. in E. G. Caserta, *Croce and Marxism: From the Years of Revisionism to the Last Postwar Period* (Naples: Morano, 1987), 15 n. 17. W. von Humboldt, "Über die innere und äußere Organisation der höheren wissenschaftlichen Anstalten in Berlin," 1809–10, first published in 1896. I cite from the version in *Die Idee der Deutschen Universität* (Darmstadt: Hermann Gentner, 1956), 375–86, at 377–8. This passage is also cited and translated in R. Vom Bruch, "A Slow Farewell to Humboldt? Stages in the History of German Universities, 1810–1945," in M. G. Ash, *German Universities Past and Future: Crisis or Renewal?* (Providence, R.I.: Berghahn, 1997), 3–27, at 10.

1. Cf. W. R. Everdell, *The First Moderns: Profiles in the Origins of Twentieth-Century*

Thought (Chicago: University of Chicago Press, 1997); and R. Safranski, *Martin Heidegger: Between Good and Evil,* trans. E. Osers (Cambridge, Mass.: Harvard University Press, 1998), 16–144.

2. Aristotle, *Poetics,* 13.1452b–1453a and 15.1454a–b.

3. Cf. P. Bourdieu, *Outline of a Theory of Practice* (Cambridge: Cambridge University Press, 1977); and D. Swarz, *Culture and Power: The Sociology of Pierre Bourdieu* (Chicago: University of Chicago Press, 1997).

4. For Croce, see, for example, B. Croce, *History: Its Theory and Practice,* trans. D. Ainslie (New York: Russell and Russell, 1960), 224: "The negation of Christian transcendency was the work of the age of the Renaissance." For Gentile, see esp. his *Il pensiero italiano del Rinascimento,* 3d ed (Florence: Sansoni, 1940); and some of the studies in idem, *Studi sul Rinascimento* (Florence: Vallecchi, 1923); see G. Turi, *Giovanni Gentile: Una biografia* (Florence: Giunti, 1995), 145; and C. Vasoli, "Gentile e la filosofia del Rinascimento," in *Croce e Gentile: fra tradizione nazionale e filosofia europea,* ed. M. Ciliberto and R. Brienza (Rome: Riuniti, 1993), 289–307.

5. I rely here on Turi, *Giovanni Gentile;* and H. S. Harris, *The Social Philosophy of Giovanni Gentile* (Urbana: University of Illinois Press, 1960).

6. G. Gentile, *La filosofia di Marx* (Pisa: Spoerri, 1899).

7. G. Gentile, *La riforma dell'educazione: Discorsi ai maestri di Trieste,* 4th ed., rev. (Florence: Sansoni, 1935), 53; Harris, *Social Philosophy,* 3.

8. Gentile, *La riforma dell'educazione,* 53.

9. Harris, *Social Philosophy,* 4–7.

10. 1 Cor. 13:2, King James Version; cf. G. Gentile, *Sistema di logica come teoria del conoscere,* 3d ed. (Florence: Sansoni, 1940), 1:34; Harris, *Social Philosophy,* 5.

11. Gentile, reviewing the Italian edition of J. E. Spingarn's *Literary Criticism in the Renaissance,* in *La critica* 3 (1905): 237–38.

12. Giordano Bruno (d. 1600) was a notable exception for Gentile, and in fact Bruno was an important influence on Gentile's thought; see G. Gentile, *Giordano Bruno e il pensiero del rinascimento* (Florence: Vallecchi, 1920), 259–355; Turi, *Giovanni Gentile,* 138–47.

13. Harris, *Social Philosophy,* 7–11; Turi, *Giovanni Gentile,* 32–34, 134–38.

14. Turi, *Giovanni Gentile,* 75–81. In this respect, Gentile worked within a by then well-established tradition in European thought, begun, really, by Gottlob Frege; see chapter 3.

15. Cf. D. Spanio, "Idealismo e dialettica dell'idea nell'attualismo di Giovanni Gentile," in *Croce e Gentile un secolo dopo* (Florence: Le Lettere, 1994); also published in *Giornale critico della filosofia italiana,* 6th ser., 14, fasc. 2–3 (1994): 428–61, with the literature cited in 435 n. 4; and G. Gentile, *La riforma della dialettica hegeliana,* 4th ed. (Florence: Sansoni, 1975; 1st ed., Messina: Principato, 1913).

16. See, in general, U. M. Miozzi, *Lo sviluppo storico dell'università italiana* (Florence: Le Monnier, 1993); G. Cives, ed., *La scuola italiana dall'Unità ai nostri giorni* (Florence: La Nuova Italia, 1990); R. Moscati, "The Changing Policies of Education in Italy," *Journal of Modern Italian Studies* 3 (1998): 55–72; and L. Minio-Paluello, *Education in Fascist Italy* (Oxford: Oxford University Press, 1946).

17. Minio-Paluello, *Education in Fascist Italy.* For the central ideas behind the Humboldt-era research university, see the collected writings in *Die Idee der deutschen Universi-*

tät: Die fünf Grundschriften aus der Zeit ihrer Neubegründung durch klassischen Idealismus und romantischen Realismus, ed. E. Anrich (Darmstadt: Gentner, 1956). A powerful critique of the program was offered by H. Schelsky, *Einsamkeit und Freiheit: Idee und Gestalt der deutschen Universität und ihrer Reformen* (Reinbek, Germany, 1963). There is a good introduction to the Humboldt-era reforms in Vom Bruch, "A Slow Farewell to Humboldt?" 3–27.

18. Religious instruction in the schools had been mandatory since 1859, the year of the *lex Casati,* the foundational set of Italian educational laws in the period of national unification; by the time of the Fascist reforms, however, this provision had dwindled. Gentile reintroduced it as the very basis of elementary education, in order to instill correct moral principles and since most Italians were in fact Catholic; but the soundest basis for secondary education he considered to be philosophical. Harris, *Social Philosophy,* 66–76; Minio-Paluello, *Education in Fascist Italy.*

19. G. Gentile, "L'unità della scuola media e la libertà degli studi," *Rivista filosofica,* fasc. 2–3 (1902); reprinted in G. Gentile, *La nuova scuola media* (Florence: Vallecchi, 1925), 9–54, at 25–26; cited and translated in Harris, *Social Philosophy,* 61–62. The text is now available in a critical edition in the *Opere complete di Giovanni Gentile,* vol.40, as G. Gentile, *La nuova scuola media,* ed. H. A. Cavallera (Florence: Le Lettere, 1988); the cited passage is on p. 15.

20. See D. D. Roberts, *Benedetto Croce and the Uses of Historicism* (Berkeley: University of California Press, 1987).

21. His thought was transmitted to the English-speaking world largely through the efforts of R. G. Collingwood; see, e.g, that author's *The Idea of History* (1946; reprint, Oxford: Oxford University Press, 1993).

22. On Croce and Laterza, see D. Coli, *Croce, Laterza e la cultura europea* (Bologna: Il Mulino, 1983).

23. *La critica* was an important voice in Italian culture; bimonthly, it ran until December 1944; Roberts, *Benedetto Croce,* 10. On the early years of the journal, see E. Garin, *Cronache di filosofia italiana, 1900–1943,* 2d ed. (Bari: Laterza, 1959), 187–240.

24. The following quotations are taken from the letter of Croce to Vossler of 19 August 1913; see B. Croce, *Carteggio Croce-Vossler, 1899–1949,* ed. V. De Caprariis (Rome: Laterza, 1982), letter 139 (pp. 165–67); the letter is also cited and analyzed in Garin, *Cronache di filosofia italiana,* 284–85.

25. Perhaps most cogently and passionately expressed in a well-known work written during in the years of Fascism, B. Croce, *La storia come pensiero e come azione* (Bari: Laterza, 1938); Eng. trans.: B. Croce, *History as the Story of Liberty,* trans. S. Sprigge (London: Allen and Unwin, 1941).

26. A. Labriola, *La concezione materialistica della storia* (Bari: Laterza, 1953); I have cited from the translation in A. Labriola, *Essays on the Materialistic Conception of History,* trans. C. H. Kerr (Chicago, 1903; reprint, New York: Monthly Review Press, 1966), 95.

27. Cf. E. Garin, introduction to A. Labriola, *Epistolario,* ed. D. Dugini and R. Martinelli, 3 vols. (Rome: Riuniti, 1983), 1:xix.

28. See M. Agrimi, "Labriola tra Croce e Gentile," in *Croce e Gentile un secolo dopo* (Florence: Le Lettere, 1994); also published in *Giornale critico della filosofia italiana,* 6th ser., 14, fasc. 2–3 (1994): 184–204; Garin puts it well, highlighting the differences between

Croce and Gentile on Marx in his "Croce e Gentile interpreti di Marx," in *Croce e Gentile fra tradizione nazionale e filosofia europea*, 3–13, at 12–13: for Croce, Marx was the "theoretician and historian of modernity"; for Gentile, "the reformer of Hegelian dialectic."

29. Cf. W. L. Adamson, *Avant-Garde Florence: From Modernism to Fascism* (Cambridge, Mass.: Harvard University Press, 1993), 67–70.

30. Roberts, *Benedetto Croce*, 18.

31. B. Croce, *History as the Story of Liberty*, trans. S. Sprigge (London: Allen and Unwin, 1941), 34–35.

32. Croce, *History: Its Theory and Practice*, 224–42; idem, *La filosofia di Giambattista Vico* (Bari: Laterza, 1911); Eng. trans.: B. Croce, *The Philosophy of Giambattista Vico*, trans. R. G. Collingwood (London: Russell and Russell, 1913).

33. Croce, *History as the Story of Liberty*, 302.

34. On this aspect of Vico's thought, see F. Fellman, *Das Vico-Axiom: Der Mensch macht die Geschichte* (Freiburg: Alber, 1976); L. Pompa, *Human Nature and Historical Knowledge* (Cambridge: Cambridge University Press, 1990); D. P. Verene, *Vico's Science of Imagination* (Ithaca, N.Y.: Cornell University Press, 1981); N. S. Struever, "Rhetoric and Philosophy in Vichian Inquiry Investigation," *New Vico Studies* 3 (1985): 131–45; idem, "Humanism and Science in the Context of Vichian Inquiry," *New Vico Studies* 11 (1993): 45–58.

35. Croce, *History as the Story of Liberty*, 59, 62.

36. In a sense, Croce recalls Hegel's master-slave dichotomy: agonistically, the master has gained a position of dominance over the slave through struggle; thus the master has the ability to exercise freedom but, possessing freedom (and concomitantly, leisure), gradually loses the ability to strive for freedom, while the slave has the ability to see its value because he is continually striving. Eventually, the slave rises up against the master but then himself falls into the danger of lassitude.

37. For recent literature, see V. Giustiniani, "Homo, Humanus, and the Meanings of 'Humanism,'" *Journal of the History of Ideas* 46 (1985): 167–95; A. Rabil, ed., *Renaissance Humanism: Foundations, Forms, and Legacy*, 3 vols. (Philadelphia: University of Pennsylvania Press, 1988); R. G. Witt, "The Humanist Movement," in *Handbook of European History, 1400–1600*, ed. T. A. Brady Jr., H. A. Oberman, and J. D. Tracy, 2 vols. (1995; reprint, Grand Rapids: Eerdmans, 1996), 2:93–125; R. Black, "Humanism," in *The New Cambridge Medieval History*, ed. C. Allmand (Cambridge: Cambridge University Press, 1998), 243–77 and 906–15; P. Richard Blum, "Was ist Renaissance-Humanismus? Zur Konstruktion eines kulturellen Modells," in *Philologie und Erkentnis: Beiträge zu Begriff und Problem frühneuzeitlicher "Philologie,"* ed. R. Häfner (Tübingen: Max Niemeyer Verlag, 2001), 227–46; F.-R. Hausmann, "Humanismus und Renaissance in Italien und Frankreich," in *Der neue Mensch: Perspektiven der Renaissance*, ed. M. Schwarze (Regensburg, Germany: Friedrich Pustet, 2000), 7–35; E. Kessler, "Humanist Thought: A Response to Scholastic Philosophy," *Res publica litterarum* 2 (1979): 149–66; D. Biow, *Doctors, Ambassadors, Secretaries: Humanism and Professions in Renaissance Italy* (Chicago: University of Chicago Press, 2002), 1–26; and R. Fubini, *Humanism and Secularization from Petrarch to Valla*, trans. Martha King (Durham, N.C.: Duke University Press, 2003). For a Europe-wide survey, see C. G. Nauert Jr., *Humanism and the Culture of Renaissance Europe* (Cambridge: Cambridge University Press, 1995).

38. W. K. Ferguson, *The Renaissance in Historical Thought: Five Centuries of Interpretation* (New York: Houghton Mifflin, 1948).

39. For some representative publications, see Garin, *Cronache di filosofia italiana;* idem, *La cultura filosofica del Rinascimento italiano: Ricerche e documenti* (Firenze: Sansoni, 1992); idem, *La cultura italiana tra '800 e '900* (Rome: Laterza, 1976); idem, *Giovanni Pico della Mirandola, vita e dottrina* (Florence: Le Monnier, 1937); idem, *L'illuminismo inglese, i moralisti* (Milan: Bocca, 1942); idem, *Scienza e vita civile nel rinascimento italiano* (Bari: Laterza, 1993); idem, *L'umanesimo italiano: Filosofia e vita civile nel Rinascimento* (orig. Italian ed., 1965; reprint, Bari: Laterza, 1994); the work first appeared in German as *Der italienische Humanismus* (Bern: Francke, 1947). There is an English translation published as *Italian Humanism: Philosophy and Civic Life in the Renaissance,* trans. Peter Munz (Oxford: Blackwell, 1965).

40. I draw here on the autobiographical account in E. Garin, *La filosofia come sapere storico* (Rome: Laterza, 1990), 119–58. For background to Florentine life in this period, see Adamson, *Avant-Garde Florence.*

41. Garin, *La filosofia come sapere storico,* 120–21.

42. Ibid., 128.

43. Garin, *L'illuminismo inglese.*

44. Garin, *La filosofia come sapere storico,* 130.

45. Garin, *Giovanni Pico.*

46. Garin, *La filosofia come sapere storico,* 136.

47. Ibid., 144.

48. P. della Mirandola, *De hominis dignitate, Heptaplus, De ente e uno, e scritti vari,* ed. E. Garin (Florence: Vallecchi, 1942); idem, *Disputationes adversus astrologiam divinatricem,* 2 vols. (Florence: Vallecchi, 1946–52); E. Garin, ed., *Prosatori latini del Quattrocento* (Milan: Ricciardi, 1952).

49. Garin, *La filosofia come sapere storico.*

50. M. Heidegger, *Brief über den Humanismus* (Bern: A. Francke, 1947); now in Martin Heidegger, *Gesamtausgabe,* vol. 9, ed. F.-W. von Hermann (Frankfurt am Main: Vittorio Klostermann, 1976), 313–64. See also the study of E. Grassi, *Heidegger and the Question of Renaissance Humanism: Four Studies,* Medieval and Renaissance Texts and Studies, 24 (Binghamton, N.Y., 1983); and for background on Grassi, see T. W. Crusius, foreword to E. Grassi, *Rhetoric as Philosophy: The Humanist Tradition,* trans. J. M. Krois and A. Azodi (Carbondale: Southern Illinois University Press, 2000), xi–xviii.

51. See Safranski, *Martin Heidegger;* H. Küschbert-Tölle, *Martin Heidegger: Der letzte Metaphysiker?* (Königstein, Germany: Forum Academicum, 1979); W. Marx, *Is There a Measure on Earth? Foundations for a Nonmetaphysical Ethics,* trans. T. J. Nenon and R. Lilly (Chicago: University of Chicago Press, 1997); G. Steiner, *Martin Heidegger* (Chicago: University of Chicago Press, 1991).

52. Heidegger, *Brief,* 320.

53. I cite from Garin, *L'umanesimo italiano.*

54. Ibid., 21.

55. Ibid., 22.

56. Ibid.

57. Ibid., 16.

58. Cf. ibid., 59–60, where he places Francesco Filelfo—whose linguistic and classicist credentials in Latin and Greek were superb—outside of the humanist tradition, because he "emptied the *studia humanitatis* of all life." Garin feels similarly about Ermolao Barbaro (84–87), who did not really care to examine deeply the real problems of the human spirit with which he came into contact and cared, in Garin's opinion, only about literary elegance.

59. His major works: H. Baron, *The Crisis of the Early Italian Renaissance: Civic Humanism and Republican Liberty in an Age of Classicism and Tyranny,* 2 vols. (Princeton, N.J.: Princeton University Press, 1955; reissued as a one-volume ed., 1966); idem, *Humanistic and Political Literature in Florence and Venice at the Beginning of the Quattrocento: Studies in Criticism and Chronology* (Cambridge, Mass.: Harvard University Press, 1955); idem, *From Petrarch to Leonardo Bruni: Studies in Humanistic and Political Literature* (Chicago: University of Chicago Press, 1968); idem, *Petrarch's Secretum: Its Making and Its Meaning* (Cambridge, Mass.: Medieval Academy of America, 1985); idem, *In Search of Florentine Civic Humanism: Essays on the Transition from Medieval to Modern Thought,* 2 vols. (Princeton, N.J.: Princeton University Press, 1988). For Baron's influence, see A. Rabil, "The Significance of 'Civic Humanism' in the Interpretation of the Italian Renaissance," in Rabil, *Renaissance Humanism,* 1:141–74; a number of the chapters in Q. Skinner, *Visions of Politics,* 3 vols. (Cambridge: Cambridge University Press, 2002), vol. 2; R. Fubini, "Renaissance Historian: The Career of Hans Baron," *Journal of Modern History* 64 (1992): 541–74; J. Hankins, "The 'Baron Thesis' after Forty Years: Some Recent Studies on Leonardo Bruni," *Journal of the History of Ideas* 56 (1995): 309–38; many of the studies in J. Hankins, ed., *Renaissance Civic Humanism: Reappraisals and Reflections* (Cambridge: Cambridge University Press, 2000); the studies of R. G. Witt, J. M. Najemy, C. Kallendorf, and W. Gundersheimer in the *American Historical Review* 101 (1996): 107–44; and M. Jurdjevic, "Civic Humanism and the Rise of the Medici," *Renaissance Quarterly* 52 (1999): 994–1020.

60. Baron did so in 1925, in *Historische Zeitschrift,* in a review of F. Engel-Jànosi, *Soziale Probleme der Renaissance;* cf. Fubini, "Renaissance Historian," 560; Hankins, introduction to his *Renaissance Civic Humanism,* 1.

61. H. Baron, "Moot Problems of Renaissance Interpretation: An Answer to Wallace K. Ferguson," *Journal of the History of Ideas* 19 (1958): 26–34.

62. On Salutati, see R. G. Witt, *Hercules at the Crossroads: The Life, Works, and Thought of Coluccio Salutati* (Durham, N.C.: Duke University Press, 1983); idem, *Coluccio Salutati and His Public Letters* (Geneva: Librairie Droz, 1976).

63. C. Salutati, *Tractatus de tyranno,* ed. F. Ercole (Berlin: Rothschild, 1914). Salutati's vacillations were the product of a complex life, and his ideas changed with his life circumstances; see Witt, *Hercules at the Crossroads.*

64. Cf. Baron, *The Crisis of the Early Italian Renaissance;* and idem, *In Search of Florentine Civic Humanism,* 1:135.

65. W. J. Connell, "The Republican Idea," in Hankins, *Renaissance Civic Humanism,* 14–29, at 16.

66. For the 1950s and 1960s in the United States, see P. Novick, *That Noble Dream: The "Objectivity Question" and the American Historical Profession* (Cambridge: Cambridge University Press, 1988), 281–411.

67. R. Fubini, "Renaissance Historian: The Career of Hans Baron." See also K. Schiller, "Hans Baron's Humanism," *Storia della storiografia* 34 (1998): 51–99; for refugee and immigrant scholars, see D. Fleming and B. Bailyn, eds., *The Intellectual Migration: Europe and America, 1930–1960* (Cambridge, Mass.: Harvard University Press, 1969).

68. Fubini, "Renaissance Historian."

69. See ibid., 550.

70. Garin, *L'umanesimo italiano*, 11.

71. Ibid.; "certain scholar" is my choice in translating. Garin in Italian uses the word *taluno* (a certain one), which can also have generalizing force, meaning something like "certain people" in general. But the explicit reference to Kristeller in the note leaves no doubt as to whom Garin primarily had in mind when he was preparing the Italian edition.

72. Garin, *La filosofia come sapere storico*, 146–47.

73. Cf. P. O. Kristeller and M. L. King, "Iter Kristellerianum: The European Journey (1905–1939)," *Renaissance Quarterly* 47 (1994): 907–29; Kristeller, "A Life of Learning," ACLS Occasional Paper, 12, now in Kristeller's *Studies in Renaissance Thought and Letters* (Rome: Edizioni di Storia e Letteratura, 1994), 4:567–83; P. O. Kristeller, introduction to his *Renaissance Thought and Its Sources*, ed. M. Mooney (New York: Columbia University Press, 1979); E. P. Mahoney, "Paul Oskar Kristeller and his Contribution to Scholarship," in *Philosophy and Humanism: Renaissance Essays in Honor of Paul Oskar Kristeller*, ed. E. P. Mahoney (New York: Columbia University Press, 1976), 1–18; W. Ludwig, "Zum Gedenken an Paul Oskar Kristeller," *Neulateinisches Jahrbuch* 2 (2000): 13–23.

74. Kristeller and King, "Iter Kristellerianum."

75. Cf. Kristeller, *Renaissance Thought and Its Sources*, 105: "Complete objectivity may be impossible to achieve, but it should remain the permanent aim and standard of the historian as well as of the philosopher and scientist."

76. Kristeller, *Studies*, 4:572.

77. J. Hankins, "Two Twentieth Century Interpreters of Renaissance Humanism: Eugenio Garin and Paul Oskar Kristeller," *Comparative Criticism* 23 (2001).

78. For the "revolt of the medievalists," see Ferguson, *Renaissance*.

79. A. Campana, "The Origin of the Word 'Humanist,'" *Journal of the Warburg and Courtauld Insititutes* 9 (1946): 60–73; P. O. Kristeller, "Humanism and Scholasticism in Renaissance Italy," *Byzantion* 17 (1944–45): 346–74, now in Kristeller, *Studies*, 1:553–83; see there, 574, for discussion of the term; see also P. F. Grendler, "Five Italian Occurrences of Umanista, 1540–1574," *Renaissance Quarterly* 20 (1967): 317–24.

80. P. O. Kristeller, "The Impact of Early Humanism on Thought and Learning," in *Developments in the Early Renaissance*, ed. B. S. Levy (Albany: State University of New York Press, 1972), 120–57, at 125–26.

81. Cf. Kristeller, *Renaissance Thought and Its Sources*, 18: "I shall not discuss the Renaissance in terms of a few outstanding and well-known thinkers and writers alone, but I shall rather try to draw a cultural map of the period, taking into account the vast amount of information hidden away in the bibliographies of early editions, in the collections and catalogues of manuscript books, and in the records of schools, universities, and other institutions."

82. W. H. Sewell Jr., "Geertz, Cultural Systems, and History: From Synchrony to

Transformation," in *The Fate of "Culture": Geertz and Beyond*, ed. S. Ortner (Berkeley: University of California Press, 1999), 335–55, at 40.

83. B. J. Kohl, "The Changing Concept of the *Studia Humanitatis* in the Early Renaissance," *Renaissance Studies* 6 (1992): 185–209.

84. P. F. Grendler, *Schooling in Renaissance Italy: Literacy and Learning, 1300–1500* (Baltimore: Johns Hopkins University Press, 1989).

85. The best introduction to Kristeller's early years is Kristeller and King, "Iter Kristellerianum."

86. He was in Italy at the time of Hitler's January 1933 racial decrees, made a brief trip back to Germany, then moved to Italy in 1934. See ibid., 917.

87. For basic orientations to Norden and Wilamowitz-Moellendorff, see *An Introductory Bibliography to the History of Classical Scholarship Chiefly in the XIXth and XXth Centuries*, ed. W. M. Calder III and D. J. Kramer (Hildesheim: Olms, 1992), s.v.; and B. P. P. Kytzler, "Eduard Norden," and R. L. Fowler, "Ulrich von Wilamowitz-Moellendorff," both in *Classical Scholarship: A Biographical Encyclopedia*, ed. W. W. Briggs and W. M. Calder III (New York: Garland, 1990), 341–45 and 489–522, respectively; for Hoffman, see P. Wilpert, "Leben und Schriften Ernst Hoffmans," in E. Hoffman, *Platonismus und Christliche Philosophie* (Zürich: Artemis-Verlag), 479–97.

88. F. Paulsen, with R. Lehmann, *Geschichte des gelehrten Unterrichts auf den deutschen Schulen und Universitäten vom Ausgang des Mittelalters bis zur Gegenwart*, 3d ed., 2 vols. (Berlin: de Gruyter, 1921), 2:210–47.

89. Von Humboldt, "Über die innere und äußere Organisation," in *Die Idee der deutschen Universität*, 377.

90. Ibid., 377–78.

91. F. Schleiermacher, "Gelegentliche Gedanken über Universitäten in Deutschem Sinn," in *Die Idee der Deutschen Universität*, 219–308, at 224–25.

92. Cf. F. K. Ringer, *The Decline of the German Mandarins: The German Academic Community, 1890–1933* (Cambridge, Mass.: Harvard University Press, 1969).

93. The term was coined in 1890 by the great historian of Roman law Theodor Mommsen but existed in practice *ante litteram;* see T. Mommsen, in *Sitzungsberichte der Königlich Preußischen Akademie der Wissenschaften zu Berlin* (Berlin, 1890), 792, cited in Vom Bruch, "A Slow Farewell to Humboldt?" 14.

94. Indeed, large-scale projects were prized in European culture for at least a century before their university-based institutionalization; one has only to recall the *Encyclopédie*. On the founding of the *MGH* and the surrounding environment, see P. Geary, *The Myth of Nations: The Medieval Origins of Europe* (Princeton, N.J.: Princeton University Press, 2002), 21–33. Though the *MGH* series owed its founding to the *Gesellschaft für ältere deutsche Geschichtskunde*, which was itself founded in 1819, the *MGH* series received new momentum in the 1870s.

95. An eloquent way into this world is provided in F. Stern, *Einstein's German World* (Princeton, N.J.: Princeton University Press, 1999), 13–164.

96. Dilthey: see J. Owensby, *Dilthey and the Narrative of History* (Ithaca, N.Y.: Cornell University Press, 1994); R. A. Makkreel, *Dilthey: Philosopher of the Human Studies* (Princeton, N.J.: Princeton University Press, 1992); T. Plantinga, *Historical Understanding in the*

Thought of Wilhelm Dilthey (Toronto: University of Toronto Press, 1980); H. A. Hodges, *The Philosophy of Wilhelm Dilthey* (Westport, Conn.: Greenwood, 1976).

97. Kristeller and King, "Iter Kristellerianum."

98. This search for manuscripts had actually begun a few years before his permanent departure from Germany, during research trips to Italy in the early 1930s; cf. ibid., 917.

99. P. O. Kristeller, *Iter Italicum: A Finding List of Uncatalogued or Incompletely Catalogued Humanistic Manuscripts of the Renaissance in Italian and Other Libraries*, 6 vols. (Leiden: Brill, 1963–95), 1:xiii; for his love and appreciation of manuscripts, see also the pieces collected in Kristeller, *Studies*, 4:381–480.

100. Kristeller, *Iter Italicum;* idem, *Latin Manuscript Books before 1600: A List of the Printed Catalogues and Unpublished Inventories of Extant Collections*, 4th rev. ed. by Sigrid Krämer (Munich: Monumenta Germaniae Historica, 1993).

101. For two cases of Kristeller's examinations of the effect of past prejudice on modern scholarship, see P. O. Kristeller, "The Origin and Development of the Language of Italian Prose," in his *Studies*, 1:473–93; and idem, "The Myth of Renaissance Atheism and the French Tradition of Free Thought," *Journal of the History of Philosophy* 6 (1968): 233–43.

102. Cf. Garin's view of Francesco Filelfo and Ermolao Barbaro, cited above.

103. For one iteration of this idea, see the comments of Michael Mooney in Kristeller, *Renaissance Thought and Its Sources*, ix.

104. For the *Iter* and *Latin Manuscript Books*, see above; for the *Catalogus*, see *Catalogus translationum et commentariorum: Mediaeval and Renaissance Latin Translations and Commentaries*, 7 vols. to date (Washington, D.C.: Catholic University of America Press, 1960-), vols. 1–3, editor-in-chief P. O. Kristeller; vols. 4–5, editor-in-chief F. Edward Cranz; vol. 7, editor-in-chief Virginia Brown. The goal of the latter project is to provide annotated lists and guides to Latin translations of and commentaries to important classical works throughout the Middle Ages and the Renaissance.

105. P. O. Kristeller, *Der Begriff der Seele in der Ethik des Plotin*, Heidelberger Abhandlungen zur Philosophie und ihrer Geschichte, 19 (Tübingen: J. C. B. Mohr, 1929), 3: Der philosophische Gehalt einer Lehre oder eines Weltbildes beruht ja auf seinem Verhältnis zu der Wirklichkeit, die zu allen Zeiten besteht und auch für uns, trotz des Abstandes an Zeit und geistiger Verfassung, in gleicher Weise faßbar ist.

106. Ibid., 4: Vor allem scheint es uns an einem festen Maßstab der Wirklichkeit zu fehlen, mit dem wir sein Bild der Wirklichkeit vergleichen könnten.

107. Ibid, 5: ihre [i.e., his account's] Wahrheit liegt in der überzeugenden Deutung des Textmaterials, so wie die Wahrheit einer naturwissenschaftlichen Hypothese in der Erklärung der Phänomene besteht. Kristeller's language of "phenomena" recalls the Aristotelian language of "saving the phenomena" in scientific explanation, that is, offering an explanation that squares with the appearances of nature as we perceive them. Empiricism was a lifelong love. In volumes 5 and 6 of the *Iter Italicum*, Kristeller chose as an epigraph the following saying attributed to Epicurus: "An opinion is valid when it is confirmed and not refuted by the evidence of a sense perception," which I believe may have been a paraphrase, though the general point about the sense-based epistemology of Epicurus is of course valid, as can be seen especially in Epicurus's "Letter to Herodotus," reported in Diogenes Laertius, *Vitae philosophorum*, 10. In the *Iter* volumes, Kristeller does

not specifically attribute the saying, but light can be shed on the question by examining his *Greek Philosophers of the Hellenistic Age,* trans. G. Woods (New York: Columbia University Press, 1993), which originally appeared in Italian as *Filosofi greci dell'età ellenistica* (Pisa: Scuola Normale, 1991). In the English version, Kristeller writes, "According to Epicurus, the truth and validity of an opinion is never intrinsic but is based entirely on perceptions and their objects. An opinion is true when it is confirmed and not refuted by perception, and is false when it is refuted or not confirmed by perception" (7). In note 3 on that page, he cites a number of sources, though none of them yield the exact phrase of the epigraph of *Iter* 4 and 5; the closest I can find of Kristeller's sources there is *Epicurea,* ed. H. Usener (Leipzig: Teubner, 1887), fr. 247, p. 181, lines 12–15, which equals Sextus Empiricus, *Adversus mathematicos,* 7.211, also known as *Adversus dogmaticos,* 1.211: οὐκοῦν τῶν δοξῶν κατὰ τὸν Ἐπίκουρον αἱ μὲν ἀληθεῖς εἰσιν αἱ δὲ ψευδεῖς, ἀληθεῖς μὲν αἵ τε ἐπιμαρτυρούμεναι καὶ οὐκ ἀντιμαρτυρούμεναι πρὸς τῆς ἐναργείας, ψευδεῖς δὲ αἵ τε ἀντιμαρτυρούμεναι καὶ οὐκ ἐπιμαρτυρούμεναι πρὸς τῆς ἐναργείας. Literally, "Therefore, of opinions, according to Epicurus, there are some that are true and some that are false. On the one hand, the true ones are positively and not negatively witnessed in the presence of the evidence [or clear vision]; the false ones, on the other hand, are negatively and not positively witnessed in the presence of the evidence [or clear vision]."

108. P. O. Kristeller, "The Renaissance in the History of Philosophical Thought," in *The Renaissance: Essays in Interpretation,* by A. Chastel et al. (London: Methuen, 1982), 128. The volume first appeared in Italian and was published by Laterza in 1979.

109. Ibid., 129–30.

110. Ibid.

111. Kristeller, *Renaissance Thought and Its Sources,* 32–49. This notion of seemingly antagonistic disciplines coexisting side by side may be something Kristeller gleaned from his early reading of the masterful study of H. von Arnim (*Leben und Werke des Dio von Prusa, mit einer Einleitung: Sophistik, Rhetorik, Philosophie in ihrem Kampf um die Jugendbildung* [Berlin, 1898]), in which von Arnim had surveyed the coexistence and occasional rivalry of philosophy and rhetoric from the fifth century B.C. to the second century A.D.; see J. Monfasani, "Toward the Genesis of the Kristeller Thesis of Renaissance Humanism: Four Bibliographical Notes," *Renaissance Quarterly* 53 (2000): 1156–73, at 1157–59.

112. For the scope of Renaissance Aristotelianism, see C. H. Lohr, *Latin Aristotle Commentaries,* 3 vols. (Florence: Olschki, 1990–99), vol. 2; C. B. Schmitt, *Aristotle and the Renaissance* (Cambridge, Mass.: Harvard University Press, 1983); D. Iorio, *The Aristotelians of Renaissance Italy: A Philosophical Exposition* (Lewiston, Maine: Mellen, 1991); D. Lines, *Aristotle's Ethics in the Italian Renaissance* (Leiden: Brill, 2002); E. P. Mahoney, *Two Aristotelians of the Italian Renaissance: Nicoletto Vernia and Agostino Nifo* (Aldershot, Eng.: Ashgate, 2000).

113. Kristeller, *Renaissance Thought and Its Sources,* 172. Ficino only very briefly held a university post, and it is not known exactly what he taught. See J. Davies, "Marsilio Ficino: Lecturer at the Studio fiorentino," *Renaissance Quarterly* 45 (1992): 785–90; J. Hankins, "Lorenzo de' Medici as a Patron of Philosophy," *Rinascimento,* 2d ser., 34 (1994): 15–53.

114. Kristeller says little about Marx; about Nietzsche he says that he was a philosopher "whom I never appreciated"; cf. Kristeller, "A Life of Learning," 4:572; he takes

potshots at analytic philosophy; and so far as I know, he never mentioned R. Rorty's *Philosophy and the Mirror of Nature* (Princeton, N.J.: Princeton University Press, 1979), the most sensible importation and rethinking of twentieth-century continental philosophical trends into the analytic tradition.

115. Cf. H. H. Gray, "Renaissance Humanism: The Pursuit of Eloquence," *Journal of the History of Ideas* 24 (1963): 497–514.

116. P. O. Kristeller, "The Study of the History of Philosophy and Its Problems," in *Filosofia e cultura: Per Eugenio Garin,* ed. M. Ciliberto and C. Vasoli, 2 vols. (Rome: Riuniti, 1991), 1:351–70, at 362–63.

117. Kristeller's position echoes Hegel, who wrote regarding the Renaissance revival of ancient thought, even ancient philosophy, "Such endeavors are, however, connected rather with the history of literature and culture, and with the advancement of the same; we do not find originality in this philosophic work, nor can we recognize therein any forward step. We have still writings of that period, by which we find that each school of the Greeks found its adherents, . . . though they were of a very different stamp from those of olden times. For true instruction in philosophy we must, however, go to the original sources, the ancients." See G. F. W. Hegel, *Lectures on the History of Philosophy: Medieval and Modern Philosophy,* trans. E. S. Haldane and F. H. Simson, vol. 3 (1840; reprint, Lincoln: University of Nebraska Press, 1995), 110–11.

118. See Rorty, *Philosophy and the Mirror of Nature,* esp. 131–38, for the "professionalization" of philosophy after Kant.

119. See A. Nehamas, *The Art of Living: Socratic Reflections from Plato to Foucault,* Sather Classical Lectures, 61 (Berkeley: University of California Press, 1998), 1–15; and P. Hadot, *What Is Ancient Philosophy?* trans. M. Chase (Cambridge, Mass: Harvard University Press, 2002).

120. Kristeller, *Renaissance Thought and Its Sources,* 36–37; again, cf. Hegel, *Lectures,* 113–14.

121. Kristeller, *Renaissance Thought and Its Sources,* 3.

122. Ibid., 113–15.

123. R. Wolin, *Heidegger's Children: Hannah Arendt, Karl Löwith, Hans Jonas, and Herbert Marcuse* (Princeton, N.J.: Princeton University Press, 2001).

124. An important initiative is under way, however: The I Tatti Renaissance Library, published by Harvard University Press and directed by James Hankins, is a new, important series that is publishing works of Renaissance Latin literature with *en face* English translations, much like the Loeb Classical Library. See the appendix for other efforts.

125. There is a marked contrast between this Anglo-American development and scholarship on the Italian Renaissance by Europeans, especially Italians, who since Garin have always taken care to integrate the manuscript heritage into their work and who often, as a first scholarly project, do an edition of a text.

126. Cf. W. Bouwsma, "The Two Faces of Humanism: Stoicism and Augustinianism in Renaissance Thought," in *Itinerarium Italicum: The Profile of the Italian Renaissance in the Mirror of Its European Transformations,* ed. H. A. Oberman and T. A. Brady, Studies in Medieval and Reformation Thought, 14, (Leiden: Brill, 1975), 3–60, at 3; W. Bouwsma, "Review Article: Renaissance Humanism: Foundations, Forms, and Legacy," *Church History* 59 (1990): 65–70; R. Starn, "Who's Afraid of the Renaissance?" in *The Past and Future*

of Medieval Studies, ed. J. Van Engen (Notre Dame, Ind.: University of Notre Dame Press, 1994), 129–47; C. Dempsey, *Inventing the Renaissance Putto* (Chapel Hill: University of North Carolina Press, 2001), 107–11.

127. T. Kuhn, *The Structure of Scientific Revolutions,* 3d ed. (Chicago: University of Chicago Press, 1996).

128. H. Holborn, "Der deutsche Idealismus in sozialgeschichtlicher Beleuchtung," *Historische Zeitschrift* 174 (1952): 359–84; G. Mosse, *The Crisis of German Ideology* (New York, 1964).

129. On this aspect in Kristeller, see Fubini, "Renaissance Historian," 573–74.

130. Garin, *La filosofia come sapere storico,* 139–40.

131. Ibid., 141–44; and cf. Minio-Paluello, *Education in Fascist Italy,* 162–66.

132. See the study of F. Cambi, *Tra scienza e storia: Percorsi del neostoricismo italiano: Eugenio Garin, Paolo Rossi, Sergio Moravia* (Milan: Edizioni Unicopli, 1992), 22–26 et passim.

133. Kristeller, in neo-Boethian fashion, in *Renaissance Thought and Its Sources,* 133.

134. Novick, *That Noble Dream,* 576.

T H R E E ✧ *A Microhistory of Intellectuals*

E P I G R A P H : D. LaCapra, *Rethinking Intellectual History: Texts, Contexts, Language* (Ithaca, N.Y.: Cornell University Press, 1983), 18. R. Rorty, *Philosophy and the Mirror of Nature* (Princeton, N.J.: Princeton University Press, 1979), 388–89.

1. R. Scruton, *A Short History of Modern Philosophy,* 2d ed. (London: Routledge, 1995), 238. See G. Frege, *Die Grundlagen der Arithmetik: Eine logisch-mathematische Untersuchung über den Begriff der Zahl* (Breslau, 1884), trans. J. L. Austin as *The Foundations of Arithmetic* (Oxford: Oxford University Press, 1950); M. Dummett, *Frege: Philosophy of Language,* 2d ed. (Cambridge, Mass.: Harvard University Press, 1981), esp. 665–84 for Frege's importance.

2. Scruton, *A Short History of Modern Philosophy,* 239.

3. L. Wittgenstein, *Tractatus Logico-Philosophicus,* German text with trans. by D. F. Pears and B. F. McGuiness (London: Routledge, 1961), sec. 7, p. 74.

4. Cf. D. Bloor, *Wittgenstein: A Social Theory of Knowledge* (New York: Columbia University Press, 1983).

5. See R. Carnap, "The Elimination of Metaphysics through the Logical Analysis of Language," in *Logical Positivism,* ed. A. J. Ayer (Chicago: University of Chicago Press, 1959).

6. See Heidegger's *Sein und Zeit,* trans. as *Being and Time* by J. Macquarrie and E. S. Robinson (New York, 1962); and for a valuable overview, in addition to the works cited in chapter 2, see A. Megill, *Prophets of Extremity: Nietzsche, Heidegger, Foucault, Derrida* (Berkeley: University of California Press, 1985), 105–80.

7. Cf. C. Lévi-Strauss, *Tristes Tropiques* (Paris: Librairie Plon, 1955), 43.

8. For recent studies, see C. Howells, ed., *The Cambridge Companion to Sartre* (Cambridge: Cambridge University Press, 1992); and D. Cooper, *Existentialism* (Oxford: Oxford University Press, 1990).

9. See J. Derrida, *Of Grammatology*, trans. G. Spivak (Baltimore: Johns Hopkins University Press, 1997; orig. French ed., 1967), 107–18.

10. Derrida's analysis of this episode in Lévi-Strauss is well treated in C. Norris, *Derrida* (Cambridge, Mass: Harvard University Press, 1987), 133–36.

11. M. Foucault, *The Order of Things: An Archaeology of the Human Sciences* (New York: Vintage, 1994; orig. French ed., 1966).

12. B. Ramberg, "Post-Ontological Philosophy of Mind: Rorty versus Davidsohn," in *Rorty and His Critics*, ed. R. B. Brandom (Oxford: Blackwell, 2000), 351–70, at 351.

13. Rorty, *Philosophy and the Mirror of Nature*, 6.

14. Ibid.

15. R. Popkin, *The History of Scepticism from Erasmus to Spinoza* (Berkeley: University of California Press, 1979); W. Bouwsma, *The Waning of the Renaissance, 1550–1640* (New Haven, Conn.: Yale University Press, 2000).

16. See R. Descartes, *Discourse on Method and the Meditations*, trans. F. E. Sutcliffe (Middlesex: Penguin, 1968).

17. I. Kant, *Critique of Pure Reason*, unified ed., trans. W. Pluhar (Indianapolis: Hackett, 1996); G. Di Giovanni, "The First Twenty Years of Critique: The Spinoza Connection," in *The Cambridge Companion to Kant*, ed. P. Guyer (Cambridge: Cambridge University Press, 1992), 417–48.

18. Johann Gottlieb Fichte (1762–1814) was important as one who theorized how this transformation from theory to practice might take place; see A. J. La Vopa, *Fichte: The Self and the Calling of Philosophy, 1762–1799* (Cambridge: Cambridge University Press, 2001), 183–230; and see J. G. Fichte, "Deduzierter Plan einer in Berlin zu errichtenden höheren Lehranstalt," in *Die Idee der Deutschen Universität*, ed. E. Anrich (Darmstadt: Hermann Gentner, 1956), 125–217.

19. J. Habermas, "Richard Rorty's Pragmatic Turn," in Brandom, *Rorty and His Critics*, 31–55, at 35.

20. E. Muir, "The Italian Renaissance in America," *American Historical Review* 100 (1995): 1095–118, at 1117.

21. There are good complementary short surveys with bibliographies on the *Annales* school in the relevant sections of G. G Iggers, *Historiography in the Twentieth Century: From Scientific Objectivity to the Postmodern Challenge* (Middletown, Conn.: Wesleyan University Press, 1997); and M. Bentley, *Modern Historiography: An Introduction* (London: Routledge, 1999). Invaluable on the *Annales* is P. Burke, *The French Historical Revolution: The* Annales *School, 1929–89* (Cambridge: Polity Press, 1990).

22. Bloch's study in Germany was important in his intellectual formation, for it is there that he may first have encountered the work of Karl Lamprecht, an enduring influence on the conception of a "total history." Iggers, *Historiography in the Twentieth Century*, 31–34 and 52.

23. For the use of the term *histoire totale*, see Burke, *The French Historical Revolution*, 114, who points out that in the founding generation it was their fellow-traveler, the anthropologist Marcel Mauss, who used the term *totale* to describe this all-encompassing version of history; later Braudel would use it commonly.

24. Ibid., 16–7; B. Müller, introduction to *Correspondance, Tome Premier, 1928–1933,*

by M. Bloch and L. Febvre, ed. B. Müller (Paris: Éditions Fayard, 1994), v–lv, at xix–xxi; J. E. Craig, *Scholarship and Nation Building: The Universities of Strasbourg and Alsatian Society, 1870–1939* (Chicago: University of Chicago Press, 1984).

25. On y a un sentiment de solidarité, d'union, d'échange qu'on ne saurait avoir au même degré nulle part. In a letter from Febvre to H. Berr, cited in Müller, introduction, xx.

26. Ce n'est pas une chimère ici à Strasbourg, nous collaborons ainsi, toutes les semaines, professeurs de toutes les disciplines littéraires, sans nous demander notre titre de spécialité. Cited in ibid.

27. Burke, *The French Historical Revolution*, 28. L. Febvre, *Le problème de l'incroyance au 16e siècle: La religion de Rabelais* (Paris, 1942).

28. Burke, *The French Historical Revolution*, 43–53; J. Revel, introduction to *Histories: French Constructions of the Past*, ed. J. Revel and L. Hunt (New York: New Press, 1995), 1–63.

29. Burke, *The French Historical Revolution*, 45; F. Braudel, *Civilization and Capitalism, 15th–18th Century*, 3 vols., trans. S. Reynolds, vol. 2, *The Wheels of Commerce* (Berkeley: University of California Press, 1992), 21–23; idem, *Afterthoughts on Material Civilization and Capitalism*, trans. P. M. Ranum (Baltimore: Johns Hopkins Univeristy Press, 1977), 110–15.

30. Braudel, *Afterthoughts*.

31. For example, see J. Delumeau, *Le péché et la peur: La culpabilisation en Occident XIIIe–XVIIIe siècles* (Paris: Fayard, 1983); J. LeGoff, *Intellectuals in the Middle Ages*, trans. T. L. Fagan (Oxford: Blackwell, 1993); R. Chartier, *The Cultural Uses of Print in Early Modern France*, trans. L. G. Cochrane (Princeton, N.J.: Princeton University Press, 1987). Paul F. Grendler makes a similar point regarding the breadth of the *Annales* movement in "The Italian Renaissance in the Past Seventy Years: Humanism, Social History, and Early Modern in Anglo-American and Italian Scholarship," in *The Italian Renaissance in the Twentieth Century: Acts of an International Conference, Florence, Villa I Tatti, June 9–11, 1999*, ed. A. J. Grieco, M. Rocke, and F. G. Superbi (Florence: Olschki, 2002), 3–23, at 7–8.

32. An idea of the debates in France for this last period can be gleaned from the readings in Revel and Hunt, *Histories*, 427–649; and see Burke, *The French Historical Revolution*, 65–93.

33. Iggers, *Historiography in the Twentieth Century*, 107. Recent surveys of microhistory with bibliographies include K. Appuhn, "Microhistory," in *Encyclopedia of European Social History from 1350–2000*, ed. P. Stearns, 6 vols. (New York: Scribner, 2001); E. Muir, "Introduction: Observing Trifles," in *Microhistory and the Lost Peoples of Europe*, ed. E. Muir and G. Ruggiero, trans. E. Branch (Baltimore: Johns Hopkins University Press, 1991), vii–xxviii; and idem, "The Italian Renaissance in America."

34. C. Ginzburg and C. Poni, "The Name and the Game: Unequal Exchange and the Historiographic Marketplace," in Muir and Ruggiero, *Microhistory and the Lost Peoples of Europe*, 1–10.

35. Iggers, *Historiography in the Twentieth Century*, 103, citing E. P. Thompson, *The Making of the English Working Class* (New York: Pantheon, 1966), 12.

36. Ginzburg and Poni, "The Name and the Game."

37. C. Ginzburg, *The Cheese and the Worms: The Cosmos of a Sixteenth-Century Miller,*

trans. A. Tedeschi and J. Tedeschi (Baltimore: Johns Hopkins University Press, 1980; reprint, New York: Penguin, 1982).

38. Ibid., xii.

39. For a bibliography on microhistory including works outside Italy, see Muir, "Observing Trifles," xxii–xxiii n. 7. With respect to the fifteenth century in Italy, one should be singled out: G. Brucker's *Giovanni and Lusanna: Love and Marriage in Renaissance Florence* (Berkeley: University of California Press, 1986).

40. R. Collins, *A Sociology of Philosophies: A Global Theory of Intellectual Change* (Cambridge, Mass.: Harvard University Press, 1998).

41. For two recent studies that make their concerns with generations an explicit part of their analysis, see M. L. King, *Venetian Humanism in an Age of Patrician Dominance* (Princeton, N.J.: Princeton University Press, 1986); and R. G. Witt, *In the Footsteps of the Ancients: The Origins of Humanism from Lovato to Bruni* (Leiden: Brill, 2000).

42. I have found helpful here R. Chartier, *The Order of Books: Readers, Authors, and Libraries in Europe between the Fourteenth and Eighteenth Centuries* (Stanford, Calif.: Stanford University Press, 1994); C. Kallendorf, *Virgil and the Myth of Venice: Books and Readers in the Italian Renaissance* (Oxford: Oxford University Press, 1999), 1–30; and J. Hankins, *Plato in the Italian Renaissance,* 2 vols. (Leiden: Brill, 1990), introduction.

43. T. Kuhn, *The Structure of Scientific Revolutions,* 3d ed. (Chicago: University of Chicago Press, 1996); the first edition appeared in 1962. Kuhn presented some modifications to his views in idem, *The Essential Tension: Selected Studies in Scientific Tradition and Change* (Chicago: University of Chicago Press, 1977).

44. G. Bachelard, *The New Scientific Spirit,* trans. A. Goldhammer (Boston: Beacon, 1984); cf. M. Tiles, *Bachelard, Science, and Objectivity* (Cambridge, 1984). I have found very useful and rely heavily on D. Swarz, *Culture and Power: The Sociology of Pierre Bourdieu* (Chicago: University of Chicago Press, 1997).

45. Swarz, *Culture and Power,* 32.

46. The notion of a "coupre epistemologique," present in Bachelard, was popularized and used systematically by Louis Althusser and thus gained greater currency in French thought than it might have; cf. L. Althusser, *For Marx* (New York: Vintage, 1970), 257; Swarz, *Culture and Power,* 32.

47. A good introduction to Bourdieu's thought is in his *Outline;* and in general in Swarz, *Culture and Power.*

48. P. Bourdieu, *The Logic of Practice* (Stanford, Calif.: Stanford University Press, 1990), 53; Swarz, *Culture and Power,* 100.

49. Bourdieu, *Outline,* 79.

50. E. Panofsky, *Architecture gothique et pensée scolastique,* trans. P. Bourdieu (Paris: Editions de Minuit, 1967), postface at 136–67.

51. For *doxa,* see Bourdieu, *Outline,* 164–71.

52. Ibid., 169.

53. Swarz, *Culture and Power,* 108.

54. See, e.g., Aristotle, *Nicomachean Ethics,* 1098b33 et seq. For the medieval use, compare Aquinas, *Summa contra gentiles,* 1.92: "habitus potentiae alicuius perfectivus est."

55. The quotation is from Swarz, *Culture and Power,* 74.

56. Ibid., 117.

57. P. Bourdieu and L. J. D. Wacquant, *An Invitation to Reflexive Sociology* (Chicago: University of Chicago Press, 1992), 96; Swarz, *Culture and Power*, 119.

FOUR ᴦ *Orthodoxy*

1. Aristotle has a verb form, *orthodoxēo, Nicomachean Ethics,* 7.9; Pollux, the late-second-century A.D. lexicographer, has *orthodoxia* in his *Onomasticon,* 4.7, but for the most part the welding together of the roots *orthos* (right, correct) and *doxa* (opinion) is a late ancient phenomenon and tends to be used in didactic contexts, such as in commentators on Aristotle (for example, Simplicius, *Comm. on Aristotle's Categories,* 2A, has the adverbial form, *orthodoxastikōs*) and commentators on Plato (Proclus, *In Platonis Alcib.,* 1.23, has the adjective *orthodoxastikos;* Olympiodorus, *In Phd.,* 113, has *orthodoxia*), or more commonly in late ancient ecclesiastical writers (though the word does not appear in the New Testament). Among the many late ancient Greek authors in which the root *orthodox-* appear are Basil, Eusebius, Gregory of Nazianzen, Gregory of Nyssa, Chrysostom, and Origen; there are a host of others in the patristic environment: see the *Thesaurus Linguae Graecae,* CD-Rom E (2001), distributed by the University of California at Irvine, Classics Department. The word does not appear in the classicizing Byzantine lexicographers Suda (5 vols., ed. A. Adler [Stuttgart: Teubner, 1928–38]) or Hesychius (ed. K. Latte [Copenhagen: Munksgaard, 1966]).

2. For example, Augustine, *De vera religione,* 5.9; Jerome, *Epistolae,* 61 (alias 75); Du Cange, *Glossarium medii aevi latinitatis,* 4:737; more commonly the Latin equivalent, *recta opinio,* is used.

3. J. B. Henderson, *The Construction of Orthodoxy and Heresy* (Albany: State University of New York Press, 1998); W. Bauer, *Orthodoxy and Heresy in Earliest Christianity* (Philadelphia: Fortress, 1971); P. Godman, *The Saint as Censor: Robert Bellarmine between Inquisition and Index,* Studies in Medieval and Reformation Thought, 80 (Leiden: Brill, 2000), 178.

4. Augustine, *De genesi ad literam contra Manichaeos,* 1.1, Patrologia Latina 34.173; Aquinas, *Summa theologiae,* 2a2ae, 11, esp. art. 3; and for evil, 1a, 49, 2, resp. The position went back to Paul, 1 Cor. 11:19: "Nam oportet et hereses esse ut et qui probati sunt manifesti fiant in vobis."

5. The same is true of many of the greatest Renaissance artists: see L. Barkan, *Unearthing the Past: Archaeology and Aesthetics in the Making of Renaissance Culture* (New Haven, Conn.: Yale University Press, 1999).

6. For Ficino, cf. M. J. B. Allen, *Synoptic Art: Marsilio Ficino on the History of Platonic Interpretation* (Florence: Olschki, 1998), 1–92.

7. Cf. C. S. Celenza, "Late Antiquity and Florentine Platonism: The 'Post-Plotinian' Ficino," in *Marsilio Ficino: His Theology, His Philosophy, His Legacy,* ed. M. J. B. Allen and V. R. Rees (Leiden: Brill, 2002), 71–97, at 74.

8. See G. Fragnito, *In museo e in villa: Saggi sul Rinascimento perduto,* La via lattea, 4 (Venice, 1988); cf. also P. Simoncelli, "Inquisizione romana e riforma in Italia," *Rivista storica italiana* 100 (1988): 5–125; E. Gleason, "Sixteenth Century Italian Spirituali and the Papacy," in *Anticlericalism in Late Medieval and Early Modern Europe,* ed. P. Dykema and H. Oberman, Studies in Medieval and Reformation Thought, 51 (Leiden: Brill, 1993), 299–307, at 306–7.

9. See the works collected in P. Athanassiadi and M. Frede, eds., *Pagan Monotheism in Late Antiquity* (Oxford: Oxford University Press, 1999); and J. Assman, "Translating Gods: Religion as a Factor of Cultural (Un)Translatability," in *The Translatability of Cultures: Figurations of the Space Between*, ed. S. Budick and W. Iser (Stanford, Calif.: Stanford University Press, 1996), 25–37; and for broader context, idem, *Moses the Egyptian: The Memory of Egypt in Western Monotheism* (Cambridge, Mass.: Harvard University Press, 1998).

10. See the editors' introduction in Athanassiadi and Frede, *Pagan Monotheism*, 1–20, at 8.

11. Ibid., 3.

12. For the curia, see C. S. Celenza, *Renaissance Humanism and the Papal Curia: Lapo da Castiglionchio the Younger's De curiae commodis*, Papers and Monographs of the American Academy in Rome, 31 (Ann Arbor: University of Michigan Press, 1999), 11–17; and for the humanists' extra-institutional intellectual status, see R. Fubini, *Humanism and Secularization from Petrarch to Valla*, trans. Martha King (Durham, N.C.: Duke University Press, 2003), esp. 44.

13. For Valla's life, see G. Mancini, *Vita di Lorenzo Valla* (Florence: Sansoni, 1891), still the most thorough biography. For changing perceptions of Valla, see J. Kraye, "Lorenzo Valla and Changing Perceptions of Renaissance Humanism," *Comparative Criticism* 23 (2001): 37–55.

14. See chapter 5, 122–23.

15. See J. Davies, *Florence and Its University during the Early Renaissance*, Education and Society in the Middle Ages and Renaissance, 8 (Leiden: Brill, 1998); Holmes, *The Florentine Enlightenment*.

16. See D. Marsh, *The Quattrocento Dialogue: Classical Tradition and Humanist Innovation* (Cambridge, Mass.: Harvard University Press, 1980); for the dialogue form in the later Renaissance, see V. Cox, *The Renaissance Dialogue: Literary Dialogue in Its Social and Political Contexts, Castiglione to Galileo* (Cambridge: Cambridge University Press, 1992).

17. L. Bruni, *Dialogi ad Petrum Paulum Histrum*, ed. S. U. Baldassarri, Istituto Nazionale di Studi sul Rinascimento, Studi e Testi, 35 (Florence: Olschki, 1994); I cite from the translation in L. Bruni, *The Humanism of Leonardo Bruni*, ed. G. Griffiths, J. Hankins, and D. Thompson (Binghamton, N.Y., 1987), 63–84; on Bruni as a best-seller, see J. Hankins, *Repertorium Brunianum: A Critical Guide to the Writings of Leonardo Bruni* (Rome, 1997).

18. *Dialogi ad Petrum Paulum Histrum*, in Bruni, *The Humanism*, 64.

19. For three perspectives, with bibliography, see D. Quint, "Humanism and Modernity: A Reconsideration of Bruni's *Dialogues*," *Renaissance Quarterly* 38 (1985): 423–45; R. Fubini, "All'uscita della scolastica medievale: Salutati, Bruni, e i *Dialogi ad Petrum Histrum*," *Archivio storico italiano* 150 (1992): 1065–103; and R. G. Witt, *In the Footsteps of the Ancients: The Origins of Humanism from Lovato to Bruni* (Leiden: Brill, 2000), 432–42.

20. See N. S. Struever, *The Language of History in the Renaissance: Rhetoric and Historical Consciousness in Florentine Humanism* (Princeton, N.J.: Princeton University Press, 1970); idem, *Theory as Practice: Ethical Inquiry in the Renaissance* (Chicago: University of Chicago Press, 1992); V. Kahn, "Humanism and the Resistance to Theory," in *Literary Theory / Renaissance Texts*, ed. P. Parker and D. Quint (Baltimore: Johns Hopkins University Press, 1986), 373–96, at 374–77. B. Vickers, *In Defence of Rhetoric* (Oxford: Oxford University Press, 1988).

21. Cf. K. Gouwens, "Perceiving the Past: Renaissance Humanism after the 'Cognitive Turn,'" *American Historical Review* 103 (1998): 55–82, esp. 65–66.

22. Cf. A. Nehamas, *The Art of Living: Socratic Reflections from Plato to Foucault,* Sather Classical Lectures, 61 (Berkeley: University of California Press, 1998).

23. Mancini, *Vita,* 10; and for background, M. Lorch, "Lorenzo Valla,"in *Renaissance Humanism: Foundations, Forms, and Legacy,* ed. A. Rabil, 3 vols. (Philadelphia: University of Pennsylvania Press, 1988), 1:332–49; and Fubini, *Humanism and Secularization from Petrarch to Valla,* 140–73.

24. Mancini, *Vita,* 14–17.

25. L. Valla, *Repastinatio dialectice et philosophie,* ed. G. Zippel, 2 vols. (Padua: Antenore, 1982), 1:2 (I, proem, 3).

26. Ibid., 2:448 (II, proem, 6–7).

27. S. Camporeale, *Lorenzo Valla, umanesimo e teologia* (Florence: Olschki, 1972).

28. Valla, *Repastinatio,* 1:1 (I, proem, 1).

29. See Camporeale, *Lorenzo Valla;* C. M. Trinkaus, *In Our Image and Likeness: Humanity and Divinity in Italian Humanist Thought,* 2 vols. (London: Constable, 1970).

30. On Alfonso, see A. Ryder, *Alfonso the Magnanimous: King of Aragon, Naples, and Sicily, 1396–1458* (Oxford: Oxford University Press, 1990).

31. Most notably Antonio Beccadelli, known as "Panormita" because he hailed from Palermo.

32. Camporeale, *Lorenzo Valla,* 15.

33. See Celenza, *Renaissance Humanism and the Papal Curia;* A. Grafton, *Leon Battista Alberti: Master Builder of the Italian Renaissance* (New York: Hill and Wang, 2000); various studies in Dykema and Oberman, *Anticlericalism.*

34. L. Valla, *De falso et ementita Constantini donatione,* ed. W. Setz, Monumenta Germaniae Historica, Quellen zur Geistesgeschichte des Mittelalters, 10 (Weimar: Hermann Böhlaus, 1976), 58.

35. See the introduction in H. Fuhrmann, *Constitutum Constantini: Einleitung und Text,* Monumenta Germaniae Historica, Fontes iuris Germanici antiqui in usum scholarum separatim editi X (Hannover: Hahn, 1968); and W. Setz, *Lorenzo Vallas Schrift gegen die konstantinische Schenkung: Die falso credita et ementita Constantini donatione: Zur Interpretation und Wirkungsgeschichte,* Bibliothek des Deutschen historischen Instituts in Rom, 44 (Tübingen: Max Niemeyer Verlag, 1975), 18 and literature in n. 1.

36. 2 Tim. 2:4; for other medieval arguments questioning the *Constitutum,* see Setz, *Lorenzo Vallas Schrift,* 18–34; and Fuhrmann's introduction cited in the previous note.

37. Camporeale, *Lorenzo Valla.*

38. Valla, *De falso et ementita Constantini donatione,* ed. Setz, 102–3 and 108–9.

39. See O. Z. Pugliese, introduction to L. Valla's *Profession of the Religious and Selections from the Falsely-Believed and Forged Donation of Constantine,* 2d ed., trans. O. Z. Pugliese (Toronto: Center for Renaissance and Reformation Studies, 1994), 24.

40. See Ryder, *Alfonso the Magnanimous,* 210–51.

41. L. Valla, *Epistole,* ed. O. Besomi and M. Regoliosi, Thesaurus Mundi, 24 (Padua: Antenore, 1984), 249–52, at 252.

42. See Valla, *De falso et ementita Constantini donatione,* ed. Setz, 62.10 and 175.18;

V. De Caprio, "Retorica e ideologia nella *Declamatio* di Lorenzo Valla sulla donazione di Costantino," *Paragone* 338 (1978): 35–56; and Pugliese, introduction, 26.

43. Valla, *De Constantini donatione,* ed. Setz, 57.18–20.

44. Ibid., 59.3–6.

45. Ibid., 148.5–6: Non desiderat sinceritas christiana patrocinium falsitatis.

46. In Valla's work, one will not find syllogistically well-argued positions concerning individual issues of importance to late medieval theologians. See J. Monfasani, "The Theology of Lorenzo Valla," in *Humanism and Early Modern Philosophy,* ed. J. Kraye and M. W. F. Stone (London: Routledge, 2000), 1–23. My argument is simply that Valla changed the way one approached questions of theology and ecclesiology—not with any programmatic statement, but simply by the force, intellectual gravity, and overall number of his works. Valla was at his best when thinking in an anticlassificatory but intellectually meaningful manner, and the very form of scholastic theological thought was classificatory in nature. So it was inevitable that, from a certain perspective, in Monfasani's words, "Valla was no theologian" (13) and indeed can seem to err or to be naive with respect to certain well-worked theological questions. But I think at times one needs to resist the temptation to cut Renaissance figures down to size by emphasizing aspects of their thought that were not central to their overall projects—a centrality that one can sometimes only see in hindsight.

47. L. Valla, *De professione religiosorum,* ed. M. Cortesi; for an English translation, see Valla, *The Profession of the Religious.*

48. Valla, *De professione,* ed. Cortesi, 3.1.

49. Ibid., 4.2–3.

50. Here Valla draws on Quintilian, *Inst.* 1. Praef. 14; see Pugliese, introduction, 48.

51. In general on early Renaissance appreciation of the Church fathers, see C. M. Stinger, *Humanism and the Church Fathers: Ambrogio Traversari (1386–1439) and Christian Antiquity in the Italian Renaissance* (Albany: State University of New York Press, 1977).

52. This is clear from the main preface to the work: "Pontifex ille maximus, qui merito beatissimus ab Hieronymo appellatur, omnium doctrinarum peritissimus, lingue tamen grece non ita peritum se fuisse significavit, cum ipsi Hieronymo delegavit decernendam *quenam latina Novi Testamenti exemplaria* cum greca veritate, tanquam cere impresse cum suo sigillo congruerent." L. Valla, *Collatio Novi Testamenti,* ed. A. Perosa (Florence: Sansoni, 1970), 3, my emphasis. The two manuscripts on which Perosa based his edition of the older version of the *Annotations,* the *Collatio,* each have two prefaces, an earlier and a final version; I am citing from the final version. As to the opinion concerning Jerome, modern scholarship is in agreement with Valla; Jerome is held to be a final redactor of a number of already existing Latin exemplars.

53. Ibid., 6–7.

54. The best introduction to Renaissance biblical philology, with a lengthy section on Valla, is J. Bentley, *Humanists and Holy Writ* (Princeton, N.J.: Princeton University Press, 1983).

55. Cf. C. S. Celenza, "Renaissance Humanism and the New Testament: Lorenzo Valla's Annotations to the Vulgate," *Journal of Medieval and Renaissance Studies* 21 (1994): 33–52.

56. L. Valla, *Collatio,* ad loc., idem, "Adnotationes in Novum Testamentum," in idem, *Opera Omnia,* 2 vols. (Basel, 1560; reprint with pref. by E. Garin, Turin: Bottega d'Erasmo, 1962), 1:859.

57. L. Valla, *De libero arbitrio,* in *Prosatori latini del quattrocento,* ed. E. Garin (Milan: Ricciardi, 1952), 522–65; I cite from the English translation in E. Cassirer, P. O. Kristeller, and J. H. Randall, *The Renaissance Philosophy of Man* (Chicago: University of Chicago Press, 1948), 155–82.

58. For background, see J. Marenbon, *Boethius* (Oxford: Oxford University Press, 2003); and M. Gibson, ed., *Boethius* (Oxford: Blackwell, 1981).

59. Camporeale, *Lorenzo Valla,* 166–69 et passim; idem, "Renaissance Humanism and the Origins of Humanist Theology," in *Humanity and Divinity in Renaissance and Reformation: Essays in Honor of Charles Trinkaus,* ed. J. W. O'Malley, T. M. Izbicki, and G. Christianson (Leiden: Brill, 1993), 101–24, at 106–7.

60. Valla, *De libero arbitrio,* ed. Garin, 544; Eng. trans., 169.

61. Ibid., ed. Garin, 550; Eng. trans., 174.

62. Livy, *Ab urbe condita,* 1.56–58.

63. Valla, *De libero arbitrio,* ed. Garin, 546; Eng. trans., 171.

64. Ibid., ed. Garin, 544; Eng. trans., 169.

65. Ibid., ed. Garin, 554; Eng. trans., 176.

66. L. Valla, "Encomium Sancti Thomae Aquinatis," ed. J. Vahlen, in Valla, *Opera Omnia,* 2:346–52, at 350: "*sed se totos ad imitandum Paulum apostolum contulerunt,* omnium theologorum longe principem ac theologandi magistrum," my emphasis. S. Camporeale, "Lorenzo Valla tra Medioevo e Rinascimento: *Encomion S. Thomae—1457,*" *Memorie Dominicane,* n.s., 7 (1976): 3–186; J. W. O'Malley, "Some Renaissance Panegyrics of Aquinas," *Renaissance Quarterly* 27 (1974): 174–92; idem, "The Feast of Thomas Aquinas in Renaissance Rome: A Neglected Document and Its Import," *Rivista di storia della Chiesa in Italia* 35 (1981): 1–27.

67. W. S. Blanchard, "The Negative Dialectic of Lorenzo Valla: A Study in the Pathology of Opposition," *Renaissance Studies* 14 (2000): 149–89.

68. Florentine humanists in the first half of the fifteenth century often began as social and economic outsiders, however; see L. Martines, *The Social World of the Florentine Humanists, 1390–1460* (Princeton, N.J.: Princeton University Press, 1963). Riccardo Fubini has recently stressed, with decidedly different emphases from Garin's, the "outsider" status of humanists; see Fubini, *Humanism and Secularization from Petrarch to Valla.*

69. Cf. A. Grafton and L. Jardine, *From Humanism to the Humanities: Education and the Liberal Arts in Fifteenth- and Sixteenth-Century Europe* (Cambridge, Mass.: Harvard University Press, 1986); for the entry of humanism into Italian universities on a wide scale in the late fifteenth and early sixteenth centuries, see P. F Grendler, *The Universities of the Italian Renaissance* (Baltimore: Johns Hopkins University Press, 2002).

70. T. J. Reiss, *Knowledge, Discovery, and Imagination in Early Modern Europe: The Rise of Aesthetic Rationalism* (New York: Cambridge University Press, 1997).

71. Cf. C. S. Celenza, *Piety and Pythagoras in Renaissance Florence: The Symbolum Nesianum,* Studies in the History of Christian Thought, 101 (Leiden: Brill, 2001), 15–51; idem, "Late Antiquity and Florentine Platonism," 71–97.

72. Cf. Oberman in Oberman and Brady, *Itinerarium Italicum,* xx.

73. See A. Grafton, *Joseph Scaliger: A Study in the History of Classical Scholarship,* 2 vols.

(Oxford, 1983–93), 1:9–100; idem, *Defenders of the Text: The Traditions of Scholarship in an Age of Science* (Cambridge, Mass.: Harvard University Press, 1991), 23–75; K. Krautter, *Philologische Methode und Humanistische Existenz: Filippo Beroaldo und sein Kommentar zum Goldenen Esel des Apuleius* (Munich: Fink, 1971); and C. S. Celenza, "Late Antiquity and the Florentine Renaissance: Historiographical Parallels," *Journal of the History of Ideas* 62 (2001): 17–35.

74. See A. Field, *The Origins of the Platonic Academy of Florence* (Princeton, N.J.: Princeton University Press, 1988); M. Bullard, "Marsilio Ficino and the Medici: The Inner Dimensions of Patronage," in *Christianity and the Renaissance: Image and Religious Imagination in the Quattrocento,* ed. T. Verdon and J. Henderson (Syracuse, N.Y.: Syracuse University Press, 1990), 467–92; A. Brown, *The Medici in Florence: The Language and Exercise of Power* (Florence: Olschki, 1992), 215–45; idem, *Bartolomeo Scala, 1430–1497, Chancellor of Florence: The Humanist as Bureaucrat* (Princeton, N.J.: Princeton University Press, 1979); R. Black, *Benedetto Accolti and the Florentine Renaissance* (Cambridge: Cambridge University Press, 1985); and N. Rubinstein, *The Government of Florence under the Medici (1434–1494),* 2d ed. (Oxford: Clarendon Press; New York: Oxford University Press, 1997). Essential reading is J. Hankins, *Plato in the Italian Renaissance,* 2 vols. (Leiden: Brill, 1990).

75. See, e.g., Ficino's letters to Cavalcanti and Filippo Contronio in M. Ficino, *Lettere,* vol. 1, ed. S. Gentile (Florence: Olschki, 1990); also in Ficino, *Opera Omnia,* 632–33.

76. See Bullard, "Marsilio Ficino and the Medici," 215–45; and the important studies of R. Fubini, "Ficino e I Medici all'avvento di Lorenzo il Magnifico," *Rinascimento,* 2d ser., 24 (1984): 3–52; idem, "Ancora su Ficino e I Medici," *Rinascimento,* 2d ser., 27 (1987): 275–91; both now contained in idem, *Quattrocento fiorentino: Politica diplomazia cultura* (Pisa, 1996).

77. For the chronology of Ficino's work, see P. O. Kristeller, *Supplementum Ficinianum,* 2 vols. (Florence: Oschki, 1937), 1:lxxvii–clxvii; idem, "Marsilio Ficino as a Beginning Student of Plato," *Scriptorium* 20 (1966): 41–54, reprinted in idem, *Studies in Renaissance Thought and Letters,* vol. 3 (Rome: Edizioni di Storia e Letteratura, 1993), 93–108; and S. Gentile, "Sulle prime traduzioni dal greco di Marsilio Ficino," *Rinascimento,* 2d ser., 30 (1990): 57–104.

78. See Allen, *Synoptic Art.*

79. One of many artists and intellectuals: see J. Hankins, "Lorenzo de' Medici as a Patron of Philosophy," *Rinascimento,* 2d ser., 34 (1994): 15–53; high affective dimension: Bullard, "Marsilio Ficino and the Medici."

80. See A. Verde, *Lo studio fiorentino, 1473–1503: Ricerche e documenti* 5 vols. to date (Florence: Olschki, 1973–94), vol. 2; and Hankins, "Lorenzo de' Medici as a Patron of Philosophy."

81. On Poliziano, see V. Branca, *Poliziano e l'umanesimo della parola* (Turin, 1983); J. D'Amico, *Theory and Practice in Renaissance Textual Criticism: Beatus Rhenanus between Conjecture and History* (Berkeley, Calif., 1988), 23–27; P. Godman, *From Poliziano to Machiavelli: Florentine Humanism in the High Renaissance* (Princeton, N.J.: Princeton University Press, 1998); Grafton, *Joseph Scaliger,* 1:9–100; and I. Maier, *Ange Politien: La formation d'un poète humaniste, 1469–1480* (Geneva: Droz, 1966); for a precise, excellent introduction to his style of miscellanistic criticism, see J. Kraye, "Cicero, Stoicism, and Textual Criticism: Poliziano on $KATOP\Theta\Omega MA$," *Rinascimento,* 2d ser., 23 (1983): 79–110.

82. A. Poliziano, "Miscellaneorum centuria prima," in idem, *Opera* (Venice: Aldus Manutius, 1498), unpaginated; and idem, *Miscellaneorum centuria secunda,* ed. V. Branca and M. P. Stocchi (Florence, 1978).

83. Godman, *From Poliziano to Machiavelli,* 3–133, is especially lucid on the manner in which Poliziano's agonistic context shaped the evolution of his scholarhip.

84. Buonincontri: see A. Field, "Lorenzo Buonincontri and the First Public Lectures on Manilius (Florence, ca. 1475–78)," *Rinascimento,* 2d ser., 36 (1996): 207–25; Poliziano and Pliny: Godman, *From Poliziano to Machiavelli,* 98–106.

85. See A. Poliziano, *Lamia: Praelectio in priora Aristotelis analytica,* ed. A. Wesseling, Studies in Medieval and Reformation Thought, 38 (Leiden, 1986); C. S. Celenza, *Piety and Pythagoras;* J. Kraye, "Ficino in the Firing Line: A Renaissance Neoplatonist and His Critics," in Allen and Rees, *Marsilio Ficino,* 377–98; A. D. Scaglione, *Essays on the Arts of Discourse: Linguistics, Rhetoric, Poetics* (New York: Peter Lang, 1998), 39–58.

86. The Medici were not despots in the sense of having absolute control over governmental policy; but they solidified control over the Florentine oligarchic regime in such a way that they were recognized by contemporaries as easily being the most influential citizens. The process happened over the fifteenth century in fits and starts; conspiracies were always afoot to overthrow them in the name of battling "tyranny," but it happened nonetheless; for Cosimo's approach, see Rubinstein, *The Government of Florence,* 144–53; for later consolidation under Lorenzo, especially after the creation of the council of Seventy in 1480, see ibid., 231–63.

87. Hankins, "Lorenzo de' Medici as a Patron of Philosophy." L. de' Medici, *Tutte le opere,* 2 vols., ed. P. Orvieto (Rome: Salerno, 1992); A. Poliziano, *Stanze per la giostra, Orfeo, Rime,* ed. B. Maier (Novara: Club del libro, 1969); A. Poliziano, *The Stanze of Angelo Poliziano,* trans. David Quint (University Park: Pennsylvania State University Press, 1993).

88. See M. J. B. Allen, "The Second Ficino-Pico Controversy: Parmenidean Poetry, Eristic and the One," in *Marsilio Ficino e il ritorno di Platone: Studi e documenti,* ed. G. C. Garfagnini, 2 vols. (Florence, 1986), 2:417–55, now in idem, *Plato's Third Eye: Studies in Marsilio Ficino's Metaphysics and Its Sources* (Aldershot, Eng.: Ashgate, 1995), as study 10; E. Garin, *Giovanni Pico della Mirandola: Vita e dottrina* (Florence: Le Monnier, 1937); and L. Valcke and R. Galibois, *Le périple intellectuel de Jean Pic de la Mirandole, suivi du Discours de la dignité de l'homme et du traité L'être et l'un* (Sainte-Foy, Quebec, 1994).

89. See D. Weinstein, *Savonarola and Florence: Prophecy and Patriotism in the Renaissance* (Princeton, N.J.: Princeton University Press, 1970); L. Polizzotto, *The Elect Nation: The Savonarolan Movement in Florence, 1494–1545* (Oxford: Clarendon, 1994); and Allen, *Synoptic Art.*

90. See the excellent material in C. V. Kaske, "Ficino's Shifting Attitude Towards Astrology in the 'De vita coelitus comparanda,' the letter to Poliziano, and the 'Apologia' to the Cardinals," in *Marsilio Ficino e il ritorno di Platone: Studi e documenti,* ed. G. C. Garfagnini, 2 vols. (Florence: Olschki, 1986), 2:371–81.

91. Ficino's letter to Poliziano, dated 20 August 1494, is in *Op.* 958. Poliziano's letter is edited in Kristeller, *Supplementum,* 2:278–79; cf. 279: "Nam nec mutare sententiam turpe philosopho, qui cottidie plus videt et ad opinionem vulgi saepe se non inutiliter accomodat, quod et Aristoteles in exotericis libris et in dialogis Plato fecit, qui quidem non dogmatici habentur."

92. The *Apologia* is edited in Kristeller, *Supplementum*, 2:76–79. For "Hypocritarum princeps," see ibid., 77.

93. On Florence and the transition to a court society, see R. Bizocchi, *Chiesa e potere nella Toscana del Quattrocento* (Bologna, 1987), 351–52; Brown, *Medici in Florence,* 247–62; and Brown, *Bartolomeo Scala.*

94. J. Hankins, "Cosimo de' Medici and the 'Platonic Academy,'" *Journal of the Warburg and Courtauld Institutes* 53 (1990): 144–62; and idem, "The Myth of the Platonic Academy of Florence," *Renaissance Quarterly* 44 (1991): 429–75.

95. Cf. Celenza, *Piety and Pythagoras,* chap. 3.

96. Cf. C. Dempsey, *The Portrayal of Love: Botticelli's Primavera and Humanist Culture at the Time of Lorenzo the Magnificent* (Princeton, N.J., 1992).

97. Cf. J.-P. Sartre, *L'idiot de la famille: Gustave Flaubert de 1821–1857* (Paris: Gallimard, 1971), 1:783.

98. I cite from M. Ficino, *De triplici vita,* ed. and trans. C. Kaske and J. Clark (Binghamton, N.Y., 1989).

99. Ficino, *De triplici vita,* proem, 102–5.

100. Cf. N. Siraisi, *Medieval and Early Renaissance Medicine: An Introduction to Knowledge and Practice* (Chicago, 1990), 68–69, 149–52.

101. Ficino, *De triplici vita,* 2.11.

102. Ibid.

103. Ibid., *Apologia.*

104. Pliny, *Nat.,* 11.39.95.

105. Ovid, *Fasti,* 6.132–68; cf. 141: "sive igitur nascuntur aves, seu carmine fiunt."

106. See the entries in L. Hain and W. A. Copinger, *Supplement to Hain's Repertorium Bibliographicum* (Milan: Gorlich, 1950), 9238–42. Witchcraft: for four approaches to the problem, very different but complementary, see S. Clark, *Thinking with Demons: The Idea of Witchcraft in Early Modern Europe* (Oxford: Oxford University Press, 1997); R. Briggs, *Witches and Neighbors: A History of European Witchcraft* (New York: Viking, 1996); B. P. Levack, *The Witch-Hunt in Early Modern Europe,* 2d ed. (London: Longman, 1995); and W. Stephens, *Demon Lovers* (Chicago: University of Chicago Press, 2002).

107. Cf. Apuleius, *Met.,* 2.21.

108. Present famously in Dante, *Purgatorio,* 19.

109. See the edition of Innocent's 1487 bull in P. della Mirandola, *De hominis dignitate, Heptaplus, De ente et uno e scritti vari,* ed. E. Garin (Florence: Vallecchi, 1942); and S. A. Farmer, *Syncretism in the West: Pico's 900 Theses (1486): The Evolution of Traditional Religious and Philosophical Systems,* Medieval and Renaissance Texts and Studies, 167 (Tempe: Arizona State University Press, 1998), 15–16, from whom the quotation is drawn.

110. See, for instance, Ficino, *De triplici vita,* 3.15, 3.18, and 3.20. *De triplici vita* is subsequently cited in the text and notes by the abbreviation *DV* and book and chapter or book, chapter, and page numbers.

111. P. Camporesi, *Bread of Dreams* (Chicago: University of Chicago Press, 1989), 40–55.

112. On the need to think carefully about the categories of "high" and "low" when approaching early modern culture, see G. Ruggiero, *Binding Passions: Tales of Magic, Marriage, and Power at the End of the Renaissance* (Oxford: Oxford University Press, 1993); and

for the classic statement of the reciprocal relationship between "low" and "high" culture, see C. Ginzburg, *The Cheese and the Worms: The Cosmos of a Sixteenth-Century Miller,* trans. A. Tedeschi and J. Tedeschi (Baltimore: Johns Hopkins University Press, 1980; reprint, New York: Penguin, 1982), xiii–xxvi in 1980 ed.

113. See B. P. Copenhaver, "Scholastic Philosophy and Renaissance Magic in the *De vita* of Marsilio Ficino," *Renaissance Quarterly* 37 (1984): 523–54; Celenza, "Late Antiquity and Florentine Platonism."

114. See Porphyry, *Vita Plotini,* 10; in Ficino's translation, *Op.* 2:1541.

115. Ficino himself is aware of the range of his hermeneutic. Cf. these two passages: "But lest we digress too long from what we initially started to do, interpreting Plotinus . . ." (*DV* 3.26: 384–85) and "Iamblichus demonstrates that true and certain prophecy cannot come from such evil daemons, nor is it produced by human arts or by nature; it is only produced in purified minds by divine inspiration. But now let us get back to Hermes, or rather Plotinus" (391).

116. Another noteworthy passage along those lines occurs at *DV* 3.22: 368–69, where Ficino discusses what he means when he says "celestial goods descend to us." One way this occurs is "that the goods of celestial souls partly leap forth into this our spirit through rays, and from there overflow into our souls and partly come straight from their souls or from angels into human souls which have been exposed to them—exposed, I say, not so much by some natural means as by the election of free will or by affection." Concluding, he writes: "In summary, consider that those who by prayer, by study, by manner of life, and by conduct imitate the beneficence, action, and order of the celestials, since they are more similar to the gods, receive fuller gifts from them." Again, the discourse is about making our soul similar to the divine through will but not about actually having a part of the soul be essentially divine, as in Plotinus.

117. Albert, *Speculum astronomiae,* ed. S. Caroti, M. Pereira, and S. Zamponi (Pisa: Domus Galilaeana, 1977), 32.103–39 and 47.1–21, cited in *DV,* Kaske and Clark's ed., 449 n. 28; T. Aquinas, *Summa contra Gentiles,* 3.104–7 (in vols. 13–15 of his *Opera Omnia,* Leonine edition, 47 vols. [Rome, 1882–1971]), cited in *DV,* Kaske and Clark's ed., 450 n. 31; see also notes 32–34 and the notes to 3.17, at 444–46. In general see Copenhaver, "Scholastic Philosophy."

118. See Copenhaver, "Scholastic Philosophy"; and idem, "Renaissance Magic and Neoplatonic Philosophy: 'Ennead' 4.3–5 in Ficino's 'De vita coelitus comparanda,'" in Garfagnini, *Marsilio Ficino,* 2:351–69.

119. See J. B. Russell, *Witchcraft in the Middle Ages* (Ithaca, N.Y.: Cornell University Press, 1972), 101–65.

120. On this point, see M. J. B. Allen, "Summoning Plotinus: Ficino, Smoke, and the Strangled Chickens," in *Reconsidering the Renaissance,* Medieval and Renaissance Texts and Studies, 93, ed. M. Di Cesare (Binghamton, N.Y.: Medieval and Renaissance Texts, 1992), 63–88, now in Allen, *Plato's Third Eye,* study 14.

121. For the way the power of images is tied to Ficino's adaptation of the seminal reasons (λόγοι σπερματικοί) of Plotinus, see Copenhaver, "Renaissance Magic and Neoplatonic Philosophy."

122. See Celenza, "Late Antiquity and Florentine Platonism."

123. *DV, Apologia,* 398–99: "Quidnam agis et tu, strenue Soderini noster? Tolerabis ne

superstitiosos caecosque nescio quos futuros, qui vitam in animalibus vel abiectissimis herbisque vilissimis manifestam vident, in coelo, in mundo, non vident?"

124. Copenhaver, "Scholastic Philosophy."

125. Cf. M. J. B. Allen, *The Platonism of Marsilio Ficino: A Study of His* Phaedrus *Commentary, Its Sources and Genesis* (Berkeley, Calif., 1984), x–xi.

F I V E ✧ *Honor*

E P I G R A P H : L. B. Alberti, *I libri della famiglia,* in idem, *Opere Volgari,* 3 vols., ed. C. Grayson (Bari: Laterza, 1960–73), 1:1–341, at 284 and 294 (bk. 4; the character speaking in each case is Adovardo); I cite from the translation of R. N. Watkins (Columbia: University of South Carolina Press, 1969), 266 and 274.

1. M. Garber, *Academic Instincts* (Princeton, N.J.: Princeton University Press, 2000). For a noteworthy exception to this tendency among Renaissance intellectual historians, see A. F. D'Elia, "Marriage, Sexual Pleasure, and Learned Brides in the Wedding Orations of Fifteenth-Century Italy," *Renaissance Quarterly* 55 (2002): 379–433.

2. J. W. Scott, "Gender: A Useful Category of Historical Analysis," in her *Gender and the Politics of History* (New York: Columbia University Press, 1988), 28–50, which originally appeared in the *American Historical Review* 91 (1986).

3. Ibid., 42.

4. J. S. Mill, *The Subjection of Women* (1869), in idem, *On Liberty* with *The Subjection of Women* and *Chapters on Socialism,* ed. S. Collini (Cambridge: Cambridge University Press, 1989), 117–217, at 138.

5. Scott, "Gender," 41.

6. C. W. Bynum, *Jesus as Mother: Studies in the Spirituality of the High Middle Ages* (Berkeley: University of California Press, 1982).

7. Cf. C. Trinkaus, *Adversity's Noblemen: The Italian Humanists on Happiness* (New York: Columbia University Press, 1940); E. Garin, *Italian Humanism: Philosophy and Civic Life in the Renaissance,* trans. Peter Munz (Oxford: Blackwell, 1965); and, most recently and incisively, R. Fubini, *Humanism and Secularization from Petrarch to Valla,* trans. Martha King (Durham, N.C.: Duke University Press, 2003).

8. L. Martines, *The Social World of the Florentine Humanists* (Princeton, N.J.: Princeton University Press: 1963). The same concern, vis-à-vis humanist economic and political enfranchisement, can be seen in Venice, as Margaret King has shown; see her *Venetian Humanism in an Age of Patrician Dominance* (Princeton, N.J.: Princeton University Press, 1986).

9. C. Salutati, *Invectivum in Antonium Luschum Vicentinum,* in *Prosatori latini del Quattrocento,* ed. E. Garin (Milan: Ricciardi, 1952), 8–37.

10. A. Grafton, *Leon Battista Alberti, Master Builder of the Italian Renaissance* (New York: Hill and Wang, 2000), 31–70. See S. Saygin, *Humphrey, Duke of Gloucester (1390–1447) and the Italian Humanists* (Leiden: Brill, 2002), esp. 205–10, for some analogous concerns.

11. It is true that European intellectuals used the term *republic of letters* in a self-conscious way much later, and it has come to designate the intellectual milieu of the *erudits* of the seventeenth and eighteenth centuries. But it is worth recalling that a very similar term was used at least as early as 1417, when Francesco Barbaro wrote to Pog-

gio Bracciolini praising him for rediscovering a number of books: "Whom then do I honor? Those men, certainly, who have given the most assistance and adornment to this literary republic" [Quos autem orno? Eos nempe, qui huic litterarie rei p. plurima adiumenta atque ornamenta contulerunt]. See F. Barbaro, *Epistolario*, 2 vols., ed. C. Griggio (Florence: Olschki, 1994), 2:71–79, at 75. An English translation of the letter can be found in P. W. G. Gordan, trans. and ed., *Two Renaissance Book Hunters: The Letters of Poggius Bracciolini to Nicolaus de Niccolis* (New York: Columbia University Press, 1974), 196–203, at 199, where the term in question is rendered as "republic of letters."

12. H. H. Gray, "Renaissance Humanism: The Pursuit of Eloquence," *Journal of the History of Ideas* 24 (1963): 497–514.

13. The most comprehensive study of this period is the eloquent G. Holmes, *The Florentine Enlightenment, 1400–1450* (London: Weidenfeld and Nicholson, 1969; Oxford: Oxford University Press, 1992).

14. For the Bruni passage, see L. Bruni, *De studiis et litteris*, in idem, *Opere letterarie e politiche*, ed. and trans. P. Viti (Turin: UTEP, 1996), 248–78, at 260; and for an English translation, idem, *The Humanism of Leonardo Bruni*, ed. G. Griffiths, J. Hankins, and D. Thompson (Binghamton, N.Y., 1987), 240–51, at 244, from which I cite. For background on the construction of masculinity, see D. D. Gilmore, *Manhood in the Making: Cultural Concepts of Masculinity* (New Haven, Conn.: Yale University Press, 1990); for an in-depth examination in late-sixteenth- and early-seventeenth-century Venice, see C. Povolo, *L'intrigo dell'Onore: Poteri e istituzioni nella Repubblica di Venezia tra Cinque e Seicento* (Verona: Cierre, 1997); and still useful on matters of honor in the Renaissance is G. Maugain, *Moeurs italiennes de la Renaissance: La vengeance* (Paris: Les Belles Lettres, 1935). Latin acquisition: see W. J. Ong, *Interfaces of the Word: Studies of the Evolution of Consciousness and Culture* (Ithaca, N.Y.: Cornell University Press, 1977).

15. In a voluminous literature, some touchstone works, in rough chronological order, include at least these: L. Martines, "A Way of Looking at Women in Renaissance Florence," *Journal of Medieval and Renaissance Studies* 4 (1974): 15–28; J. Kelly-Gadol (who also wrote as J. Kelly), "Did Women Have a Renaissance," in *Becoming Visible: Women in European History*, ed. R. Bridenthal and C. Koonz (Boston, 1977), 137–64, reprinted in J. Kelly-Gadol, *Women, History, and Theory: The Essays of Joan Kelly* (Chicago: University of Chicago Press, 1984), 19–50; R. Trexler, "Celibacy in the Renaissance: The Nuns of Florence," in his *The Women of Renaissance Florence* (Binghamton, N.Y., 1993), 6–30 (the essay originally appeared in French in 1977); P. Labalme, ed., *Beyond Their Sex: Learned Women of the European Past* (New York, 1980); P. O. Kristeller, "Learned Women of Early Modern Italy: Humanists and University Scholars," in Labalme, *Beyond Their Sex*, 91–116; A. Rabil, *Laura Cereta: Quattrocento Humanist* (Binghamton, N.Y.: MRTS, 1981); D. O. Hughes, "Sumptuary Law and Social Relations in Renaissance Italy," in *Disputes and Settlements: Law and Human Relations in the West*, ed. J. Bossy (Cambridge: Cambridge University Press, 1983), 69–99; M. King and A. Rabil, eds., *Her Immaculate Hand: Selected Works by and about Women Humanists of Quattrocento Italy* (Binghamton, N.Y.: MRTS, 1983); M. King, *Women in the Renaissance* (Chicago: University of Chicago Press, 1991); O. Niccoli, ed., *Rinascimento al femminile* (Rome, 1991); L. Panizza, ed., *Women in Italian Renaissance Culture in Society* (Oxford, 2000), esp. the study of D. Robin, "Humanism and Feminism in Laura Cereta's Public Letters," 368–84; L. Panizza and S. Wood, eds., *A History of Women's*

Writing in Italy (Cambridge: Cambridge University Press, 2000), esp. Panizza, "Humanism," 25–30. See also the texts in the University of Chicago Press series The Other Voice in Early Modern Europe, for a discussion of which see the appendix.

16. Monica Chojnacka, using a broad definition of "agency" and a focus on non-elite women, has studied the way sixteenth- and early-seventeenth-century Venetian women created lived identities that in certain ways were not tied to men, but rather to social, often local communities; see M. Chojnacka, *Working Women of Early Modern Venice* (Baltimore: Johns Hopkins University Press, 2001). Joanne M. Ferraro, in her *Marriage Wars in Late Renaissance Venice* (Oxford: Oxford University Press, 2001), has also argued that women had more agency than often assumed, here in the way marriages were dissolved in the same period.

17. None of this is to say that the Latin literature of the lost Renaissance is irrelevant for an age that has claimed to leave certain underlying assumptions regarding gender behind. It is to say that, to understand the value of Renaissance ideas, one must give up the fiction that ideas are culturally embedded to such an extent that they can never have any meaning outside of the immediate context within which they were produced.

18. L. Martines, *April Blood: Florence and the Plot against the Medici* (Oxford: Oxford University Press, 2003), 98.

19. Gilmore, *Manhood in the Making*, 35.

20. R. G. Witt, *In the Footsteps of the Ancients: The Origins of Humanism from Lovato to Bruni*, Studies in Medieval and Reformation Thought, 74 (Leiden: Brill, 2000), 230–91; C. E. Quillen, *Rereading the Renaissance: Petrarch, Augustine, and the Language of Humanism* (Ann Arbor: University of Michigan Press, 1998); C. M. Trinkaus, *The Poet as Philosopher: Petrarch and the Formation of Renaissance Consciousness* (New Haven, Conn.: Yale University Press, 1979).

21. Witt, *In the Footsteps of the Ancients,* argues that Petrarch was a third-generation humanist whose religious concerns shaped the humanist movement definitively; in the next generation, with Coluccio Salutati, the religious concern continues but is modified, and in the following generation, the era of Bruni, the movement becomes resecularized.

22. See Holmes, *The Florentine Enlightenment,* esp. chaps. 2 and 3.

23. C. S. Celenza, *Renaissance Humanism and the Papal Curia: Lapo da Castiglionchio the Younger's De curiae commodis,* Papers and Monographs of the American Academy in Rome, 31 (Ann Arbor: University of Michigan Press, 1999), chap. 1.

24. See G. Mollat, *The Popes at Avignon, 1305–1378,* trans. J. Love from the 9th French ed. (Edinburgh: Thomas Nelson and Sons, 1963); for Constance, see P. H. Stump, *The Reforms of the Council of Constance (1414–1418),* Studies in the History of Christian Thought, 53 (Leiden: Brill, 1994), with full bibliography at 429–44; A. Franzen and W. Müller, eds., *Das Konzil von Konstanz: Beiträge zu seiner Geschichte und Theologie* (Freiburg, 1964); for some documents, see N. P. Tanner, ed., *Decrees of the Ecumenical Councils,* 2 vols. (London: Sheed and Ward; Washington, D.C.: Georgetown University Press, 1990), 1:403–51; and C. M. D. Crowder, *Unity, Heresy, and Reform, 1378–1460: The Conciliar Response to the Great Schism* (New York: St. Martin's Press, 1977), 1–145; and see also B. Tierney, *Foundations of the Conciliar Theory: The Contribution of the Medieval Canonists from Gratian to the Great Schism,* rev. ed., Studies in the History of Christian Thought, 81 (Leiden: Brill, 1998).

25. Celenza, *Renaissance Humanism and the Papal Court,* 11–17; J. D'Amico, *Renaissance*

Humanism in Papal Rome: Humanists and Churchmen on the Eve of the Reformation (Baltimore: Johns Hopkins University Press, 1983); P. Partner, *The Pope's Men: The Papal Civil Service in the Renaissance* (Oxford: Oxford University Press, 1990); idem, "Ufficio, famiglia, stato: Contrasti nella curia romana," in *Roma capitale (1447–1527),* ed. S. Gensini (Pisa, 1994).

26. See Partner, "Ufficio, famiglia, stato." It was really not until the pontificate of Nicholas V (1447–55), pope after Eugenius IV, that the papal court took on a predominantly humanist flavor, for Nicholas, as his humanist biographer Giannozzo Manetti put it, "summoned to himself some of the men most distinguished in erudition and the humanist discplines and most learned in both tongues [Latin and Greek], with annual payments and regular wages" [. . . atque aliquot insuper doctrine et humanitatis studiis prestantes viros utriusque lingue peritissimos annuis mercedibus et ordinariis salariis ad sese evocasset]. See Manetti's *Vita* of Nicholas, Book 2, ed. and trans. J. O'Connor and C. Smith, in their *Building the Kingdom: Giannozzo Manetti on the Material and Spiritual Edifice* (Tempe: Arizona State University Press, forthcoming), sec. 13.

27. Cf. C. S. Celenza, "Lapo da Castiglionchio il Giovane, Poggio Bracciolini e la *vita curialis:* Appunti su due testi umanistici," *Medioevo e Rinascimento* 14, n.s., 11 (2000): 129–45.

28. Celenza, *Renaissance Humanism and the Papal Court;* R. Fubini, "Castiglionchio, Lapo da, detto il Giovane," *Dizionario biografico degli Italiani* (Rome, 1979), 22:44–51; Grafton, *Leon Battista Alberti,* 31–70, 193–94.

29. See Celenza, *Renaissance Humanism and the Papal Court;* and Fubini, "Castiglionchio, Lapo da." For literature on Orsini, see C. S. Celenza, "The Will of Cardinal Giordano Orsini (ob. 1438)," *Traditio* 51 (1996): 257–86; and see the classic biography by E. König, *Kardinal Giordano Orsini + 1438: Ein Lebensbild aus der Zeit der großen Konzilien und des Humanismus,* Studien und Darstellungen aus dem Gebiete der Geschichte, 5.1 (Freiburg im Breisgau, 1906).

30. See C. S. Celenza, "'Parallel Lives': Plutarch's *Lives,* Lapo da Castiglionchio the Younger (1405–1438), and the Art of Italian Renaissance Translation," *Illinois Classical Studies* 22 (1997): 121–55; M. Pade, "The Latin Translations of Plutarch's *Lives* in Fifteenth-Century Italy and Their Manuscript Diffusion," in *The Classical Tradition in the Middle Ages and the Renaissance,* ed. C. Leonardi and B. M. Olsen (Spoleto, 1995), 169–83; idem, "A Checklist of the Manuscripts of the Fifteenth-Century Latin Translations of Plutarch's Lives," in *L'eredità culturale di Plutarco dall'Antichità al Rinascimento,* ed. I. Gallo (Naples, 1998), 251–87; idem, "Sulla fortuna delle Vite die Plutarco nell'umanesimo italiano del Quattrocento," in *Fontes* 1 (1998): 101–16.

31. MS Paris, Bibliothèque Nationale, Par. Lat. 11,388, fols. 6v–9.

32. Lapo da Castiglionchio the Younger, *De curiae commodis,* edited and translated in Celenza, *Renaissance Humanism and the Papal Curia.*

33. Ibid., 7.22–24.

34. Ibid., 4.11–12.

35. The text of the letter is in E. Walser, *Poggius florentinus: Leben und Werke* (Leipzig, 1914; reprint, Hildesheim: Olms, 1974), 502–3; an excellent account of the episode is in J. Monfasani, *George of Trebizond: A Biography and a Study of His Rhetoric and Logic,* Columbia Studies in the Classical Tradition, 1 (Leiden: Brill, 1976), 109–11.

36. Monfasani, *George*, 121–22.

37. Lapo, *De curiae commodis*, ed. Celenza, 4.24.

38. Ibid.

39. Ibid., 7.25–26.

40. MS Vatican City, Biblioteca Apostolica Vaticana, Ottob. Lat. 1677, fol. 178: et ad te perbrevem epistolam scripsi, quo facilior tibi responsio videretur. Atqui ad eam tu ad hunc diem nihil respondisti. Cited in Celenza, *Renaissance Humanism and the Papal Curia*, 20 n. 86.

41. Ibid., fol. 178v, cited and trans. in Celenza, *Renaissance Humanism and the Papal Curia*, 20.

42. D. Robin, *Filelfo in Milan: Writings, 1451–1477* (Princeton, N.J.: Princeton University Press, 1991).

43. See V. da Bisticci, *Le vite*, 2 vols., ed. A. Greco (Florence: Istituto Nazionale di Studi sul Rinascimento, 1970–74), 1:465–66. For Bruni's report, see his letter to Salutati, ed. L. Mehus, I, II, cited by Greco, ibid., at 465 n. 2: "Hic ego letatus mihi occasionem praestitam cum illo, ut optabam, in comparationem veniendi, rescripsi uti praeceptum fuerat, biduoque post constituto tempore meae illiusque litterae Pontifici, Patribusque recitatae sunt. Quibus lectis, quantum interesse visum sit, nescio, illud tantum scio, fautores illius, qui tam arroganter illum mihi praeferebant, aperte iam confiteri se falsa nimium opinione ductos errasse. Pontifex certe ipse mihi statim gratulatus, reiecto illo, me ad officium dignitatemque recepit."

44. Lapo, *De curiae commodis*, ed. Celenza, 5.14.

45. J. Huizinga, *The Autumn of the Middle Ages*, trans. R. J. Payton and U. Mammitzsch (Chicago: University of Chicago Press, 1996), 1.

46. On Biondo Flavio, see R. Fubini, "Biondo, Flavio," in *Dizionario biografico degli Italiani* (Rome, 1968), 10:536–59, with full bibliography at 557–59; and M. Miglio, *Storiografia pontifica del Quattrocento* (Milan, 1975).

47. The text of the letter is in M. Regoliosi, "'Res gestae patriae' e 'res gestae ex universa Italia': La lettera di Lapo da Castiglionchio a Biondo Flavio," in *La memoria e la città*, ed. C. Bastia and M. Bolognani (Bologna: Il Nove, 1995), 273–305; cited and translated in Grafton, *Leon Battista Alberti*, 54.

48. Grafton, *Leon Battista Alberti*, 55.

49. Ibid., 51–57.

50. The quotation is from ibid., 52; for an account of Valla's thrashing of Poggio's Latinity, see R. Pfeiffer, "Küchenlatein," *Philologus* 86 (1931): 455–59, reprinted in idem, *Ausgewählte Schriften: Aufsätze und Vorträge zur griechischen Dichtung und zum Humanismus* (Munich: Beck, 1960), 183–87; on the low status of cooks, an ancient source that Valla and his cohort would have had in mind was Terence, *Eun.* 257 as this was mediated through Cicero, *De officiis*, 1.150.

51. See M. Regoliosi, introduction to *Antidotum in Facium*, by L. Valla, ed. M. Regoliosi (Padua: Antenore, 1981), lxxxiii.

52. See Poggio's letter of 21 May 1455 to a certain Johannes Bartholomeus (perhaps Giovanni di Bartolomeo Guida, according to Arthur Field), in P. Bracciolini, *Lettere*, 3 vols., ed. H. Harth (Florence: Olschki, 1984–87), 3:340–41, at 340: "Sed difficile est, mi

Ioannes, sententiam eius ferre artis quam quis ignorat. Ego facultatis dicendi sum ignarus et *philosophiae ars a me abest,*" my emphasis; see A. Field, *The Origins of the Platonic Academy of Florence* (Princeton, N.J.: Princeton University Press, 1988), 42–44.

53. S. I. Camporeale, "Poggio Bracciolini versus Lorenzo Valla: The *Orationes in Laurentium Vallam,*" in *Perspectives on Early Modern and Modern Intellectual History: Essays in Honor of Nancy S. Struever,* ed. J. Marino and M. Schlitt (Rochester, N.Y.: University of Rochester Press, 2001), 27–48; Mancini, *Vita,* 279–301; see Poggio's various *Invectivae in Vallam,* in P. Bracciolini, *Opera* (Basel, 1538), reprinted, with preface by R. Fubini, in P. Bracciolini, *Opera Omnia,* 4 vols., ed. R. Fubini (Turin: Bottega D'Erasmo, 1964–66), 1:188–251 and 4:867–85.

54. P. Bracciolini, *De vera nobilitate* (written in 1440), ed. D Canfora (Padua, 1999).

55. Poggio, letter to Pietro Tommasi, in Poggio, *Lettere,* 3:291–96, at 292: Si mihi amicus esset, reicerem talis monstri omnem non solum amicitiam, sed vite consuetudinem abscinderemque a me omnem eam corporis partem, que mihi suam benevolentiam suaderet. Nam qui vir bonus posset amicus esse Valle, fanatico, scurre, maledico, iactatori, heretico, omnium clarissimorum doctrina virorum tum presentium, tum preteritorum detractatori contumelioso?

56. Ibid., 293: Non solum in gentiles sed etiam in Augustinum, Hieronymum, Lactantium omnesque insuper philosophos hec demens insana et execranda bestia investa est.

57. Ibid., 294: "At illud perversum animal ea est natura et stultitia, ut non verbis admonenda sed carcere esset et fustibus coercenda."

58. D. Weinstein, *The Captain's Concubine: Love, Honor, and Violence in Renaissance Tuscany* (Baltimore: Johns Hopkins University Press, 2000), 9.

59. Lapo, *De curiae commodis,* ed. Celenza, 4.10.

60. Ibid., 6.4–5.

61. Ibid., 7.15.

62. Grafton, *Leon Battista Alberti,* 50–51.

63. Grafton, *Leon Battista Alberti.*

64. Alberti, *I libri della famiglia,* in idem, *Opere volgari,* ed. Grayson, 1:333–34; L. B. Alberti, *I libri della famiglia,* trans. R. N. Watkins (Columbia: University of South Carolina Press, 1969), 310.

65. Grafton, *Leon Battista Alberti,* 32–33.

66. Ibid., 61–62; see the annotated translations of some of Alberti's *intercenales* ("dinner pieces" intended to be read "inter cenam et pocula" [between dinner and drinks]) by D. Marsh in L. B. Alberti, *Dinner Pieces* (Binghamton, N.Y.: Medieval and Renaissance Texts, 1987).

67. See G. Ponte, "Lepidus e Libripeta," *Rinascimento* 12 (1972): 237–65, cited by Marsh in Alberti, *Dinner Pieces,* 225 n. 1. Niccoli raised the ire of many: see M. C. Davies, "An Emperor without Clothes? Niccolò Niccoli under Attack," *Italia medioevale e umanistica* 30 (1987): 95–148.

68. Alberti, *Dinner Pieces,* 16.

69. Alberti, *I libri della famiglia,* in idem, *Opere volgari,* ed. Grayson, 1:294 and 1:338; Alberti, *I libri della famiglia,* trans. Watkins, 274 and 314; cf. also Watkins's introduction, 8.

six ᭡ *What Is Really There?*

1. See S. Timpanaro, *La genesi del metodo del Lachmann,* 2d ed. (Padua: Liviana Editrice, 1981); P. L. Schmidt, "Lachmann's Method: On the History of a Misunderstanding," in *The Uses of Greek and Latin,* ed. A. C. Dionisotti, A. Grafton, and J. Kraye, Warburg Institute Surveys and Texts, 16 (London: Warburg Instutute, 1988), 227–36; E. J. Kenney, *The Classical Text: Aspects of Editing in the Age of the Printed Book,* Sather Classical Lectures, 44 (Berkeley: University of California Press, 1974), esp. 103–10 and 130–42; and see now the comprehensive G. Fiesoli, *La genesi del Lachmannismo* (Florence: Sismel, 2000).

2. Schmidt, "Lachmann's Method," 229.

3. Ibid. A stemma is a detailed diagram created to illustrate the relationship among different manuscripts. An excellent guide to the practicalities of classical text editing is M. West, *Textual Criticism and Editorial Technique* (Stuttgart: Teubner, 1973); and a fine introduction is in L. D. Reynolds and N. G. Wilson, *Scribes and Scholars: A Guide to the Transmission of Greek and Latin Literature,* 3d ed. (Oxford: Clarendon; New York: Oxford University Press, 1991), 207–41; see esp. 211–16 for stemmatics and its limitations.

4. Kenney, *The Classical Text,* 108.

5. Kenney, *The Classical Text;* Timpanaro, *La genesi;* G. Pasquali, *Storia della tradizione e critica del testo,* 2d ed. (Florence: Le Monnier, 1952).

6. Kenney, *The Classical Text,* 133–36.

7. West, *Textual Criticism,* 5; also cited in Kenney, *The Classical Text,* 143.

8. P. O. Kristeller made a number of these points regarding the uniqueness of Renaissance material in "The Lachmann Method: Merits and Limitations," in *Text: Transactions of the Society for Textual Scholarship,* vol. 1 for 1981 (1984), 11–20; and see also the various pieces in idem, *Studies in Renaissance Thought and Letters* (Rome: Edizioni di Storia e Letteratura, 1956–94), 4:381–480.

9. The manuscripts are MS Florence Bibl. Naz. Magl. XXIII, 126 (fols. 1–96), which I shall refer to as F, and MS Florence Bibl. Ricc. 142, which I shall refer to as R. The dialogue is in F, at fols. 65–93, and in that manuscript only the first 96 folios are autograph. For suggestive thoughts concerning the use of of autograph manuscripts in the realm of medieval studies, see A. Petrucci, *Writers and Readers in Medieval Italy: Studies in the History of Written Culture,* ed. and trans. C. M. Radding (New Haven, Conn.: Yale University Press, 1995), 145–68.

10. See F, fols. 46v–48v, 63–64v, 93v–94v, and the description of the MS in C. S. Celenza, *Renaissance Humanism and the Papal Curia: Lapo da Castiglionchio the Younger's De curiae commodis,* Papers and Monographs of the American Academy in Rome, 31 (Ann Arbor: University of Michigan Press, 1999), 87–90.

11. F, fol. 19: *Cum Arati Sicyonii clarissimi ducis res domi militiaeque gestas ex Plutarcho latine interpretatus essem, easque ad aliquem principem—pro mea consuetudine—mittere statuissem, dubitanti mihi diu ac deliberanti cuinam nostrorum principum potissimum dedicarem has lucubratiunculas meas* [my emphasis], *nullus sane occurebat cui consilio prudentia cum magnitudine, integritate, constantia, tum bellicis rebus et gloria militari Arati vita convenire videretur.* The dedication is of Plutarch's *Life of Aratus,* to Cardinal Cesarini; there is

an edition of the preface in C. S. Celenza, "'Parallel Lives': Plutarch's *Lives,* Lapo da Castiglionchio the Younger (1405–1438), and the Art of Italian Renaissance Translation," *Illinois Classical Studies* 22 (1997): 152–55, and the cited passage is on 152; I have taken the liberty of altering my own punctuation there to better reflect the grammar.

12. See Celenza, "Parallel Lives," 135–36.

13. Ibid., 141; and M. Cortesi, "Umanesimo greco," in *Lo spazio letterario del medioevo: 1. Il medioevo latino,* vol. 3, *La ricezione del testo* (Rome, 1995), 457–507, esp. 462–70.

14. Celenza, "Parallel Lives," 139.

15. The fifteenth-century Florentine bookseller and biographer Vespasiano da Bisticci says that Lapo was "melancholic, and of a nature that rarely laughed." See his *Le vite,* ed. A. Greco, 2 vols. (Florence: Istituto Nazionale di Studi sul Rinascimento, 1970–74), 1:582.

16. Lapo da Castiglionchio, *De curiae commodis,* edited and translated in Celenza, *Renaissance Humanism and the Papal Curia,* 3.13.

17. F, fol. 69v, my emphasis.

18. Lapo da Castiglionchio, *De curiae commodis,* ed. Celenza, 7.23.

19. Ibid., 7.25–27.

20. Ibid., 7.27.

21. Ibid., 7.28; F, fol. 82.

22. MS Florence, Biblioteca Nazionale, Ser. Pan. 123. See P. O. Kristeller, *Iter Italicum: A Finding List of Uncatalogued or Incompletely Catalogued Humanistic Manuscripts of the Renaissance in Italian and Other Libraries,* 6 vols. (Leiden: Brill, 1963–95), 1:145. The frontispiece lists the following works "Leonis Baptistae Alberti" (of Leon Battista Alberti): *Philodoxis,* an *Apologia pro Romana Curia* (this is Lapo's dialogue), *De re uxoria,* and *Oratio funebris pro cane suo.*

23. L. Valla, *Repastinatio dialectice et philosophie,* ed. G. Zippel, 2 vols. (Padua: Antenore, 1982).

24. B. Platina, *De falso et vero bono,* ed. M. G. Blasio (Rome: Edizioni di Storia e Letteratura, 1999).

25. Cf. L. Jardine, *Erasmus, Man of Letters: The Construction of Charisma in Print* (Princeton, N.J.: Princeton University Press, 1993), introduction.

26. J. Hankins, *Repertorium Brunianum: A Critical Guide to the Writings of Leonardo Bruni* (Rome: Edizioni di Storia e Letteratura, 1997), preface; J. Soudek, "Leonardo Bruni and His Public: A Statistical and Interpretative Study of His Annotated Latin Version of the ps.-Aristotelian *Economics,*" *Studies in Medieval and Renaissance History* 5 (1968): 49–136; idem, "A Fifteenth-Century Humanistic Bestseller: The Manuscript Diffusion of Leonardo Bruni's Annotated Latin Version of the ps.-Aristotelian *Economics,*" in *Philosophy and Humanism: Renaissance Essays in Honor of Paul Oskar Kristeller,* ed. E. P. Mahoney (Leiden: Brill, 1976), 129–43.

27. John Najemy has recently looked into the fifteenth-century background to Machiavelli's culture of letter-writing; see J. Najemy, *Between Friends: Discourses of Power and Desire in the Machiavelli-Vettori Letters of 1513–15* (Princeton, N.J.: Princeton University Press, 1993), 18–57. But accounts like Najemy's are rare; if one looks at the overall amount of Machiavelli scholarship, the number of scholars who have given more than a cursory glance to the fifteenth-century background out of which Machiavelli emerged

is stunningly small. Another exception to the tendency to treat Machiavelli in a historical vacuum is the still unsurpassed J. G. A. Pocock, *The Machiavellian Moment: Florentine Political Thought and the Atlantic Republican Tradition* (Princeton, N.J.: Princeton University Press, 1975).

28. I am thinking of V. Cox, *The Renaissance Dialogue: Literary Dialogue in Its Social and Political Contexts, Castiglione to Galileo* (Cambridge: Cambridge University Press, 1992); P. N. Miller, *Peiresc's Europe: Learning and Virtue in the Seventeenth Century* (New Haven, Conn.: Yale University Press, 2000); T. J. Reiss, *Knowledge, Discovery, and Imagination in Early Modern Europe: The Rise of Aesthetic Rationalism* (New York: Cambridge University Press, 1997); J. R. Snyder, *Writing the Scene of Speaking: Theories of Dialogue in the Late Italian Renaissance* (Stanford, Calif.: Stanford University Press, 1989); S. Toulmin, *Cosmopolis: The Hidden Agenda of Modernity* (New York: Free Press, 1989); and V. Kahn, *Rhetoric, Prudence, and Skepticism in the Renaissance* (Ithaca, N.Y.: Cornell University Press, 1985).

29. The classic study is E. Eisenstein, *The Printing Press as an Agent of Change* (Cambridge: Cambridge University Press, 1979); there is an excellent survey of printing and the Italian Renaissance in B. Richardson, *Printing, Writers, and Readers in Renaissance Italy* (Cambridge: Cambridge University Press, 1999).

30. Eisenstein, *The Printing Press.*

31. Ibid., 26 ff. See also, for many connected issues: A. C. De la Mare and L. Hellinga, "The First Book Printed in Oxford," *Transactions of the Cambridge Bibliographical Society* 7 (1978): 184–244; the relevant studies in J. B. Trapp, ed., *Manuscripts in the First Fifty Years after Printing* (London: Warburg Institute, 1983); and A. Grafton, "The Importance of Being Printed," *Journal of Interdisciplinary History* 11 (1980): 265–86.

32. M. Ficino, *De triplici vita,* ed. and trans. C. Kaske and J. Clark (Binghamton, N.Y., 1989), 3.19; and S. Toussaint, "Un orologio per il De vita: Meccanica e metafisica in Marsilio Ficino," in *Marsilio Ficino: Fonti, Testi, Fortuna,* ed. S. Gentile and S. Toussaint, Atti del Convegno Internazionale di Studio, Istituto Nazionale di Studi sul Rinascimento, forthcoming (Florence); and idem, "Ficino, Mercurius, Archimedes, and the Celestial Arts: Modern Outlines of Ficino's Magic," in *Marsilio Ficino: His Theology, His Philosophy, His Legacy,* ed. M. J. B. Allen and V. Rees (Leiden: Brill, 2002), 307–26.

33. For the beginnings of this process in Petrarch, see S. Rizzo, "Il latino del Petrarca," in Dionisotti, Grafton, and Kraye, *The Uses of Greek and Latin,* 41–56; see also Rizzo's fundamental work *Il lessico filologico degli umanisti* (Rome: Edizioni di Storia e Letteratura, 1973), for a minute understanding of how humanists used and transformed the Latin language. For the ramifications of the turn toward classicizing Latin, see R. G. Witt, *In the Footsteps of the Ancients: The Origins of Humanism from Lovato to Bruni* (Leiden: Brill, 2000).

34. See the meticulously argued study of R. Black, *Humanism and Education in Medieval and Renaissance Italy: Tradition and Innovation in Latin Schools from the Twelfth to the Fifteenth Century* (Cambridge: Cambridge University Press, 2001).

35. For Garin, see chapter 2 of this book; for Greene, see T. Greene, *The Light in Troy: Imitation and Discovery in Renaissance Poetry* (New Haven, Conn.: Yale University Press, 1982), esp. 9–11. R. Fubini, *Humanism and Secularization from Petrarch to Valla,* trans. Martha King (Durham, N.C.: Duke University Press, 2003); Witt, *In the Footsteps of the Ancients.*

36. There is a substantial literature on this problem; for a start, one can see C. Gray-

son, *A Renaissance Controversy: Latin or Italian* (Oxford: Oxford University Press, 1960); A. Mazzocco, *Linguistic Theories in Dante and the Humanists* (Leiden: Brill, 1993); M. Tavoni, *Latino, grammatica, volgare: Storia di una questione umanistica,* Medioevo e Umanesimo, 53 (Padua: Antenore, 1984); Fubini, *Humanism and Secularization,* 9–43; I. D. Rowland, *The Culture of the High Renaissance: Ancients and Moderns in Sixteenth-Century Rome* (Cambridge: Cambridge University Press, 1998), 199–211; and the excellent studies of M. L. McLaughlin, *Literary Imitation in the Italian Renaissance: The Theory and Practice of Literary Imitation in Italy from Dante to Bembo* (Oxford: Oxford University Press, 1995); and idem, "Histories of Literature in the Quattrocento," in *The Languages of Literature in Renaissance Italy,* ed. P. Hainsworth (Oxford: Oxford University Press, 1988), 63–80.

37. P. Burke, *The Art of Conversation* (Ithaca, N.Y.: Cornell University Press, 1993); F. Waquet, *Latin, or the Empire of a Sign: From the Sixteenth to the Twentieth Centuries,* trans. J. Howe (London: Verso, 2001); for early modern England, see J. W. Binns, *Intellectual Culture in Elizabethan and Jacobean England: The Latin Writings of the Age* (Leeds: Francis Cairns, 1990). The best overall survey of postmedieval Latin (i.e., neo-Latin, which has been the term for post-1300 Latin accepted by the International Association for Neo-Latin Studies since 1973) is in the two volumes of J. IJsewijn, *Companion to Neo-Latin Studies* (Louvain: Louvain University Press, 1990 and 1998).

38. A. D. Scaglione, *Classical Theory of Composition* (Chapel Hill: University of North Carolina Press, 1972); G. Mazzacurati, *Misura del classicismo rinascimentale* (Naples: Liguori, 1967); Greene, *The Light in Troy,* 171–96.

39. P. Bembo, *Prose della Volgar lingua,* 1st ed. (Venice, 1525); now also in idem, *Prose e Rime,* 2d ed., ed. C. Dionisotti (Turin: UTEP, 1966), 73–309.

40. Ibid., 128–29.

41. W. J. Kennedy, *Authorizing Petrarch* (Ithaca, N.Y.: Cornell University Press, 1994), 82–102; V. De Caprio, "Dal Latino al volgare: Bembo e la ricostituzione della norma," in *Interpreting the Italian Renaissance: Literary Perspectives,* ed. A. Toscano (Stony Brook, N.Y.: Forum Italicum, 1991), 99–112.

42. See J. Monfasani, "The Ciceronian Controversy," in *The Cambridge History of Literary Criticism,* vol. 3, *The Renaissance,* ed. G. P. Norton (Cambridge: Cambridge University Press, 1999), 395–401; and G. W. Pigman, "Imitation and the Renaissance Sense of the Past: The Reception of Erasmus' *Ciceronianus,*" *Journal of Medieval and Renaissance Studies* 9 (1979): 155–77, at 169–71, cited in Monfasani, "The Ciceronian Controversy," 397 n. 3.

43. McLaughlin, *Literary Imitation in the Italian Renaissance,* 278.

44. T. Tunberg, "Neo-Latin Literature and Language," in *The Encyclopedia of the Renaissance,* ed. P. Grendler, 6 vols. (New York: Scribner, 1999), 4:289–94, at 292.

45. Ibid., 4:291–92. See also IJsewijn, *Companion to Neo-Latin Studies,* 1:39–53; Greene, *The Light in Troy,* 6; S. Rizzo, "Petrarca, il latino e il volgare," *Quaderni petrarcheschi* 7 (1990): 7–40. And see the classic statement of Lorenzo Valla in the preface to book 1 of his *On the Elegances of the Latin Language,* his best selling-book in early modern Europe: "For wherever the Roman language is dominant, there you will find Roman *imperium*" [Ibi namque Romanum imperium est, ubicunque Romana lingua dominatur]. L. Valla, *De linguae latinae elegantia,* 2 vols., ed. S. L. Moreda (Madrid: Universidad de Extremadura, 1999), 1:60. For the *Elegantiae,* see M. Regoliosi, *Nel cantiere del Valla: Elaborazione e montaggio delle 'Elegantie'* (Rome: Bulzoni, 1993).

46. See G. Lepschy, "Mother Tongues and Literary Languages," *Modern Language Review* 96 (2001): xxxiii–xlix, esp. xxxix–xlii with bibliography.

47. For a start on this problem, see G. Lepschy, *Mother Tongues and Other Reflections on the Italian Language* (Toronto: University of Toronto Press, 2002); the classic work is T. De Mauro, *Storia linguistica dell'Italia unita*, 2d ed. (Rome: Laterza, 1979); and see Burke, *The Art of Conversation*, 66–88.

48. I. Wallerstein, *The Modern World-System: Capitalist Agriculture and the Origins of the European World-Economy in the Sixteenth Century* (New York: Academic Press, 1974).

49. Among the critiques are that Wallerstein's perspective does not satisfactorily account for the success of the United Provinces of the Netherlands, that it starts with a conceptual model rather than building toward one, that the temporal origins are murky, and so forth. See T. Skocpol, *Social Revolutions in the Modern World* (Cambridge: Cambridge University Press, 1994), 55–71; and R. Brenner, "Agrarian Class Structure and Economic Development in Preindustrial Europe," *Past and Present* 70 (1976): 30–75.

50. For a start, see J. Kirshner, ed., *The Origins of the State in Italy, 1300–1600* (Chicago: University of Chicago Press, 1996), with ample bibliography in the introduction; and K. Appuhn, "Inventing Nature: Forests, Forestry, and State Power in Renaissance Venice," *Journal of Modern History* 72 (2000): 861–89.

51. P. Schiera, "Legitimacy, Discipline, and Institutions: Three Necessary Conditions for the Birth of the Modern State," in Kirshner, *The Origins*, 11–33, at 33.

52. R. Fubini, "The Italian League and the Policy of the Balance of Power at the Accession of Lorenzo de' Medici," in Kirshner, *The Origins*, 166–99.

53. J. Marino, "The Italian States in the 'Long Sixteenth Century,'" in *Handbook of European History, 1400–1600*, ed. T. A. Brady, H. A. Oberman, and J. D. Tracy, 2 vols. (1995; reprint, Grand Rapids: Eerdmans, 1996), 1:331–67.

54. See P. Herde, "Politik und Rhetorik in Florenz am Vorabend der Renaissance: Die ideologische Rechtsfertigung der Florentiner Aussenpolitik durch Coluccio Salutati," in *Archiv für Kulturgeschichte* 47 (1965): 141–220; E. Muir, *Civic Ritual in Renaissance Venice* (Princeton, N.J.: Princeton University Press, 1981); idem, *Mad Blood Stirring: Vendetta and Factions in Friuli during the Renaissance* (Baltimore: Johns Hopkins University Press, 1993); G. Ruggiero, *Violence in Early Renaissance Venice* (New Brunswick, N.J.: Rutgers University Press, 1980); idem, *The Boundaries of Eros: Sex Crime and Sexuality in Renaissance Venice* (Oxford: Oxford University Press, 1985). Stressing Venice's interests on terra firma is J. S. Grubb, *Firstborn of Venice: Vicenza in the Early Renaissance State* (Baltimore: Johns Hopkins University Press, 1988). For the premodern Italian south, see T. Astarita, *Village Justice: Community, Family, and Popular Culture in Early Modern Italy* (Baltimore: Johns Hopkins University Press, 1999).

55. This is a point well made, apropos of Machiavelli, by David Laven, in his "Machiavelli, *Italianità*, and the French Invasion of 1494," in *The French Descent into Renaissance Italy, 1494–95: Antecedents and Effects*, ed. D. Abulafia (Aldershot, Eng.: Ashgate, 1995), 355–69; see also a number of the studies in *The World of Savonarola: Italian Elites and Perceptions of Crisis*, ed. S. Fletcher and C. Shaw (Aldershot, Eng.: Ashgate, 2000), esp. L. Martines, "Literary Crisis and the Generation of 1494," 5–21; A. R. Ascoli, *Ariosto's Bitter Harmony: Crisis and Evasion in the Italian Renaissance* (Princeton, N.J.: Princeton University Press, 1987), 3–42; and see the discussion with references in F. Gilbert, *Machiavelli and Guicciar-*

dini: Politics and History in Sixteenth-Century Florence (Princeton, N.J.: Princeton University Press, 1965).

56. E. Cochrane, *Italy, 1539–1630,* ed. J. Kirshner (London: Longman, 1988); idem, *Florence in the Forgotten Centuries, 1527–1800* (Chicago: University of Chicago Press, 1973); idem, ed., *The Late Italian Renaissance* (New York: Harper and Row, 1970); and K. Gouwens, *Remembering the Renaissance: Humanist Narratives of the Sack of Rome* (Leiden: Brill, 1998). A good evocation of the end of a sense of cultural vitality in early-sixteenth-century Rome can be found in Rowland, *The Culture of the High Renaissance,* 245–54.

57. P. Burke, *The European Renaissance: Centres and Peripheries* (Oxford: Blackwell, 1998), 1–17. For earlier statements of similar types, see E. Gombrich, "From the Revival of Letters to the Reform of the Arts: Niccolò Niccoli and Filippo Brunelleschi," in idem, *The Essential Gombrich: Selected Writings on Art and Culture,* ed. R. Woodfield (London: Phaidon, 1996; essay originally published in 1967), 411–35; and M. Baxandall, *Giotto and the Orators* (Oxford: Oxford University Press, 1971).

Appendix

1. See, for example, P. Bracciolini, *De infelicitate principum,* ed. D. Canfora (Rome: Edizioni di Storia e Letteratura, 1998); and B. Platina, *De falso et vero bono,* ed. M. G. Blasio (Rome: Edizioni di Storia e Letteratura, 1999).

2. For surveys, see the relevant studies in E. Follieri, ed., *La filologia medievale e umanistica greca e latina nel secolo XX: Atti del congresso internazionale . . . 11–15 dicembre 1989,* 2 vols. (Rome: Università di Roma, 1993); and the relevant sections of J. IJsewijn, *Companion to Neo-Latin Studies,* 2 vols. (Louvain: Louvain University Press, 1990 and 1998). The term *neo-Latin* has been used since 1973 by the International Association for Neo-Latin Studies to indicate all postmedieval Latin up to the present.

3. See V. D. Hanson and J. Heath, *Who Killed Homer? The Demise of Classical Education and the Recovery of Greek Wisdom* (New York: Free Press, 1998), 81–86. For remarks on translation and the classics, see P. Burian, "Translation, the Profession, and the Poets," *American Journal of Philology* 121 (2000): 299–307.

4. Hanson and Heath, *Who Killed Homer?*

5. Cf. G. Most, "'With Fearful Steps Pursuing Hopes of High Talk with the Departed Dead,'" *Transactions of the American Philological Association* 128 (1998): 311–24.

6. E. Cassirer, P. O. Kristeller, and J. H. Randall, eds., *The Renaissance Philosophy of Man* (Chicago: University of Chicago Press, 1948).

7. B. G. Kohl and R. G. Witt, eds., *The Earthly Republic: Italian Humanists on Government and Society* (Philadelphia: University of Pennsylvania Press, 1978).

8. See M. King and A. Rabil Jr., "Editors' Introduction to the Series," in H. C. Agrippa, *Declamation on the Nobility and Preeminence of the Female Sex,* ed. and trans. A. Rabil Jr. (Chicago: University of Chicago Press, 1996), ix–xxviii, at ix. For a list of titles with descriptions, see www.press.uchicago.edu/Complete/Series/OVIEME.html.

9. Ficino's Greek-to-Latin translations and paraphrases of the later Platonist Iamblichus, work that Ficino did at the outset of his career and which had a discernible influence on his overall outlook on the problem of integrating religion and philosophy, are available only in manuscript; see MSS Vatican City, Biblioteca Apostolica Vaticana,

Vat. Lat. 5953 and 4530. See C. S. Celenza, "Late Antiquity and Florentine Platonism: The 'Post-Plotinian' Ficino," in *Marsilio Ficino: His Theology, His Philosophy, His Legacy,* ed. M. J. B. Allen and V. R. Rees (Leiden: Brill, 2002); and for the dating, the excellent study of S. Gentile, "Sulle prime traduzioni dal greco di Marsilio Ficino," *Rinascimento,* 2d ser., 30 (1990): 57–104. The standard edition still used for many of Ficino's works is M. Ficino, *Opera Omnia,* 2 vols. (Basel, 1576; reprint, Turin, 1959).

    10. See www.IterGateway.org.

    11. MS Florence, Biblioteca Nazionale, Magl. VIII. 7, fols. 92v–94; cf. P. O. Kristeller, *Iter Italicum: A Finding List of Uncatalogued or Incompletely Catalogued Humanistic Manuscripts of the Renaissance in Italian and Other Libraries,* 6 vols. (Leiden: Brill, 1963–95), 1:132. This mansucript was also noticed by E. Garin, "La cultura milanese nella prima metà del secolo XV," in *Storia di Milano,* 16 vols. (Milano: Fondazione Traccani degli Alfieri per la storia di Milano, 1953–66), vol. 6 (1955), pp. 545–608, at 604 n. 3 and 605 n. 2; and V. Zaccaria, "Summe opere di Pier Candido Decembrio," *Rinascimento* 8 (1956): 13–74, at 19–20. The manuscript is primarily a collection of works by Pier Candido Decembrio and Guarino da Verona.

    12. MS Florence, Biblioteca Nazionale, Magl. VIII. 7, fol. 92v: Philosophi Graeca appellatione vocantur, qui Latine amatores sapientiae interpretantur.

    13. Isidore of Seville, *Etymologiae,* 8.6.

    14. There are so many initiatives already begun that it would be pointless to attempt a listing here, especially since many are still quite new and likely to change considerably. A good model in classical studies can be found in the Perseus Digital Library, www.perseus.tufts.edu.

Index

Agrippa, Henricus Cornelius, 116
Alberti, Leon Battista, 114, 132–33, 139–40;
    Libri della famiglia (On the Family), 114, 133
Albert the Great, 110–11
Alfonso of Aragon, "the Magnanimous," 89,
    90, 92, 94, 98. *See also* Naples
Allen, Michael J. B., 104
Altertumswissenschaft, 4, 6
Althusser, Louis, 181
analytical philosophy, 59–60, 65
Annales movement, 70–73; *Annales d'histoire
    économique et sociale*, 70
Aquinas, St. Thomas, 42, 66, 81, 92, 98,
    110–11, 141
Ariosto, 10
Aristotle, 17, 35, 36, 40, 41, 47, 49, 50, 51, 54,
    56, 80, 88, 90, 102, 104, 167, 175; and hexis,
    77–78
Athanassiadi, Polymnia, 84
Augustine, Saint, xv, 21, 81, 130
Aurispa, Giovanni, 91, 100
Averroes, 36, 102, 103, 167
Avignon, 122

Bach, Johann Sebastian, 141
Bachelard, Gaston, 75–76; and idea of
    epistemological break, 76
Bacon, Francis, 150
Bade, Josse, 94
Barbaro, Ermolao, 172
Barbaro, Francesco, 130, 153, 191
Baron, Hans, xiv, xvii, 36–39, 40, 43, 153
Beard, Mary, xvi
Beaufret, Jean, 33
Becker, Marvin, xix
Belles Lettres, 7, 151
Bembo, Pietro, xiii, 10, 143, 145, 147; *Prose
    della vulgar lingua (On vernacular prose)*, 145
Ben-Yehudah, Eliezer, 146
Berlin, Isaiah, 99
Berlin, University of: and philosophical fac-
    ulty, 4, 5, 44–45, 68. *See also* philology,
    classical; *Wissenschaft*

Beroaldo, Filippo, 101, 142
Berr, Henri, 70
Biblioteca Teubneriana, 7
Biddick, Kathleen, xvii
Bildung, 5
Blasio, Maria Grazia, 140
Bloch, Marc, 70–72. *See also Annales* move-
    ment
Bloch, R. Howard, xvii
Böckh, August, 2, 5
Boethius, 93, 96; *Consolatio philosophiae
    (Consolation of Philosophy)*, 96
Borgia family, 98
Bourdieu, Pierre, 14, 62, 75–78, 106; and idea
    of capital, 76–78, 102–3, 125; and idea of
    doxa, 14, 77, 106; and idea of field, 76–
    78, 81, 85, 99, 100–106, 113; and idea of
    habitus, 14, 76–77, 85, 87, 93, 116, 127
Bracciolini, Poggio, 14, 94, 98, 125–26,
    129–30, 131, 132, 153, 191–92
Braudel, Fernand, 70–73, 147; *Civilization and
    Capitalism*, 71–72
Brill Academic Publishers, 155
Brown, Peter, xv, 52
Brucker, Gene, xix
Brunelleschi, Filippo, xi
Bruni, Leonardo, 5, 14, 37, 86, 101, 120, 127–
    28, 130, 141, 153; *Dialogi ad Petrum Paulum
    Histrum*, 86–87; *De studiis et litteris (On
    Studies and Literature)*, 120
Bullen, J. B., xvii
Buonincontri, Lorenzo, 104
Burckhardt, Jacob, xi, xii, xvii, xviii, 1, 2,
    4, 7, 11–13, 42, 44, 84; *Die Cultur der Ren-
    aissance in Italien (The Civilization of the
    Renaissance in Italy)*, xi–xii, xviii, 12–13
Burke, Peter, xvii, 70, 71, 149
Burkert, Walter, xv, 52
Bynum, Caroline Walker, xv, 52, 117–18; *Jesus
    as Mother*, 117

Caeneus, 125
Calder III, William M., xvi

Calixtus III, Pope, 98
Campana, Augusto, 42
Canfora, Luciano, xvi
Cantor, Norman, xvii
capitalism, xviii, 71, 74, 147
Carrara family, 122
Castiglionchio the Younger, Lapo da, 123–28, 130–33, 137–40; *De curiae commodis (On the Benefits of the Curia)*, 125, 126–27, 128, 130–31, 137–39
Castiglione, Baldassare, xix, 106, 131, 141, 150
Charles V, Habsburg Emperor, 149
Charles VIII, King of France, 148
Chartier, Roger, 72
Christ, Jesus. *See* Christianity
Christianity, xv, 6, 19, 20–21, 30, 80–85, 88–99, 101–2, 106, 112–14, 116, 144
Cicero, 11, 36, 43, 101, 146
codices descripti, 136
"Cogito, ergo sum." *See* Descartes, Réne
Cohn, Samuel, xix
Collins, Randall, 74
Columbia University, 41
Conrad, Joseph, 13
Constantine, Emperor, 89–90
continental philosophy, 59, 60–64. *See also* Heidegger, Martin
Corpus Scriptorum Latinorum Paravinianum, 7
Cortesi, Paolo, 145
Croce, Benedetto, 16, 18, 19, 20, 22, 23–28, 29, 39, 55, 170
culture, reciprocity of high and low, 74, 109, 143–44

D'Alembert, Jean le Rond, 3
Damasus I, Pope, 94
Dante Alighieri, 121, 145, 149
deconstruction, 61–63
Delminio, Giulio Camillo, 145–46
Delumeau, Jean, 72
De Roover, Raymond, xix
Derrida, Jacques, 61–63, 66
De Sanctis, Francesco, 26
Descartes, Réne, 66–67, 75. *See also* foundationalism, Cartesian
Dewey, John, 41, 66
Diderot, Denis, 3
Dilthey, Wilhelm, 7, 45
disputatio, culture of, 86–88, 91, 99
Dostoyevsky, Fyodor, 31
Dreyfus Affair, 55
Droysen, Johann Gustav, 2

Eco, Umberto, 3, 46; *Name of the Rose*, 46–47
Ecole Pratique des Hautes Etudes, 71
Edizione Nazionale dei Testi Umanistici, 151
Egyptians, wisdom of, 110, 112
eliminatio codicum descriptorum, 135
emendatio, 129, 135
Encyclopédie, 3
Enlightenment, 2–3, 8, 30, 32, 71
Epicurus, 175
Erasmus, Desiderius, 94, 129, 150
Eugenius IV, Pope, 86, 90, 122
existentialism, 33–35, 44, 60–62, 66

Fascism, 20, 22–25, 28, 30, 54
Fazio, Bartolomeo, 129
Febvre, Lucien, 70–72; *The Problem of Unbelief in the Sixteenth Century*, 71. *See also* *Annales* movement
Fedele, Cassandra, 153
Ferguson, Wallace, xvii
Fichte, Johann Gottlieb, 179
Ficino, Marsilio, 50, 80, 82, 83, 99, 100–114, 142, 143–44, 151, 153, 154, 167; *De christiana religione (On the Christian Religion)*, 101, 102, 144; *Consiglio contro la peste (Counsel against the Plague)*, 101, 144; and idea of *prisca theologia* (ancient theology), 102, 110; *Theologia platonica (Platonic Theology)*, 101, 102, 113, 144; *De triplici vita (On the Triple Life)*, 106–13
Field, Arthur, 101
Filelfo, Francesco, 100, 127, 137, 172
Flashar, Helmut, xvi
Flavio, Biondo, 128
Florence, xi, xiii, xiv, 5, 14, 20, 30, 31, 32, 33, 36, 37, 38, 39, 42, 86, 101–6, 113, 118, 119, 121, 123, 127, 140, 143, 152, 156
Foucault, Michel, 63–64
foundationalism, Cartesian, 66–67
Franc, Abel, 71
Franco, Veronica, 153
Frede, Michael, 84
Frege, Gottlob, 59–60
Freud, Sigmund, 99, 154
Freytag, Gustav, 4
Friuli, 73
Fubini, Riccardo, 38, 145

Galileo Galilei, 150
Garin, Eugenio, 15, 16–19, 28–36, 38, 39, 40, 46, 48, 50, 54–57, 76, 80, 85, 99, 118, 145, 172, 173; *Italian Humanism*, 35
Geary, Patrick, xvii

Gellius, Aulus, 103; *Noctes atticae (Attic Nights)*, 103
gender theory, xv, 115–18; and masculinity, 118–21
Gentile, Giovanni, 18, 19–25, 27, 28, 29, 46, 169
George of Trebizond, 125, 129
Gerrard, Christopher, xvii
Gibbon, Edward, 8–9; *Decline and Fall of the Roman Empire*, 8
Gigante, Marcello, xvi
Gilmore, David, 121
Ginzburg, Carlo, 73–74. *See also* microhistory
Giolitti, Giovanni, 22
Goethe, Johann Wolfgang von, 34
Goetz, Walter, 39
Goldthwaite, Richard, xix
Grafton, Anthony, 128–29
Gramsci, Antonio, 26, 55
Grassi, Ernesto, 33–35
Gray, Hanna H., 119
Greece, xii, 3, 6, 7–11, 28, 30, 34, 37, 42, 44, 51, 81, 83, 91, 94–95, 101, 102, 124, 137, 149, 154, 156
Greene, Thomas, 145
Grossforschung, 5, 7, 45, 46, 53, 71
Guicciardini, Francesco, 148

Habermas, Jürgen, 68
Hankins, James, 103, 105
Harvard University Press, 151–52
Hebrew, modern, 146
Hegel, Georg Wilhelm Friedrich, 2, 19, 20, 21, 27, 33, 170, 177
Heidegger, Martin, 33–35, 44, 51–52, 61, 66
Heisenberg, Werner, 63
Hellenism, 3, 10–12, 33–35, 44, 45, 51. *See also* nationalism
Heraclitus, 27
Herder, Johann Gottfried von, 4
Herlihy, David, xix
Hermetic Corpus, 101, 112. *See also* Egyptians, wisdom of
histoire totale, 70
historicism, 2–3, 17, 23–28, 35, 55, 161
history and historiography, xiv–xvi, xix, 1–4, 6–7, 8–13; deep historiography, xvi–xvii; diachronic style, 17–18, 28–30, 36, 38–39, 47; synchronic style, 17–18, 29–30, 42–43, 47–48, 53; combining synchrony and diachrony, 76
Hitler, Adolf, 46
Hoffman, Ernst, 44

honor, xviii, 115–33
Huizinga, Johan, 128
humanism, 27, 33–34, 41, 42, 44, 53, 55; civic, xiv, 36–39, 153; German neohumanism, 4, 34, 35, 44. *See also* Renaissance humanism
Humanistica lovaniensia, 152
Humanistische Bibliothek, 152
Humboldt, Wilhelm von, 2, 3, 13, 16, 44, 68
Hunt, Lynn, xvi

Iamblichus, 110–12, 144
idealism, philosophical, xx, 19, 25, 41, 45, 53, 56
IJsewijn, Joseph, 152
immanentism, 19, 27, 28, 32, 33, 41
Innocent VIII, Pope, 32, 108
intellectual communities, 69, 74–75
Isidore of Seville, 156
Istituto Nazionale di studi sul Rinascimento, 33, 152
Italian vernacular, xiii
I Tatti Renaissance Library, 151–52

Jaeger, Werner, 44
Jaja, Donato, 19, 20
Jerome, Saint, 81, 94, 98, 130
Journal of the Warburg and Courtauld Institutes. *See* Warburg Institute

Kant, Immanuel, 19, 21, 29, 33, 40, 50, 54, 59, 65, 67–68, 75, 110
Kessler, Eckhard, 152
Kohl, Benjamin, 43
Krämer, Heinrich, 108
Kristeller, Paul Oskar, 13, 15, 16–19, 23, 28, 29, 30, 31, 32, 34, 35, 36, 40–57, 59, 68, 76, 85, 140, 152, 155, 173, 175–76, 177; *Catalogus translationum et commentariorum*, 47, 175; *Iter Italicum*, 46, 47, 155–56; *Latin Manuscript Books*, 46, 47
Kuhn, Thomas, xv, 53, 75–76; and idea of normal science, xv, 53, 75; and idea of paradigm shift, 75; and idea of revolutionary science, 75

Labriola, Antonio, 25–26
LaCapra, Dominick, 58
Lachmann, Karl Konrad Friedrich Wilhelm, 134–36; and the Lachmann method, 134–35
La critica (journal), 24
Lactantius, 130
Lamprecht, Karl, 179
Lane, Frederic, xix

Laterza publishers, 24
Latin language, xiii, xiv, 22, 23; neo-Latin, 152, 200. *See also* Renaissance Latin
lectio recepta, 136
lectio tradita, 136
LeGoff, Jacques, 72
Lévi-Strauss, Claude, 60–63; *Tristes Tropiques,* 63
lex casati, 169
Limentani, Ludovico, 31
linguistics, structural. *See* structuralism
Livy, 10, 97
Lodi, Peace of, 101, 148
Loeb, James, 7
Loeb Classical Library, 7
long fifteenth century, xiii, 142, 147–49; as opposed to long sixteenth century, 147
Loschi, Antonio, 119
Lucretia, 97
Lucretius, 134
Luther, Martin, 84

Machiavelli, Niccolò, xix, 132, 141, 148, 149, 150, 154
Malatesta, Battista, 120
Manilius, Marcus, 104
manuscript study, 136–40
Martines, Lauro, xix, 118–19, 121; *The Social World of the Florentine Humanists,* 118
Martin V, Pope, 122
Marx, Karl, 4, 19, 25, 26, 27, 50, 62, 73, 76, 78
Mauss, Marcel, 179
McLaughlin, Martin, 146
Medici family, 102, 104, 188; Cosimo de', 43, 101–2, 148, 188; Lorenzo de', 102, 103, 104
Meinecke, Friedrich, 161
Melanchthon, Philip, 150
Menander, 154
Mendelssohn, Felix, 141
Menocchio. *See* Ginzburg, Carlo
Michelet, Jules, 42
microhistory, 69–70, 73–74
Milan, 36, 39, 121
Mill, John Stuart, 116
Molho, Anthony, xix
Momigliano, Arnaldo, xvi, 4, 13
Mommsen, Theodor, 4, 5, 6, 7
monotheism, 82–85, 99
Montaigne, Michel de, 150
Monumenta Germaniae Historica, 45, 174
Morrissey, Robert, xvii
Most, Glenn, xvi

Muir, Edward, 69
Muratori, Lodovico Antonio, 14

Nabokov, Vladimir, 13
Naples, 19, 25, 89, 98, 125, 129. *See also* Alfonso of Aragon
nationalism, xiii, 2, 3, 4, 6, 23, 30; Latin language and, 2, 8, 9, 13
National Socialism, 18, 34, 38, 40, 43, 46
native language. *See* vernacular
Neoplatonism. *See* Ficino, Marsilio; Iamblichus; Plotinus; Porphyry; Proclus
Niccoli, Niccolò, 132
Nicholas V, Pope, 43, 94, 98
Nichols, Stephen, xvii
Niebuhr, Barthold, 2, 4–5
Nietzsche, Friedrich, 6, 7, 44, 50
Norden, Eduard, 43
Novick, Peter, 57

Oberman, Heiko, xvi
Orsini, Cardinal Giordano, 123
orthodoxy, xviii, 77, 80–114, 134, 143
Other Voice in Early Modern Europe, the (series), 153–54
Ovid, 108
Oxford Classical Texts (series), 7

Padua, 122
paganism, 83–85
Palermo, 33
Pannartz, Arnold, 142
Panofsky, Erwin, 13, 77
papal court, 86, 98, 122–23, 126–28, 130–31, 138–39
Parentucelli, Tommaso. *See* Nicholas V, Pope
Paris, 70
Pascal, Carlo, 7
Paul, Saint, 21, 88, 89, 90, 94–95, 97, 98, 114
Pavia, 7
Petrarch, xiv, 9, 37, 43, 100, 121–22, 143, 144, 145, 146, 153, 154
Pfeiffer, Rudolph, xvi
philology, xix, 2, 4, 15, 35–36, 39, 101, 103; classical, 2, 4–5, 134–36; as model for other historical sciences, 2. *See also* Berlin, University of
philosophische Fakultät. See Berlin, University of
philosophy, 4, 18–28, 30–34, 39, 48–52, 59–69, 87; as regulative discipline, 29, 40–41, 45, 49–52, 66–68

Piccolomini, Francesco, 167
Pico della Mirandola, Giovanni, 32, 33, 104, 108, 153, 167; *De ente et uno (On Being and the One)*, 104
Pirenne, Henri, 70
Pisa, 19, 20, 33
Pizan, Christine de, 116
Platamone, Battista, 92
Platina, Bartolomeo, 140
Plato, xx, 11, 23, 40, 41, 47, 49, 50, 51, 55, 56, 59, 65, 80, 87, 101–2, 104, 105, 112, 113, 143, 144, 154, 167
Pliny the Elder, 104, 108
Plotinus, 48, 52, 102, 107, 109–13, 144
Plutarch, 10, 124, 137
Poliziano, Angelo, 101, 103–4, 105, 142, 143, 146, 153; *Lamia*, 104; *Miscellanea (Miscellanies)*, 103–4
Pomponazzi, Pietro, 153
Porphyry, 110–11; *Letter to Anebo*, 111
poststructuralism, 61–64, 70. *See also* microhistory
pragmatism, 41, 66
printing, xiv, 142–43
Proclus, 111, 144
Pulci, Luigi, 104, 143
Pythagoras, 87, 88, 104

quantum theory, 75
questione della lingua, 145–47
Quintilian, 88, 90, 114
Quirini, Lauro, 130

Rabelais, François, 71
Ramberg, Bjørn, 65
Ranke, Leopold von, 2, 4, 9–10, 13, 14; *Geschichte der Päpste (History of the Popes)*, 9–10
recensio, 135
Reformation, xvi, 95
Reiss, Timothy, 100
Renaissance, xi–xiv, xvi–xx, 1, 2, 8–15, 16, 17, 19, 21, 26, 28–44, 46–57, 58–59, 65, 66, 68, 69, 74, 75, 76, 77, 78, 79, 80–87, 100, 107, 115–18, 120–21, 124, 129, 130, 134, 136, 139, 140–44, 147, 149, 150, 151–56
Renaissance humanism, 30, 31, 34–36, 56, 80, 86, 118, 121, 143; classic phase of, 99–100, 118–22; and the *studia humanitatis*, 42, 43, 47, 54, 85, 100, 118, 122
Renaissance Latin: significance of, ix, xiv, 1, 13–14, 17, 57, 86, 101, 119–21, 128–29, 134,

136, 143–47, 151–56, 193; as *relatively*, not *absolutely*, understudied, xix–xx, 8, 46, 151–52, 154
Renaissance Society of America, 151
representationalism, 65–66, 68
republic of letters, 119, 191–92
Rerum Italicarum Scriptores, 14. *See also* Muratori, Lodovico Antonio
rhetoric, 11, 35, 39, 42, 43, 50–51, 86–88, 89
Riehl, W. H., 4
Ritschl, Wilhelm, 4
Roberts, David D., 26
Robinson, Annabel, xvi
Rome, xii, 5, 8–11, 20, 30, 32, 34, 36, 40, 42, 44, 51, 83, 86, 90, 96, 97, 98, 104, 108, 121, 122–24, 146, 149, 154; 1527 Sack of, 149
Rorty, Richard, 50, 51, 58, 65–66, 68–69, 78, 142
Rubinstein, Nicolai, xix
Russell, Bertrand, 31, 60

Salutati, Coluccio, 37, 86–87, 100, 119, 153; *Invectivum in Antonium Luschum Vicentinum (Invective against Antonio Loschi of Vicenza)*, 119; *De saeculo et religione*, 37; *De tyranno*, 37
Sandys, Sir John, xvi
San Lorenzo, xi
Santa Maria del Fiore, xi
Santa Maria sopra Minerva, 98
Sartre, Jean-Paul, 62
Saussure, Ferdinand de, 61–62
Savonarola, Girolamo, 104–6, 143
Schiera, Pierangelo, 148
Schiller, Friedrich, 34
Schism, Great, 86, 122
Schlegel, Friedrich, 9
Schleiermacher, Friedrich, 44–45
Schmidt, P. L., 135
Schoemann, Georg Friedrich, 6
Scott, Joan Wallach, 116–17
Scrivani, Melchior, 86, 87
Scruton, Roger, 60
Scuola normale superiore di Pisa, 33
Seneca, 11
Seurat, Georges, 95
Sextus Empiricus, 66
Sextus Tarquinius, 97
Sforza, Francesco, 148
Sicily, 19, 89
Sismondi, Simonde de, 9; *Histoire de la renaissance de la liberté en Italie*, 9
Socrates, 6, 26

Spaventa, Bertrando, 19
Spiegel, Gabrielle, xvii
Sprenger, Jakob, 108
structuralism, 61–64, 70–73
Studio fiorentino, 103
Swarz, David, 76
Sweynheym, Conrad, 142
Sylvester I, Pope, 89–90
Symonds, John Addington, 13
Synesius, 111

Tarquinius Superbus, 97
Teubner series of classical texts. *See* Biblioteca Teubneriana
Theodoric, Ostrogothic King, 96
Thompson, E. P., 73
Timpanaro, Sebastiano, 135
Tiresias, 125
Tolstoy, Leo, 31
Tommasi, Pietro, 130
transcendentalism, 19, 21, 26, 28, 41, 87
Trexler, Richard, xix
Troeltsch, Ernst, 39
Tunberg, Terence, 146
Tuscan. *See* vernacular

University of Chicago Press, 153
Utrecht, Union of, 149

Valla, Lorenzo, 80, 82, 83, 84, 85–100, 113–14, 118, 129–30, 140, 141, 146, 153; *Adnotationes in Novum Testamentum (Annotations on the New Testament),* 93–95; *Encomium Sancti Thomae Aquinatis,* 96; *De falso credita et ementita Constantini donatione (On the falsely believed and fraudulent Donation of Constantine),* 89–91; *De libero arbitrio (On Free Will),* 95–98; *De professione religiosorum (On the Profession of the Religious),* 91–93; *Repastinatio dialectice et philosophie* (The *Dialectical Disputations*), 88
Van Engen, John, xvii
Van Gogh, Vincent, 141
Venice, 121, 142, 148
Verde, Armando, 103
vernacular, xiii, 2, 3, 8, 9, 10, 11, 13, 56, 57, 73, 101, 104, 133, 136, 144, 145–47
Vico, Giambattista, 26, 27, 150
Villa I Tatti (The Harvard University Center for Italian Renaissance Studies), 151
Visconti family, 36, 121
Vives, Juan Luis, 153
Voigt, Georg, 10–11
Volpaia, Lorenzo della, 144
Vossler, Karl, 24

Wallerstein, Immanuel, 147
Warburg Institute, 152
Weber, Max, 4
Welcker, Friedrich Gottlieb, 4
West, Martin L., 136
Wilamowitz-Moellendorff, Ulrich von, xvi, 6, 7, 43
William of Orange, 149
Winckelmann, Johann Joachim, 3, 11, 13, 34
Wissenschaft, 5, 44–45, 47, 49, 55, 68
Witt, Ronald G., 145
Wittgenstein, Ludwig, 60, 66
Wolf, Friedrich August, 5
Wolin, Richard, 52
women in the Italian Renaissance, 120–21, 152–53. *See also* gender theory

Zabarella, Francesco, 167
Zippel, Gianni, 140